FOUR REASONABLE MEN

FOUR REASONABLE MEN

Marcus Aurelius

John Stuart Mill

Ernest Renan

Henry Sidgwick

Brand Blanshard

WESLEYAN UNIVERSITY PRESS ⬥ Middletown, Connecticut

Parts of the section on Henry Sidgwick appeared in *The Monist,* 58 (July 1974):
349–70. They are reprinted here with permission of that journal.

All inquiries and permissions requests should be addressed to the Publisher,
Wesleyan University Press, 110 Mt. Vernon Street, Middletown, Connecticut 06457

Distributed by Harper & Row Publishers, Keystone Industrial Park, Scranton,
Pennsylvania 18512

LIBRARY OF CONGRESS CATALOGING IN PUBLICATION DATA
Blanchard, Brand, 1892–
   Four reasonable men.

  Includes index.
   1. Philosophers—Biography. I. Title.
B104.B58 1984 109 [B] 84-2195
ISBN 0-8195-5100-7 (alk. paper)
ISBN 0-8195-6102-9 (pbk.: alk. paper)

Manufactured in the United States of America

First Edition

First Wesleyan Paperback Edition

To all who, like this quartet,
try to follow the rocky road of Reason.

Contents

Illustrations

Preface

This book brings together a group of men who have surely never appeared in company before: an emperor of the civilized world, a poverty-stricken son of a Breton fisherman, an intellectual boy wonder who barely survived his Draconian education, and a modest Cambridge professor of the Victorian era. I have tried to show that they were all great men, which was the easiest part of my task. I have tried to show also—a more precarious task—that they were great for the same reason, the government of their lives by a quiet, habitual reasonableness. I have tried to show finally—and this was the hardest task of all—that reasonableness, so often painted in dull, unattractive gray, is the most desirable of all human virtues. Though it involves discipline and restraint, which are always unpopular, its restraints are tickets of admission to a wider world of happiness, understanding, and effectiveness. It is indeed the great need of mankind.

I have made no attempt to analyze in a technical way the nature of reasonableness. If anyone should want such an analysis, he will get a surfeit of it in four earlier books of mine: *The Nature of Thought* (2 vols. Allen & Unwin), *Reason and Goodness* (Humanities Press), *Reason and Analysis* (Open Court), and *Reason and Belief* (Yale University Press). This book is not philosophy, but biography, though I have added a chapter on the most universal enemy of the reasonable temper, prejudice.

My debt is deep to the company over many years of these wise and serene companions. I owe much also to my wife, Roberta Yerkes Blanshard, who, through her expert editing, has saved me from missteps without number.

BRAND BLANSHARD

New Haven, Connecticut
August 1, 1983

MARCUS AURELIUS

Marcus Aurelius
Piazza del Campidoglio, Rome

Marcus Aurelius

*T*hat "Power tends to corrupt; absolute power corrupts absolutely," the statement by which Lord Acton is chiefly remembered, has not always proved true. There is at least one conspicuous exception to it, a man who was both the most powerful person living and also completely incorruptible: Marcus Aurelius Antoninus, who for nineteen years stood at the head of the civilized world.

Besides this combination of power and principle there was another paradox about Aurelius, namely his combination of philosophy and practice. This union is perhaps harder to find than the first. To be sure, it is not unknown. Masaryk was a professional philosopher and a distinguished statesman. But the philosopher-king remains a fragile, synthetic, and chiefly imaginary being. Philosophy requires brooding; it needs long periods of gestation; it cannot be done on the run or in occasional moments of freedom. It calls for leisure and abstraction from the immediate, not immersion in it. Men of action too need some freedom of this kind, for they must rise far enough above the immediate to foresee the consequences of this or that line of action; they must be able to select from a welter of decisions which demands must be met at once and which will admit of some delay. But if, like Socrates, a man forgets the world about him and stands all night under the stars thinking about justice, or stands before his window for hours together, like Hegel, lost in the Absolute, what is oddly called absence of mind does not conduce to getting things done. Philosophy and practice pull in opposite directions. While the nature of rightness has a profound bearing on what we ought to do now, if we hold up action until we are clear what exactly rightness is, we shall be about as active as the Sphinx. It is therefore the more remarkable that Aurelius, in

3

addition to being commanding general of the Roman armies and so loaded with official duties that he dictated business letters during the games in the Colosseum, was also the author of one of the enduring classics of reflection.

The *Meditations*

His book is like no other. It is not a work of systematic speculation, nor is it a sustained analysis of any philosophical question; so he did not after all combine practice with philosophy in its full rigor. Indeed it is hardly a book at all. It is for the most part a series of jottings made by candlelight in his tent while he was commanding the armies of the north against the ever-pressing barbarians. When the camp had gone to sleep, the emperor, who was late to bed and early to rise, sat at his table and took stock, not of battles, sieges, and fortunes, of which there is little mention, but of himself, his state of mind, his lapses from justice or from speaking the truth or from command of his temper. He used these night hours to conjure up the ideals he had set before himself as a man and as a ruler of men, to see them more clearly, to consider what they demanded of him, to consider what he was in the light of what he might have been and in reason ought to be. Tacked on to his meditations by way of introduction is a roster of his teachers, of those who had shaped his mind and body, together with hosannas of gratitude toward them and benediction on them. The journal is broken rather arbitrarily into twelve books. No sure date can be attached to any of them, though the second, signed in Moravia, must come from the expedition against the Quadi, and the third, signed at Carnuntum near Vienna, from his campaign on the Danube. Marcus writes as an old man—and the *Meditations* clearly sprang from his later years, though he died a little short of his fifty-ninth birthday.

The book was never published by its author, nor did he give it its name. He called it Τὰ εἰς ἑαυτόν, literally "things to oneself," or, more intelligibly, "thoughts addressed to oneself." One would expect a book by a Roman to be written in Latin. It was in fact written in Greek. The Emperor was at home in both tongues, but Greek was the language of culture in his day, and he chose to write in it, much as Frederick the Great chose to write in French rather than in his own (as he thought) less elegant German. Nevertheless Marcus, writing for himself rather than for the public, was careless of order, continuity, and finish. He is often obscure; he sometimes breaks out into ejaculations, or stops in the middle of a sentence and does not bother to resume it.

The work has a strange history. Though it was presumably given to the public soon after the Emperor's death, "Hardly a notice of it occurs," says Farquharson, its scholarly editor, "until the days of Suidas, in the ninth century."[1] Finally, after many centuries more, it came into its own. The seventeenth century produced some 26 editions, the eighteenth 58, the nineteenth 81, and the twentieth 28 in its first eight years. The little book was a favorite of Sir Thomas Browne. Pascal's famous passage about living on a narrow edge between two eternities, past and future, seems to have been suggested by the *Meditations,* to which indeed his own *Pensées* is in some ways strikingly similar. Pope used Marcus's book in his *Essay on Man.* Jeremy Collier translated it. Frederick the Great, who used it constantly, said: "Marcus Aurelius, of all human beings, perhaps carried virtue to its highest point."[2] Matthew Arnold, in a well-known essay on him, says that he is "perhaps the most beautiful figure in history."[3] An author whose disjointed midnight musings in the second century can still speak to cultivated minds the world over must have something of interest to say. What that is we shall try to see. Meanwhile let me sketch the comparatively little that is known about his outward life.

The Boy

Marcus Aurelius was not born to the purple, but he was born (A.D. 121) to just about every other advantage one could name—of blood, environment, and education. He was a grandson of the pre-

siding prefect, or mayor, of Rome, who served three times as consul
of the empire. His father, who died while Marcus was a child, was
praetor of the city. Marcus's mother, Domitia Lucilla, who was a
consul's daughter and heiress to a large fortune, was a scholar at
home in both Greek and Latin literature. Roman morals in those
days were lax, and with such opportunities for self-indulgence as
were open to the young Marcus, most boys would probably have
burnt the candle at both ends and so burnt themselves quickly out.
But Marcus the boy was father to Aurelius the man. He got hold
of some manuals of the stern and masculine philosophy of Stoicism,
became a convert to it, and at the age of eleven took to wearing its
plain clothing, eating its frugal diet, and sleeping on the ground
wrapped in animal skins. His good mother Domitia, not knowing
what to make of such austerity in a boy who could have anything
he wanted, took counsel on whether he should be sent away to
school. The decision was against it, and she proceeded, with her
almost unlimited resources, to employ a series of the most distinguished scholars and lecturers in the empire to teach her oddly
wayward son. The boy, instead of resenting their exacting regimen,
was delighted to find logical fencers to argue with and masters in
philosophy and literature to emulate.

The most prominent of these was Cornelius Fronto, a leader of
the Roman Senate, who had developed a style of oratory considered
by many to rival that of Cicero. When Marcus was given the title
of caesar at eighteen and of consul at nineteen, he had to address
the Senate in speeches that were eagerly listened to as premonitions
of his course as emperor. Here he owed much to Fronto, who for
years had been making the young man write essays which he cor-
rected meticulously, adding long notes of advice and commentary.
A cache of letters between Fronto and his pupil was discovered in
the early nineteenth century and naturally excited great hopes.[4]
These were hardly realized, since Fronto's criticisms of royalty were
too gingerly and his pupil's responses too docile to be of much interest. But they do suggest that after a time Marcus wearied of Fronto's

insistence on linguistic minutiae and hungered for something more solid.

This more solid diet was provided by another distinguished senator, Junius Rusticus. Rusticus was a Stoic who instructed Marcus in the logic and theory of Stoicism. His greatest influence was indirect and lay in the gift to his pupil of the discourses of Epictetus. This remarkable book served as a guide to Marcus for the rest of his life. Epictetus had been a brutally treated slave, exiled from Rome by Domitian a generation before Marcus's birth, but Marcus quotes him oftener than he does any other writer. To the annoyance of Fronto, Marcus learned from Rusticus "to eschew rhetoric and fine language," for the Stoics attached small value to such things. "He taught me to read accurately, and not to be satisfied with vague general apprehension . . . ."[5] Rusticus went on to become prefect of Rome, but little is known of his use of this office except one repellent fact. The aged Christian leader, Justin Martyr, was brought before him, and the brief interview between them is still on record.[6] It ended with the inquiry by Rusticus whether Justin and his fellow Christians would or would not show their loyalty to the state by joining in sacrifice to the Roman gods. They replied that they could honor the Christian God only. Whereupon they were led away by order of Rusticus and decapitated. On matters of political and religious loyalty, mercy was hardly to be expected from a magistrate who was both a Roman and a Stoic. Marcus himself would later be confronted with the same problem.

When Marcus was seventeen, an extraordinary event took place that changed the course of his life. Apart from it, he might have become a forgotten local lecturer on philosophy. As it was, there fell on him, no one knows how, the keen and dangerous eye of the emperor Hadrian. Though capable of cruelty, Hadrian was one of the few emperors of Rome who could be called a great man. He knew by personal visitation every province of his immense empire; as a soldier he watched his frontiers like a jealous eagle; he was an indefatigable builder of temples, aqueducts, bridges, and palaces;

and sometimes the soldier and builder combined energies to notable effect, as when, with his conspicuous white head (he would never wear headgear), he appeared among the hills of Scotland building a Chinese wall from the Firth of Forth to the Firth of Clyde to keep out the marauding Highlanders. In his later years his restless spirit was turned irritable by illness and made anxious by the pressing problems of the succession.

The Prince

The Roman method of filling the throne, established by Augustus, was the election of the emperor by the Senate and its ratification by the army. But before the first century was over, the emperors had hit upon a device for taking this matter into their own hands. They would associate with themselves in office a son or other near relative, and give him sufficient power to make him the inevitable choice when the Senate, itself a hereditary body, came to act. But Hadrian was unhappily married, childless, and homosexual. On somewhat dubious grounds he adopted to succeed him a young man who shortly afterward died. Hadrian for a while considered his brother-in-law, Servianus, who admitted aspirations to the throne both on his own part and that of his grandson, but Hadrian turned against them and forced them to commit suicide. Then he made an unpredictable move. Without being impelled, so far as is known, by mixed motives, he recognized in Marcus the sort of mind and will that Rome particularly needed. He himself might die at any moment, and he knew that no boy of seventeen could govern the Roman Empire. So Hadrian adopted as his son a man of about fifty, Antoninus Pius, who was Marcus's uncle and a person of rare mind and character, on the express condition that he in turn would adopt Marcus as his own son, apprentice him to the imperial office, and assure his succession. This strange last testament of Hadrian was probably the best act he ever performed. His scheme worked to perfection and produced the forty-two years' reign of the uncle and nephew who have come to be known as the two Antonines. On the first of these, Antoninus Pius, Gibbon remarks: "His reign is marked by the rare advantage of furnishing very few materials for history; which is, indeed, little more than the register of the crimes, follies, and misfortunes of mankind."[7] Of the age of the Antonines as a whole he says: "If a man were called to fix the period in the history of the world, during which the condition of the human race was most happy and prosperous, he would, without hesitation, name that which elapsed from the death of Domitian to the accession of Commodus."[8] This is the period of Nerva, Trajan, Hadrian, and the two Antonines.

The two understood each other and worked together in apparently perfect harmony; the reign was a triumph in the cooperation of two reasonable men. For eight years, till Marcus was twenty-five, he was in daily attendance on his uncle, never missing, it is reported, as much as two consecutive days. The young prince was eager to learn from any source. He disliked tension with others and had a remarkable gift for affection, which shows itself in the showers of benediction he pours upon his teachers. Meanwhile he was absorbing from his uncle the arts of diplomacy, of efficiency in the dispatch of business, of compromise where needed, of appeasing frayed tempers, of selecting secretaries, generals, and governors, and of keeping his own poise under all circumstances.

With his love of learning and his distinguished panel of flattering teachers, Marcus was probably something of a prig, but he had a lean, athletic body, liked to box, swim, fish, and hunt, and as he grew became a handsome man of gracious speech and manners. There are few figures in the ancient world whose looks we know so well, for he was idolized from one end of the civilized world to the other, and numerous busts and statues of him have come down to us. I have sometimes thought that if he were to walk at the present moment into the room, dressed in modern coat and trousers, with his reddish hair and beard, his prominent blue eyes, and his look of abstracted, grave authority, I should recognize him at once.

Faustina

In the midst of his studies with his senatorial tutors, Marcus had an experience that deeply affected his own happiness and probably that of the empire itself. At seventeen he was betrothed to Faustina, daughter of the emperor Antoninus, then aged eight or nine. In our eyes the engagement seems an odd one in more than one way. For one thing, the fiancée was too young to make such a choice herself; the marriage was obviously arranged, and the one who arranged it was the emperor himself. For another thing, Marcus was her first cousin; in fact he was legally her brother, since he was the adopted son of Antoninus. Finally, the young Faustina was already engaged to another person. But such difficulties were cobwebs for a Roman emperor, and Antoninus simply issued the necessary decrees; indeed betrothals to kin and at early ages were common in Rome. Marcus waited for seven years till Faustina was adjudged ready, at fifteen or sixteen, for marriage, which meant, by his own account, that he really waited, young Stoic that he was, and did not, as a Roman prince was rather expected to do, dally along the primrose path. Faustina, the only child of Antoninus to reach maturity, was an attractive young lady, whose father was very proud of her. He once wrote to Fronto: "I would rather live on Gyara with her than in this palace without her"[9] (Gyara was an island where exiles were imprisoned).

Faustina presented her husband with at least twelve children, though most of them died in childhood owing to the Roman ignorance of hygiene. Marcus was devoted to her to the end. But she has had a curious fate at the hands of history. It fell to the lot of Marcus to be much away from home, leading the Roman legions that were guarding the Danube against the barbarians; at one period he was absent from Rome for three or perhaps four years continuously. Faustina was not a Stoic like himself; indeed it has been remarked that there is no record of a woman Stoic. She liked the theaters, the dancers, even the gladiators of Rome. Stories arose and

soon spread through the city that she admitted some of these favorites to her private chambers, and the stories in due time penetrated
to the camp of the Emperor beyond the Alps. He seems to have dis-
believed them stolidly and scornfully, but, perhaps by way of check-
ing their increase, he called upon Faustina to join him in the north.
By her solicitude for the welfare of the soldiers serving in that in-
hospitable climate, she earned the title "Mother of the Camp."

It is reported that before one of her confinements—numerous
enough in themselves, one would suppose, to restrain both her and
the tongue of slander—she dreamed that she was giving birth to
two serpents, one more vicious than the other. Shortly afterward
twins were born, of whom one died in infancy. The other grew up
to be one of the most cruel and irresponsible monsters ever to oc-
cupy a throne, the infamous Commodus, who was so unlike his
father as to give color to the rumor that some gladiator had spawned
him, rather than Marcus. Nor was the rumor of such infidelity the
worst that was said of her. Late in life, Marcus had to meet the
totally unexpected revolt of one of his ablest commanders, Avidius
Cassius, who attempted to turn the eastern armies against him. The
historian Cassius Dio records that Cassius was actually encouraged
in his revolt by Faustina, who, considering that Marcus was too old
and weak to hold the rule much longer, conspired to turn over to
Cassius both her person and the empire. This insinuation too Marcus totally rejected. When the revolt failed and Cassius committed
suicide, Marcus, with characteristic generosity toward a respected
foe, burnt all the correspondence that might further have incrimi-
nated him or have compromised Faustina. She started out with him
on the long march from the Danube against the rebels, but she
never finished the journey. She died in a village of the Taurus
mountains. Marcus showered her memory with honors. He issued
new coins bearing her likeness, changed the name of the town
where she died to Faustinopolis, and spurred the Senate to pass a
decree of deification.

We shall probably never know with certainty the truth about

Faustina. Most of the historians and much of the empire passed harsh judgments on her. And it may be that Marcus, with his disdain of emotion and his indifference to pleasure, had too much ice in his veins to make the most congenial partner for a woman of ardent impulse and warm Italian blood. Her temptations to waywardness may have been stronger than we know. In any case, the man who knew her best was unswervingly loyal to her and rejected the indictment with contempt. The verdict should be innocent until proven guilty.

Death of Antoninus

In A.D. 161, when Marcus was nearing forty, the old emperor Antoninus Pius died. He had not been, like Hadrian, a traveler and an empire builder; in a long reign he had hardly left the vicinity of Rome. But he was one of the best of rulers, living simply, though in a palace, dispensing justice evenly, and revered by his people. Cassius Dio, his ancient biographer, describes his end as "very sweet, and like the softest sleep."[10] When he realized that death was at hand, he called in his friends and the members of the imperial council, commended Marcus to them as his successor, and ordered that the gold statue of Fortune, which by custom was placed in the bedroom of the emperor, be now transferred to that of Marcus. Having to name a watchword for his guard that night, he chose the word *Aequanimitas,* then turned away as if to sleep, and never woke.

Seldom have a father and son, let alone adopted son and adoptive father, lived together in such unity of mind; and throughout the remainder of his life Marcus held the character of Antoninus as a light to his own path. Many years later, in his *Meditations,* he jotted down what this memory meant to him.

In all things the disciple of Antoninus. Remember his resolute championship of reason, his unvarying equability, his holiness, his serenity of look, his affability, his dislike of ostentation, his keenness for certitude about the facts; how he would never drop a subject, till he saw into it thoroughly and understood clearly; how he bore unjust reproaches without a word; how he was never in a hurry; how he gave no ear to slander; how accurately he scrutinised character and action; never carping, or craven, or suspicious, or pedantic; how frugal were his requirements, in house and bed and dress and food and service; how industrious he was and how long-suffering . . . . Remember his constancy and evenness in friendship, his forbearance to outspoken opposition, his cheerful acceptance of correction . . . . Remember all this, that so your last hour may find you with a conscience clear as his (6.30).

Problems of an Emperor

When Antoninus died, he expected, as did the Senate, that Marcus should succeed him as sole emperor. There was one objector to this plan, and strangely enough this was Marcus himself. He seemed genuinely averse to so much power and responsibility, even when invested with incomparable honor. He pointed to an expressed wish of Hadrian that when Pius died the power should be shared by Marcus with another adopted son of Pius, Lucius Verus. Marcus refused to accept the headship of the empire unless the Senate agreed that Lucius should share it with him. The astonished Senate complied. Perhaps Lucius's best qualification for the office was a clear perception that Marcus was so much his superior in every respect that he should have the final word.

The imperial pair came to power in a troubled time. The Parthians, whose capital was near the present Baghdad on the distant Tigris, were making forays against the easternmost settlements of Rome, and were invading the Roman province of Armenia at the eastern end of the Black Sea. Marcus appointed Lucius commander of the Roman armies of the east with the commission to drive the invaders back. Fortunately Lucius had as his deputies three of Rome's ablest generals, who recovered Armenia for the empire and turned back the Parthian invaders both in the center and in the south. In these triumphs Lucius had little part. He spent most of his time enjoying the sports and debauches of Antioch, which he made his wartime capital, while his generals and their soldiers did the bitter work of war. But he claimed the glory of their victories. He had some new coins issued in which he took the name of Armeniacus, and he cautioned the historian of his campaign, who was none other than Marcus's old tutor Fronto, to stress his own part in the triumph. Later Roman historians painted him in somber colors, even insinuating that he plotted the death of Marcus. This was probably false. But he was certainly no great aid to his co-emperor, whose burdens were lightened when Lucius suffered a fatal stroke in A.D. 168.

The victory in the east was bought at a heavy price. The returning soldiers brought back with them a plague with which Roman medicine was entirely unable to cope. Marcus called Galen into consultation, the physician who, after Hippocrates, stood first in the ancient world. But the terrible disease eluded even Galen's skill, and he fled from Rome to his home in distant Pergamum. What exactly the disease was no one knows. It has been identified by different modern scholars as bubonic plague, smallpox, and a peculiarly deadly form of typhus. Since Rome was the most densely populated spot in the empire, the population was cut down as with a gigantic scythe. Bodies were piled into carts like logs for removal; and Marcus had to issue an edict against digging up the occupants of old graves to make room for the victims. In the soldiers' barracks military units were decimated. The people thought that Apollo, the god of health, must have been offended, and the front doors of houses were decorated with pitiful offerings designed to induce him to spare those within. Marcus declined to leave, and in his capacity as Pontifex Maximus encouraged these and all other means of protection. To the plague was added another tragic scourge, an overflow of the Tiber, which burst its banks and flooded the city with mud and filth. Marcus was kept busy issuing decrees and trying cases of people driven to crime by desperation. He treated them with characteristic clemency.

War on the Danube

Concern about the plague and flood, however, soon had to give way to the military safety of the empire. The Quadi, Marcomanni, and other tribes that occupied the present Yugoslavia, Hungary, and Rumania were being pressed by the tribes to the north of them, and were restlessly moving south across the Danube. They threatened to engulf the Roman provinces that stood in their way, and unless they were stopped they might soon pour like another flood into Italy itself. Much of the Roman army in Italy had been wiped out by the plague; new troops had to be raised; and the people were too poor to pay for them by taxation. So Marcus held a vast auction of contents of the imperial palace, and "'sold gold, crystal and myrrhine drinking vessels, even royal vases, his wife's silk and gold-embroidered clothing, even certain jewels in fact, which he had discovered in some quantity in an inner sanctum of Hadrian's.'"[11] Marcus adopted similarly extreme methods for filling the depleted ranks of the legions. Slaves were invited to join, with a promise of freedom at the end of their term; criminals were conscripted; special units were formed for gladiators; even policemen from Greek cities were called to service. Marcus concerned himself with the drill and discipline of this motley mass into the likeness of Roman legions.

The effort worked out badly. In the autumn of A.D. 169, he set out at the head of a considerable army from Italian headquarters at Aquileia, near the present Venice, and crossed the Alps, making his winter quarters on the river Save in what is now Yugoslavia. In the spring he undertook a massive crossing of the Danube to deal with the predatory Quadi who lived north of the river. Over this great endeavor silence falls in Roman records, but stray sentences indicate that the advance was in truth a disaster to the Roman arms that probably cost some twenty thousand men. Moreover, the barbarians, exultant with success, let loose a vengeful attack of their own, which took them across the Danube and the Alpine passes into the Italian plain; there, within a few months, they were laying siege to Aquileia itself. Since the enemy controlled the mountain passes, Marcus and his army were cut off and had to send their communications to Rome down the eastern coast of the Adriatic and across that sea in order to keep their connections with Rome. But in the next year the barbarian army, trying to get back to their homeland with immense booty from Italy, were surrounded by the imperial army and largely destroyed.

Marcus Aurelius bore the official title of Caesar, but he was no Julius Caesar, no Napoleon or Wellington. To the reader of his *Meditations,* the thought of his leading legions into battle seems like putting Thomas à Kempis or John Woolman at the head of a band of hardened killers. No doubt Marcus detested his role. But to him that would have been irrelevant if he conceived it to be his duty as head of state, as head indeed of a civilization threatened with drowning under the deluge of barbarism from the north. Though the deluge did finally break the dam and wash Italy and Greece into the Dark Ages, it was not in Marcus's time. He learned strategy rapidly, and between A.D. 171 and 175 he gained such a succession of notable victories over the Quadi and Marcomanni, followed by treaties of peace with them, that the name of Germanicus was conferred upon him. In spite of increasingly frail health, he stayed winter after winter north of the Alps. One of his battles with the savage Jazyges had to be fought on the surface of the frozen Danube, the legionaries holding their formation but keeping one foot on their shields turned turtlewise on the ice to prevent their falling.

Revolt in the East

In the summer of A.D. 175 Marcus was engaged with the Sarmatians, intending to unite their territory into a single Roman province which would include the Quadi and Marcomanni. The campaign was just getting under way when the news reached him that his trusted commander in the east, Avidius Cassius, had raised the standard of revolt. He had gone further, for, hearing the rumor that Marcus had died, he had proclaimed himself the new emperor, with the support of the legions he commanded. This was a challenge with which only Marcus himself could deal adequately. His troops were loyal to him and far outnumbered those of Cassius, so there could be little doubt of the issue if it came to civil war. He at once abandoned the Sarmatian campaign and began the long march from central Europe through Thrace, Asia Minor, and Syria to Cassius's capital in Alexandria. It was while the army was crossing the Taurus mountains on this journey that Faustina died.

According to Cassius Dio's reconstruction, Marcus before setting out made a speech to his troops that no one else would or could have made. Civil war, he said, was perhaps the worst of all evils, and to avoid it he would willingly have put the issue to the vote of the army or the Senate and been ready to abide by the result. But the Senate, on hearing of the revolt, had promptly outlawed Cassius, and Marcus knew that the army was on the whole behind him; nor did he think that his abdication would be for the common good: "it is for the common good that I continue to labour and undergo danger, and have spent so much time here outside Italy, although I am already old and weak, and unable to take food without pain or sleep undisturbed." He had no personal ill will against Cassius; and he hoped that when Cassius learned that the armies of the Danube were marching against him, he would not slay himself or be slain by others, for that would cut Marcus off from the satisfaction of showing the mercy he would like to show; "for surely goodness has not completely perished among men, but a fragment of the ancient virtue remains."[12] Apparently Marcus still thought of Cassius as a friend who had gone wrong through ingratitude and error; his feeling was sorrow rather than anger; and nothing would tempt him into personal vilification.

The long march ended in Alexandria, the second city in the empire, which he had never visited. It had been one of the centers of rebellion. The leading rebels sought him out, gave themselves up, and received extraordinary clemency. Though the popular feelings were not of the friendliest, Marcus helped to win the citizens over by unpretentious conduct. He dressed and behaved like an ordinary Alexandrian. The city was a stronghold of Greek culture, of which Marcus was a devotee, and he was delighted with its museums, its stately buildings, and no doubt with its great library, the treasure house for the literature of the ancient world. On his way home he seized the opportunity to visit Athens, where he established and endowed a professorship in each of the chief reigning philosophies, the Platonic, Aristotelian, Stoic, and Epicurean, besides a fifth in rhetoric. He reached Rome happy to be at home again, but exhausted; except for brief intervals he had been absent nearly eight years. The triumph accorded to him and his army was tremendous.

For two years, A.D. 176–178, Marcus resumed the old life at Rome. He was acclaimed by the people as first in war and first in peace; his military boldness on the frontiers had guaranteed the peace of the homeland. He sat as the supreme judge in many cases; he respectfully addressed the Senate when their approval was required, and sometimes for courtesy's sake when it was not; in accordance with Roman tradition he held public carnivals in the Colosseum; and he was again able to pursue philosophy with zest in his villa at Lanuvium. This period of quiet was not to last long. In the north his old enemies, the Quadi and the Marcomanni, were again threatening to flood downward into Roman territory. The Emperor conceived a new tactic for dealing with them. He would try to make friends and even Romans of them, convert them with arms and suasion into Roman provincials, and help them to bear a share in the protection of what would now be their own empire. He set forth at the head of his legions on the third of August, A.D. 178, and pitched his camp at Vindobonum, the present Vienna. The campaign went well and success seemed imminent when in March of A.D. 180 the Emperor suddenly fell ill. No one knows what the illness was; it may have been the plague. Marcus seems to have realized early that it was serious and might be mortal, and, not wishing to postpone an inevitable end, declined food and drink. Asked on his last night for a watchword, he said, "Go to the rising sun. For I am already setting."[13]

The Other Aurelius

This brief summary is of the outward Aurelius, the man of power and action, who makes the sort of history that historians write. But it is the other Aurelius that the world has been unwilling to let go. Few care now about the marches and countermarches of the Roman commanders. What the centuries have clung to is a notebook of thoughts by a man whose real life was largely unknown to his contemporaries, a man who put down in the midnight dimness of his tent not the events of the day or the plans of the morrow, but something of far more permanent interest, the ideals and aspirations that a rare spirit lived by. "Rare spirit" is indeed too trite a description of this second Marcus, for if we exclude the New Testament, he is unique in the ancient world—unique in his inwardness, in the rigor of his self-scrutiny and of his standards, in his humility, in what Christians would call "the hunger and thirst after righteousness." Marcus was not a philosopher in the sense that the other three men in this book were philosophers. He had no system in the sense of a closely reasoned and logically articulated body of belief; he had nothing like the strenuous precision of Mill, the intellectual subtlety of Sidgwick, or the massive erudition of Renan. The attraction of his little book lies in its being an "Imitatio Christi" without Christ, the impassioned seeking of a pagan after a most exacting kind of goodness. And what makes him of special interest to this study is his profound conviction that to be right is to be reasonable and to be reasonable is to be right.

Stoicism

This principle, like so much else in his creed, Marcus took from Stoicism, and since, without familiarity with the teachings of this school his mind would be unintelligible, we must say a little about it. It was founded by Zeno, probably a Semite who was born in Cyprus but emigrated in early life to Athens, where he started teaching his new doctrine about 300 B.C. He had been exposed both to the intense moralism of the Hebrew prophets and to the eccentric asceticism of the Cynics; and the way from the one to the other he owed largely to Socrates. Unfortunately, while we have the Platonic Socrates before us almost in his entirety, we have only fragments of the distinguished line of Stoic thinkers. We do know that Zeno was followed as head of the Stoic school in Athens by Cleanthes the poet, one of whose poems has come down to us, and by Chrysippus the logician. We know that a later or middle school was led by Panaetius of Rhodes and Posidonius of Syria; the latter in person taught Cicero. And we know that in the later or Roman period the leaders were Seneca the essayist, Epictetus the slave, and Marcus the emperor. Most of these men wrote voluminously, and presumably their books were in the great repository at Alexandria which went up in flames in the sixth century. It is ironic, if it is true, that the Saracen incendiary used—or abused—Greek logic in defense of his action: either these books agree with the Koran and are therefore superfluous, or they do not agree and are therefore pernicious; hence, away with them. So we are left with only odds and ends from a series of splendid minds.

Stoicism as it remains for us is chiefly an ethics, a theory of the way to live. Its central maxims were two: first, live according to nature, and second, live according to reason; live naturally and live reasonably. Both these maxims are so vague that they mean little unless interpreted by the larger background of Stoic speculation.

Though the Stoics were more interested in practice than in specu-lation, they had developed over the years a fairly comprehensive philosophy. Oddly enough when we consider the almost devotional cast of Marcus's *Meditations,* they were materialists. They believed, like most modern scientists, that nature was a single all-embracing system governed by law. This system was composed of matter. Matter in turn embraced four kinds of elements—earth, water, air,

and fire. It was the last element, fire, ethereal but active, that provided the life, warmth, and awareness of conscious bodies. It was
diffused everywhere in varying degrees, so that the world itself was
alive. Gilbert Murray points out that the Greek word *phusis,* usually
translated "nature," really meant for the Greeks, and particularly
for the Stoics, not just the sum of things, but that which animated
all things, something like the élan vital of Bergson. "It is like a soul,
or a life-force, running through all matter as the 'soul' or life of a
man runs through all his limbs. It is the soul of the world."[14]

The World of the Stoics

This world, for Marcus, was a perfect unity; everything was linked
both logically and causally to everything else. "Constantly picture
the universe," he wrote, "as a living organism, . . . and note how
all things are assimilated to a single world-sense, all act by a single
impulse, and all co-operate towards all that comes to pass; and mark
the contexture and concatenation of the web" (4.40). . . . "you
cannot sever any fragment of the connected unity, without mutilat-
ing the perfection of the whole" (5.8). The world was not merely a
system as Euclid's geometry was a system, with everything necessitating everything else, though in fact it was that. Nor was it merely
a great machine in which every part worked smoothly with every
other part in accordance with law, though it was that too. For Marcus it was an object of worship, and one cannot worship either
geometry or a machine. The world was a unity of a further kind.
Because of its order and unity, because of that system of unbroken
law which governed every organ of the body and every star in the
sky, the whole could only be the manifestation of mind. It was one
because it manifested a single world soul.

For Marcus the world was not only ordered and alive, but good.
That is a proposition that many philosophers would regard as
dubious and many others as plainly false. Marcus preferred not to
argue the assertion out beyond saying that in a rational world, the

more one saw, the more certain its goodness became. "All that happens, happens aright. Watch narrowly, and you will find it so. Not merely in the order of events, but in just order of right, as though some power apportions all according to worth" (4.10). "Though I and both my sons be spurned of God, there is be sure a reason" (7.41). What that reason was he might not know, but he was convinced that if one contemplated a rational world with a vision wide enough to embrace the whole, one would see that it is and must be good. I suspect with regret that there is confusion here. "Rational" is an ambiguous term. It may mean in this context that the parts of a whole are logically interconnected, or it may mean that the whole is morally good. But the two meanings are not the same, nor does the first seem to entail the second. Marcus did not clearly distinguish them.

Suppose, however, that he was right in holding the universe to be not only logical but good; what was his duty? Plainly to accept it, not to fight against it. His loyalty to that duty as he saw it was unswerving; it remains, we may fairly say, one of the most striking achievements of the ancient world. Here is a man who may be defeated on the field of battle, who may hear of plots by supposed friends against his life and rule, who is called on with frail health to face the snows of the Alps and the furnace of the eastern desert, who sees most of his children taken from him by death, who may himself be seriously, even mortally ill, but who never whines or protests or complains. Instead there is only the voice of a humble and grateful compliance. "I am in harmony with all, that is a part of thy harmony, great Universe. For me nothing is early and nothing late, that is in season for thee. All is fruit for me, which thy seasons bear, O Nature! from thee, in thee, and unto thee are all things. 'Dear City of Cecrops!' saith the poet: and wilt not thou say, 'Dear City of God'" (4.23).

In recording his musings, Marcus sometimes speaks of God, sometimes of the gods. Is there inconsistency here? Not necessarily. For him, as we have seen, the world was governed by a cosmic con-

sciousness which was a single immanent spirit. But that world was also a congeries of differing areas and elements and activities, and it was natural enough that the Greeks, whom the Romans followed in such matters, should think of these separate components as governed by specialized deities. Poseidon, the Roman's Neptune, was lord of the waters; Apollo was god of the sun and the realm of light; Demeter, or her Roman equivalent, Ceres, was goddess of the earth and harvests and fertility. Of these gods there was no fixed number, and as the empire extended it took in, with a curious religious democracy, the gods of its new subjects. In this respect, Marcus was a singularly catholic theologian. Did he believe that all these motley figures, often beautifully embodied in Greek and Roman statuary, were real existences? Officially he did, for he was not only Emperor but Pontifex Maximus, the head of the Roman religion, who presided at celebrations of these deities and sacrifices to them. But one can only suspect that he did so with tongue in cheek. To a mind as sophisticated as his, these lesser deities were probably symbols of the one divine activity which manifested itself throughout all these domains. If he insisted, as he did, on retaining old forms of Roman worship, it was probably because he saw that myth, besides being a powerful preservative of a people's unity, may carry a truth in metaphorical form that the more correct philosophic formulae may fail to convey.

"Live According to Nature"

Against this background the first Stoic maxim, "Live according to nature," attains more force and meaning. This meaning adds a religious sanction to that of morality, and makes more intelligible Marcus's readiness to accept with thanks whatever nature brings. For after all, the gifts of nature were the gifts, not of chance, but of an Eternal Wisdom.

The maxim, however, bore another and more congenial sense: it

enjoined not only conformity to nature at large but conformity to one's own nature. Marcus would have had some sympathy with a movement of recent days that is sometimes an excuse for self-absorption, but at its best is the main business of life, the search for one's own identity. That identity may not be easy to discover. Every man, according to Marcus, is a little eruption of Deity, "a bright shoot of everlastingness," so he can say that his duty in a deep sense lies in becoming himself. The Commander in Chief of the universe has an immense number and variety of troops at his disposal—carpenters and blacksmiths, cooks and physicians, foot soldiers and cavalrymen, staff officers and officers of the line. His aim is to assign to each man the post he can fill best. The assignment of the cook is to be a good cook, of the carpenter to use his saw and hammer as efficiently as he can, of the staff officer to draw up an adroit and well-judged strategy. In the far-flung campaign of man on earth, our station may be fixed for us, but what we make of ourselves in that station is ours to determine. As Marcus puts it with quaint vividness: "Whatever any one else does or says, my duty is to be good; just as gold or emerald or purple for ever says, Whatever any one else does or says, my duty is to be emerald and keep my proper hue" (7.15). "No one can stop you from living according to the principle of your own nature: nothing will happen to you contrary to the principle of the universal nature" (6.58).

A society in which everyone had a dominant gift that served a socially needed function would be something of a Utopia. There would be no "mute, inglorious Miltons," no Spinozas grinding lenses for a precarious living, none of the graduate students that William James yearned over, who stubbornly pursued the Grail of a doctorate, though they were "the ruins of excellent farmers." Hazlitt's encomium on John Cavanagh, a plain undistinguished man except for one thing, that he played the game of handball better than anyone else on earth, could be widely conferred. Each round peg would gravitate to its round hole, and each square hole would attract its particular square peg. Unhappily, things never work out that way.

Then what? Marcus Aurelius gave much the same stern answer as Carlyle. Our prime business in the world is not to be happy but to do our job, whether it is our own choice or not. If Marcus had had his choice, he would probably have chosen to be a researcher in a great library and an occasional lecturer on philosophy; he had no particular desire to be Emperor of Rome and commanding general of its legions. But he had been selected and sedulously trained for the post, and he chose to be a good soldier in both a literal and a cosmic sense. His ethics was an ethics of "my station and its duties," to use Bradley's phrase. He seems to have felt no exultation in his power, no pride of place; he was carrying out an assigned mission, just as the cook and the carpenter were, and if it happened to be one of enormous responsibility, that made him all the more self-critical of the way he was doing it. If he succeeded, the highest praise he would have accepted was that given to George Herbert's housewife:

> Who sweeps a room, as for thy laws,
> Makes that and th' action fine.

"Live in Accordance with Reason"

The first of the Stoic maxims, then, "Live according to nature," is less simple than it sounds and has long roots in Stoic soil. The same must be said of the second maxim, "Live according to reason." Indeed, since it is Marcus's application of this maxim that is the ground of my present interest in him, I must examine it with some care.

What did he mean by "reason"? He meant the faculty that chiefly distinguishes man from beast. It was a complex of the higher faculties involved in knowing—the power of looking before and after and laying plans for what is not; the ability to dissect a thing into its attributes, of abstracting and attending to each singly, of grasping its connections with others, of making inferences, and weaving things and characters into systems. He conceived of reason much as did Aristotle, who regarded it as the highest of human endowments, an activity which at its best seemed to play free from bodily functions and to have no bodily basis at all. For Marcus it was not only the activity that put man above the beast, but also the activity that he shared with the divine. Human thought at its best, as Socrates showed in the *Meno,* was often concerned with things that never were on sea or land, such as points and straight lines, numbers and logical necessities. We have never seen or felt these things, as we have seen rocks and trees, but we have knowledge of them as certain as of anything that flows in through the senses.

This was the sort of knowledge that God, who was pure intelligence, possessed of all things. Fittingly enough, therefore, it was timeless knowledge. The multiplication table did not begin to be valid when men began to use it in their counting, nor will it lose its validity when man's counting is forever done. No wonder that Kepler when, many centuries later, he felt dawning upon him the mathematical laws that govern the movements of the planets, exclaimed in ecstasy that he was thinking God's thoughts after him. To Western thought, affected so deeply by Christianity, it was natural to make revelation the special channel of *moral* guidance after the manner of the Hebrew prophets and the Sermon on the Mount. That was not the view of the Greek thinkers or of Marcus Aurelius. All knowledge at its best and clearest was revelation. "God sees men's Inner Selves stripped of their material shells and husks and impurities. Mind to mind, his mental being touches only the like elements in us derivative and immanent from him" (12.2). Since the structure of the universe consists of an order of divine reason, he who understands it repeats or participates in God's understanding. "To the reasoning being the act which is according to nature is likewise according to reason" (7.11).

We are ready for the next step in the Stoic line of thought. If reason is man's highest faculty and a reflection in him of the divine wisdom, it should be made the guide of life. Of course there are other claimants for the position of guide and judge of conduct. Pleasure is perhaps the most powerful one, but our passions for wealth, for power, for fame, for athletic prowess, for commercial success may and do take complete command in the minds of many. None of these interests will stand examination as the true guide, and in every chapter of his book Marcus comes back to his emphasis on reason as the sole reliable judge. In one of his opening paragraphs he thanks an early instructor for teaching him "never, for one instant, to lose sight of reason" (1.8). He reminds himself to "suffer this governing part of you no longer to be in bondage, no longer to be a puppet pulled by selfish impulse, no longer to be indignant with what is allotted in the present or to suspect what is allotted in the future" (2.2, Farquharson's translation).[15] He insists: "it is a property of reasonable and intelligent movement to limit itself and never to be worsted by movements of sense or impulse; for each of those belong[s] to the animal in us, but the movement of intelligence resolves to be sovereign and not to be mastered by those movements outside itself" (7.55, Farquharson). The court life of an emperor stands in particular need of this restraint. "Had you a stepmother and a mother too, you would be courteous to the former, but for companionship would turn continually to your mother. For you the court is one, philosophy the other. To her then turn and turn again, and find your refreshment, for she makes even court life seem bearable to you, and you in it" (6.12).

Marcus went so far as to hold that to act reasonably was always to act rightly. It is reason that tells us what is right and what is wrong. To many modern readers this would seem an absurd overrating of intellect in practical life. The orthodox Christian would say that his ultimate guidance comes from revelation through Scripture; many others would say that it comes through conscience, an organ variously conceived; the logical positivists who were flourishing in the mid-1900s held that there was no objective right or wrong to discover, that when I called an action right or wrong, I was merely making an exclamation of liking or aversion. But it is significant that the outstanding moralists of the last hundred years—I mean such men as Sidgwick, Bradley, Rashdall, Prichard, Ross, and

Moore—all agreed that moral insight was intellectual. For most of them such insight lay in the weighing against each other of the goods and bads produced by conduct, and, though fallible, was an attempt at objective truth. Marcus conceived it in essentially the same way, though he flatly rejected the utilitarianism of his time, made popular by Epicurus. A good man, before keeping a promise or returning a borrowed book or paying a debt, does not calculate what profit there will be in it for himself or others; he chooses honesty not as the best policy, but because he sees it to be right and reasonable. "What more do you want in return for a service done? Is it not enough to have acted up to nature, without asking wages for it? Does the eye demand a recompense for seeing, or the feet for walking?" (9.42.) "Reasonable acts are called right acts" (5.14, Farquharson) because they are the natural functions of reasonable minds.

Wrongdoing as Wrong Thinking

Having made reason thus the judge and guide of conduct, it was easy for Marcus to take a further step, in which he was following, at a distance of six centuries, a far more penetrating thinker than himself. One of the favorite teachings of Socrates had been that virtue is knowledge, and its corollary that vice is ignorance. Both the views at first glance seem absurd. Socrates maintained that if a man looked clearly at a proposed action in the light of its conditions and consequences, and saw plainly that it was right, he would be drawn to it as inevitably as the bee is drawn to the flower. Human nature is essentially good, in the sense that if its highest part is given sway, it will go right automatically. "But surely," it will be said, "there are any number of people who know that they cannot afford a new car but buy it nevertheless; many who know that sweets are fattening and have set out to reduce their weight, yet, with a box of chocolates at their elbow, allow the resolution to evaporate in ignominy." "Yes, of course," Socrates (and Marcus) would have answered, "but that is because they have allowed their vision to be clouded. At the moment of buying the car, the buyer is *not* seeing the act in the light of what it means to his exchequer, family, and future. The person who reaches out for the chocolates has allowed the connection between sweets and obesity to fall out of focus. He takes a worse course because at the moment of decision he is acting in ignorance."

Now this is anything but absurd. It covers by far the larger number of cases where, supposedly knowing the right, we do the wrong.[16] It was clear to Marcus, as it was to Plato, that men are only brokenly and partially rational, that their reason is seated atop a volcano of seething feelings and desires, and that these lower parts of human nature are continually pushing aside the counsels of reflective foresight. Such foresight, as a modern evolutionist would put it, is a recent and fragile addition to the complement of human faculties; and, as Marcus insists, we are cousins of the animals in the nonrational parts of our being. In most men still the animal impulses of hunger, fear, lust, anger, gregariousness, and the emotions that form part of them, dominate conduct and make impartial judgment all but impossible. It was the realization of this fact of human nature that made Marcus the compassionate mind that he was. Men did not choose evil as evil; their passions first gilded it for them into the guise of something good, and thus they acted under illusion. "'*No soul*,' says the philosopher [Plato], '*willfully misses truth*'; no, nor justice either, nor wisdom, nor charity, nor any other excellence. It is essential to remember this continually; it will make you gentler with every one" (7.63). For "every wrongdoer is really misguided and missing his proper mark" (9.42). And Marcus seems to have practiced what he preached. We have already seen that when his best general, Avidius Cassius, committed first treason and then suicide, Marcus's comment was that he was sorry to have missed the chance to meet and pardon him.

Whether one agrees or not with Socrates and Marcus in this matter, one must agree with both that the secret of controlling

action lies in controlling thought. If one thinks of an act exclusively, one tends to do it. To take a familiar example, who of us had not stood on some precipice or other height and thought of falling or jumping over? Even though one is perfectly normal, if one gives oneself to the thought exclusively, one feels one's legs tingling with the impulse to jump, and it may be prudent to sit down and think of something else. Emile Coué, after many experiments, said that if a person stood erect and gave himself entirely to the thought of fall- *
ing backward, he invariably did. The thought, if really exclusive, carried the action with it. James held that such "ideo-motor action" was the fundamental form of will.[17] In short, "as a man thinketh in his heart, so is he." But just as the exclusive thought of something tends to the doing of it, so the investment of it by thought with its complicated results inhibits the action. Hamlet is the classic case. Moved powerfully to action, he stops and thinks:

> And thus the native hue of resolution
> Is sicklied o'er with the pale cast of thought . . . .

Though the reflective man is far more likely to act judiciously than the man of impulse, some few persons are in danger of thinking so much that they are unable to act at all. Philosophy, says Royce, is not for everyone.

The Stoic War on Emotion

No one would now deny that reasonable living requires the control of emotion by thought. Unfortunately the Stoics tried not merely to control feeling but to annihilate it. Anger, fear, grief, pity were for them not the allies but the enemies of reason, and it was better to get rid of them altogether than to try to tame and harness them. That so extreme an attitude should be regarded as conformable to human nature is not easy to sympathize with or to understand. It is true that anger often leads to the unleashing of tongue and fists and to vindictive forms of punishment, which the Stoics rejected in principle. But, as McDougall pointed out, anger is sometimes essential, as in putting the fear of the law into those who would take advantage of others. As to fear, it is what such people ought to feel, and the fear of illness, extreme pain, and death are at least eminently natural, even though the Stoics found it easy to show that they were often groundless. It is hardest of all to go along with the Stoics about such emotions as grief and pity. When Anaxagoras was told that his son had died, his detached comment was: "I never supposed that I had begotten an immortal." The scholar Anthony Birley remarks that what we call "natural affection" was "a quality which the Roman upper-classes lacked—in fact, as Fronto pointed out to Lucius, there was no word for it in Latin."[18] Pity too was an emotion to be avoided. In Seneca's *De Clementia* elaborate distinctions are drawn between clemency, as a rational disposition to be moderate in imposing punishments, and pity, which is set down as a feeble emotional flinching at the sight of suffering. "The sage will console those who weep, but without weeping with them   He will feel no pity. . . . His countenance and his soul will betray no emotion as he looks upon the withered legs, the tattered rags, the bent and emaciated frame of the beggar."[19] He will help the beggar as a suffering human being; but he will not share the suffering himself.

Marcus read Seneca and the other Stoics, and seems to have given a formal assent to this inhuman theory of emotion as disease. He aims at freedom from "passions that estrange from reason's dictates" (2.5); he holds that "to be vexed or angry or afeared, is to make oneself a runaway" (10.25) from the life of reason. But the eyes that peer through this iron mask are those of a warmhearted human being, even while he is preaching his ruthless doctrine. In recounting with characteristic gratitude what he owed to one of his teachers, Sextus, he records: "From Sextus, kindliness; . . . the universal cordiality, which made his society more agreeable than any flattery, . . . avoiding all display of anger or emotion, and showing a perfect combination of unimpassioned yet affectionate concern" (1.9). His "whoops of blessing" over his teachers, his "affectionate concern" about his friends shown in the letters to Fronto, his desolation at the loss of his children, and his love for Faustina, apparently maintained through life and death, are not the behavior of a man with a stone where his heart should be.

Pain

Better known than their attitude toward the emotions is the Stoics' attitude toward pain. Here they faced a supreme test, and they met it, if not with complete wisdom, at least with extraordinary courage. Pain they regarded as an affair of the body; but if intense, it could subvert the equanimity and control of the mind. They did not deny its reality like the present-day Christian Scientists; it was an obtrusively existent bodily evil; but it could be mitigated by prudent strategy. Marcus's main concern about it was that it should not reach and distort his soul, his higher faculties. "In sickness or pain remind yourself that it cannot demean or vitiate your pilot understanding; it does not impair it on the universal or the social side. In most cases you may find support in the saying of Epicurus, that 'pain cannot be past bearing or everlasting, if only you bear in mind its limits, and do not let fancy supplement them'" (7.64). Again, "the soul can maintain its own unclouded calm, and refuse to view [pain] as evil. For every judgment or impulse or inclination or avoidance is within, and nothing evil can force entrance there" (8.28).

Such philosophic considerations do not seem very powerful as analgesics, and a sharp toothache can end abruptly the profoundest philosophizing. Nevertheless Marcus had hold of an important truth when he said that in the presence of pains we should "not let fancy supplement them." Pain is a puzzle. Consider that a football player can receive a serious injury and not even be aware of it until after the game is over. What does that say about pain? Surely this, that the mere direction of attention can make a great difference; that when attention is strongly focused in another direction, what would normally arouse intense pain may cause none at all. Surgical opera-

tions have been successfully performed under the hypnotic suggestion that they will be painless. On the other hand, persons who go
to a dentist with the expectation of intense pain and concentrate on
the first prick of the anesthetic needle as its herald are far more likely
to experience it. Marcus was surely right in maintaining that the
power of thought over pain, though its exact laws are unknown, is
much greater than is generally supposed. He went so far as to say:
"If you are pained by anything without, it is not the thing [that]
agitates you, but your own judgment concerning the thing; and
this it is in your own power to efface" (8.47). To be sure, this is
Sparta speaking, not Athens. It is a doctrine for heroes, but hardly
for plain persons with normal nerves.

The tragedy of Stoicism is that in its very dedication to man's
highest faculty, reason, it developed an inhuman scorn for his lower
experiences. It made one or two helpful suggestions, as we have
seen, for countering pain, but its main suggestion was that of Keble
to Pusey about dealing with doubt: put it down by main force. The
Stoic heroes were men like Posidonius, who once when he was ill
and in much pain was called upon by Pompey in the hope of hearing a lecture on philosophy. When Pompey found the philosopher
in such extremities, he saluted him and started to leave, expressing
his disappointment that he was not able to hear him lecture. "But
you are able," was the reply, "nor can I allow that bodily pain
should cause so great a man to come to me in vain." Whereupon
Posidonius poured out a discourse with his usual eloquence, only
pausing occasionally when interrupted by paroxysms of pain to exclaim, "You are making no impression, pain! . . ."[20] Marcus thanks
Providence for having introduced him to the works of Epictetus,
the knowledge of which he regarded as one of the chief blessings of
his life. He must have been familiar with the story of how the slave
Epictetus was once being beaten by a sadistically cruel master. He
warned his master that continuing might break his leg. The man did
go on and did break the leg. Epictetus merely remarked, "I told
you you would do so," but refused to descend to his master's level

of anger or abuse, holding that, being what he was, he was bound to act in accordance with his nature. "Not to do likewise," Marcus observed, "is the best revenge" (6.6).

Reasonableness about Death

For most people the greatest of evils is probably not illness or pain, but death. The *Meditations* are thickly strewn with reflections on the transiency of life and the imminence of death; Marcus seems almost obsessed by them. "A free man thinks of nothing less than death," said Spinoza;[21] but to this Marcus is a conspicuous exception. What is interesting about his thought of death is not so much his conception of it, which followed that of other Stoic philosophers, but his inward attitude toward it. The event itself was prosaic enough—earth to earth, dust to dust, oblivion. It was clear that the body dissolved away; the soul too, though invisible, was material, a sort of fiery ether, and was presumably reabsorbed into the cosmic ether. Personality ceased. Marcus obviously did not like this conclusion and hints at the possibility of some kind of survival. "Death, in a universe of atoms, is dispersion; but if all is a unity, death is either extinction or transmutation" (7.32). But what such "transmutation" meant remained a mystery.

Death was in effect a dreamless sleep. Was there anything to be feared in that? Marcus thought not. We knew what it was like; we had spent many nights in it, and before our births many thousands of years in it. Peace and repose deserved welcome rather than fear. Among the pagan philosophers, who for the most part took death as the end, the alternative was the continuance of one's old personality, as Socrates thought; but the idea that this continued life might be one of penance and torture seems not to have entered their heads. It is strange that the introduction of endless terror should have been contributed by Christianity, which, ignoring the doctrine that God is love, consigned all who lacked faith to unending misery. Untroubled by such nightmares, Marcus took death as he tried to take other events, with equanimity. "Dying after all is but one among life's acts; there too our business is 'to make the best of it'" (6.2). By this he did not mean that we should take it lightly. As an important and certain event, we should prepare for it. He thought, for example, that our higher faculties, those of judgment, analysis, and inference, were the first to go, and that it was prudent, therefore, to make our plans regarding death and its consequences early, while yet those powers were fresh (3.1). On this point of the early decline of the higher powers, Marcus has, I think, been proved wrong: the life of the athlete is a short one, while much of the best work of philosophers has been done in later years. Marcus spoke with more authority when he held that the thought of death was a good medicine for pride. One can hardly be the first man in the civilized world without strong temptations to self-glorification. But "Death put Alexander of Macedon and his stable boy on a par" (6.24). It is the archdemocrat, with no trace of respect for persons.

There is much in the *Meditations* about how we should live in light of the transiency of life. We do not know when "time's winged chariot," which is never far behind us, will catch up, and this should lead us to sit down and order our "priorities." Dr. Johnson grimly remarked that nothing so concentrated the mind as the knowledge that one was to be hanged a day or two later. Johnson himself was terrified of death; Marcus was not; but still he mused on the transiency of life again and again. "He who realizes that at any moment he may be called on to leave the world and to depart from among men, commits himself without reserve to do justice in all his actions, to Nature in all that befalls. To what will be said or thought of him, to what will be done against him, he does not give a thought; but is content with two things only—to be just in his dealings and glad at his apportioned lot" (10.11). Men should so order their affairs as to be ready at any time for their discharge from service. The last of Marcus's jottings is: "Serenely take your leave; serene as he who gives you the discharge" (12.36). And he fortified this serenity by the curiously cogent and simple argument of Epicurus to prove that we never meet death at all: while we are here, it is not, and when it is here, we are not.

Bacon, in his little essay "Of Death," criticizes the Stoics for making too much of death. It is well, he holds, to think about it enough to make one's peace with it, but not so constantly as to cast a long shadow of morbidity over one's life. Life is for achieving certain great goods, and what is most important about them is their goodness, not the time they last. Death haunts the *Meditations* and accounts for much of its pervasive melancholy.

Is it permitted us to leave life when we will? According to the Western religious tradition, God has "fixed his canon 'gainst self-slaughter," and suicide commonly brings not only disapproval from others but a taint of the macabre that may hang about a family. Things were otherwise in ancient Rome. Life was cheaper and death more familiar; it was called for by the crowds at gladiatorial shows; the rate of infant deaths was appalling; and people were far more helpless against disease. Furthermore death did not bear the eschatological terror that it bore for Jonathan Edwards' "sinners in the hands of an angry God." If death was repose, the Stoic teachers felt that one had a right to it if for any reason life had hopelessly lost its savor or become a crushing burden to others. Stoicism laid stress on this right to part with life when it had become a liability, and held in admiration, not in contumely, those who exercised that right. Zeno, the founder of the sect, Cleanthes, his successor, Cato the younger, a symbol of probity and courage to the Romans, and Seneca the moralist were all Stoics, and all ended their own lives at the time and in the way that seemed to them fitting. Marcus himself seems to have hastened the end when he saw it was inevitable. Needless to say, he was not in favor of playing fast and loose with life, throwing it away romantically or impulsively; that would clearly be against reason. But sometimes reason approved. "The cabin smokes—so I take leave of it. Why make ado? But so long as there is no such notice to quit, I remain free, and none will hinder me from doing what I will; that is, to conform to the nature of a reasonable social being" (5.29).

Pleasure and Happiness

Was life for the Stoic, then, all a matter of grim and military self-control, with no place for spontaneous happiness or pleasure? If these things were taken as ends, after the manner of the fashionable Epicureans, the Stoics did repudiate them. But in order to understand their view, one needs to see that there is a difference between pleasure and happiness: pleasure is the satisfaction of the short-range impulses like hunger, thirst, sex, the seeing of a play, the winning of a game; happiness attends the satisfaction of the long-range endeavors of a life, finding oneself through a vocation, developing a system of thought, raising a family, intercourse with other minds. For a creature endowed with reason, that is, with ability to see what was important and what was not, the deliberate pursuit of the satisfactions of the moment was a prostitution of its powers. Not that one was never to relax in the enjoyment of these things; but man was a being who lived on various levels, pleasure of a sensual kind is something shared with the animals, and belonged on the lower levels of one's constitution. It was the teaching of Zeno that virtue was self-sufficient for happiness, and of Seneca that "Pleasure [or, as we should say, happiness] is the companion, not the guide, of our course." "We do not love virtue because it gives us pleasure, but it gives us pleasure because we love it."[22]

Marcus Aurelius took a similar view. To follow reason was to gain the happiness of peace within and a lasting self-respect. "In the constitution of the reasoning being I perceive no virtue in mutiny against justice; in mutiny against pleasure I see self-control" (8.39). And self-control brought the highest happiness. In line with this conviction that man was a stratified creature with reason at the top, Marcus accepted unprotestingly the extreme view of the Stoics that virtue was an affair of all or nothing. Either an act conformed to reason and was therefore perfectly right, or it did not, and then it fell into the dark region where all acts are black. This was not wholly without evidence. If you use your reason to add 7 and 5, there is only one right answer, and if you say 11, you are just as truly wrong as if you say 1,000. So Marcus and his school refused, at least formally, to recognize degrees of virtue, although of course he did not treat others or administer justice in accordance with this theory. Aurelius was obviously a better man and a better ruler than Nero, even though both fell short of perfection. Indeed the Stoics would have been nearer the truth if they had said that all rightness is a matter of degree. A respected former teacher of mine, Professor H. A. Prichard, said he doubted whether he had ever done a right act in his life, and though he was a very good man, this was quite possibly true. A right act depends, in part at least, upon its consequences in the way of intrinsic values, and such consequences extend so far into the future that one can never be sure one has exhausted them or therefore where the action lies on the ethical scale. Probability, as Butler said, is the guide of life.

The Passionless Sage

What would the perfect Stoic be like? He would be the famous "passionless sage," whose inward life was untouched by the seductions of pleasure or the assaults of pain. He would not be ambitious for wealth or reputation or power or property, for these were unnecessary to the health of the inward man and might prove more distracting than helpful. Anger, envy, jealousy, and malice would be cut off by his understanding that human nature is what it is, and that aberrations will only be worsened by retorts in kind.

A man so minded, and committed finally to the pursuit of virtue, is indeed a priest and minister of gods, true to that inward and implanted power, which keeps a man unsoiled by pleasure, invulnerable by pain, free from all touch of arrogance, innocent of all baseness, a combatant in the greatest of all combats, which is the mastery of passion, steeped in justice to the core, and with his whole heart welcoming all that befalls him as his portion . . . . He forgets not his bond of brotherhood with every rational creature; nor that the law of man's nature implies concern for all men; and that he must not hold by the opinion of the world, but of those only who live conformably to nature (3.4).

The Stoic, it must be admitted, sounds at times like the Pharisee who was concerned with nothing but his own inward purity and conformity to law. He was not a good Samaritan, melting with sympathy for suffering, and Christian love remains a blank in Roman ethics. But it did have its own substitute. Marcus wrote of the "bond of brotherhood with every rational creature," by which he meant that among men there was a network of rights and duties constructed by reason. If I prize a book for the illumination it gives me or a statue for the beauty I find in it, then I must admit, if I am reasonable, that a like illumination or a like experience of beauty in someone else is also to be prized; it is the quality of the experience that makes it good, not the fact that it is mine or yours. If wisdom and beauty are good in my own life, then it is my rational duty to grant they are the same in others' lives; and it is the rational right of others to demand that I do so. And these reciprocal relations of rights and duties do not hold between you and me merely; they hold between all men everywhere. Here in bud is the idea of a world city with a world citizenship, an international brotherhood that knows no fences of nation, sex, or race. "You are part of a social whole, a factor necessary to complete the sum; therefore your every action should help to complete the social life. Any action of yours that does not tend, directly or remotely, to this social end, dislocates life and infringes its unity. It is an act of sedition . . ." (9.23). "Socially, as Antoninus, my city and country is Rome, as a man, the world" (6.44). It is hardly possible to overrate the importance of this idea. It carries in germ the conception of the brotherhood of men as rational beings, of a United Nations appealing to a common reason, of world law, of a world city or state.

Determinism

Marcus carried much farther this notion of a world community bound together by reason. The whole universe was such a community. Every event that happens issues from converging lines of causation that run back into the infinite past, and every event will contribute to forming an indefinite future. And Marcus believed, truly I think, that the connection of causality is not just one of uniform sequence, or *B* always following *A,* though for no intelligible reason. "Subsequents follow antecedents by bond of inner consequence; it is no merely numerical sequence of arbitrary and isolated units, but a rational interconnexion" (4.45). That implies that the world is an intelligible whole, whether we succeed in understanding it or not; indeed that has been the postulate of the great tradition of rationalism in philosophy. Marcus was an emphatic determinist. "Whatever befalls was fore-prepared for you from all time; the woof of causation was from all eternity weaving the realisation of your being, and that which should befall it" (10.5). "Does aught befall you? It is well—a part of the destiny of the universe ordained for you from the beginning; all that befalls was part of the great web" (4.26).

Now if the world is a system of this sort, there are no rifts in nature, no miracles, no luck good or bad, no accidents, nothing that with sufficient knowledge would not be predictable. Such determinism was for Marcus a ground for general compassion. If you destroyed yesterday a picture or a reputation, and in doing so did what you could have avoided, what the indeterminist says to you is: "You did what was wrong, what you knew to be wrong, and what you need not have done. What ground for compassion do you leave me?" The determinist says: "Poor fellow, given your nature and nurture, I knew you only did what you had to do. There but for the grace of genes go I."

William James once said in his whimsical way that the best attitude to take toward free will and determinism was to claim freedom for yourself and count everyone else as determined. One can then say of the rest of the world, *Tout comprendre c'est tout pardonner.* This is an incoherent position, and it certainly sounds inconsistent for the Stoics to urge determinism while insisting that the passionless sage is free. To this, however, Marcus had an answer. Suppose that what a man wants above all is to behave reasonably; suppose that at a certain point his reason makes the right act clear, and he does it. Did he act freely or not? The answer is, Yes and No. The self that wanted to act reasonably was the highest self, the rational and distinctively human self. It looks forward, sees the greatest good, and is irresistibly drawn to it. Is he determined? Yes, for his choice had been appointed by a rational insight. Is he free? Yes, for his choice issued from his highest self; he has done what that self wanted to do. A self thus acting from rational insight is acting freely. When the mathematician is making his deductions, and his thought is caught up and carried along by logical necessity to a valid conclusion, is he thinking freely? Yes again, though he is under the constraint of the necessity he is following. This is at once a paradox of the rationalist system and its solution, not only for Marcus but for such great successors as Spinoza and Hegel.

It will be clear by now that Marcus Aurelius did have a system of thought, its parts fairly firmly cemented together. But in the one small book he has left us, this system must be read between the lines, developed from stray hints, and woven together from cryptic aphorisms, detached and incomplete sentences, and even exclamations. He was not a philosopher at all in the sense that the other three masters in this book were philosophers. He was a thinker of the intuitive, the Emersonian type. It is said that Emerson in his later years was lecturing on a summer's day when a breeze came in at the window and scattered the leaves of his manuscript on the floor. He leaned down, shuffled them together as they came, without noticing page numbers, and went peacefully on. His utterances did not need to follow any one sequence; they stood on their own feet; why worry? The *Meditations* is that sort of whole. Marcus was a Roman, not greatly drawn to discursive thought, but fascinated by the problems of action, of dealing with people, of adjustment to work, of maintaining serenity and reasonableness in a whirl of exacting business. He was not one of the "intellectual athletes" whom Arnold admired from a distance and distrusted; he was a moralist whom people read to imbibe more courage and quiet of mind. His book, said one of his admirers, Renan, was "the most human of all books." It may not have seemed so from our discussion. Let us try to get a more balanced view of it by turning to some of the practical musings that are typical of both the book and the man.

A Miscellany of Teachings

Getting Things Done. Marcus advises himself: "seldom and only when driven to it, to say or write, 'I have no time'; and not to indulge the tendency to cry off from duties arising out of our natural relations with those about us, on the pretext of press of business" (1.12); "nowhere to be in a hurry or to procrastinate"; "no bustle, complete order, strength, consistency" (1.15, 16, Farquharson). Marcus felt the need, if he were to make decisions wisely, to bring all his powers to bear on a problem; this he could not do in an atmosphere of hurry; so he strove for the inner peace that would enable him to contemplate things clearly.

Serenity. He recognized that many men, to secure this inner peace, need to "seek retirement in country house, on shore or hill"; but such withdrawal was not necessary to one who was master of his own mind. If you attain such mastery, "at what hour you will, you can retire into yourself. Nowhere can man find retirement more peaceful and untroubled than in his own soul; specially he who hath stores within . . . . Ever and anon grant yourself this retirement, and so renew yourself" (4.3). Marcus could quietly retire into himself amid the roar of the Colosseum and conduct business as if he were at home.

Simplicity. Marcus's serenity was due in part to his insistence on simplicity, the trimming away of superfluities. Arnold translates from the *Meditations:* "The greatest part of what we say or do being unnecessary, if a man takes this away, he will have more leisure and less uneasiness. Accordingly, on every occasion a man should ask himself: 'Is this one of the unnecessary things?' Now a man should take away not only unnecessary acts, but also unnecessary thoughts, for thus superfluous acts will not follow after."[23]

Optimism. The courts of most Roman emperors were sinks of depravity, and even Marcus was surrounded by a motley set of characters. Without being blind to their faults, he had his own way of getting on with them. "At dawn say to yourself first: 'I shall meet inquisitive, ungrateful, insolent, treacherous, slanderous men.'" But he reminds himself at once of the principle of which Socrates had persuaded him, that these men at least meant well in the sense that they were trying to live up to such light as they had: "all these qualities come from their ignorance of good and evil." And if a person has his redeeming qualities, why not attend to them rather than to his shortcomings. He tells himself: "think of the good qualities of those around you, when you want to cheer yourself up: the energy of one, the modesty of another, the generosity of another, and so on. For there is nothing so cheering as the images of the virtues shining out in the character of one's contemporaries . . . ."[24] And something of the Rembrandt eye shows itself at times: "The old woman and the old man will have an ideal loveliness, as youth its ravishing charm, made visible to eyes that have the skill" (3.2).

Pride and Humility. Lecky, the historian of Roman morals, writes: "Take away pride from the ancient Stoic or the modern Englishman, and you would have destroyed the basis of many of his noblest virtues . . . ."[25] One of the most striking things about Marcus was his curious absence of pride—curious because pride was endemic to the people whose boast was *civis Romanus sum,* and all the more curious in a man who, as head of the civilized world, was greeted on every side with adulation. He knew the danger of pride, even of pride in virtue, and was on his guard against it. "Be just and temperate and a follower of the gods; but be so with simplicity, for the pride of modesty is the worst of all" (12.27).[26] The only achievement that would have given him genuine pride was reasonableness, but that was an ideal of impossible difficulty, which incited both constant striving and constant failure. "If any one can convince and

show me that some view or action of mine is wrong, I will cheerfully change: I seek the truth, which never yet hurt any man. What
hurts is persisting in self-deceit and ignorance" (6.21).

The fact is that, as boy and man, he had a singularly docile and
teachable spirit; he was the antithesis of an Alexander, a Danton, or
a Napoleon. In his correspondence with Fronto, he records receiving
in the same post two letters from the master, one of them citing a
humiliating list of blunders he had made in a recent essay, the other
a letter of unqualified praise. ". . . I swear to you . . . ," he writes,
"that the first letter gave me the greater pleasure and that as I read
it I exclaimed several times 'How lucky I am!' "[27] He felt lucky in
having a master who would frankly put him in his place on his
knowledge of Greek. This is an odd reaction of schoolboy to teacher,
though there is no reason to doubt its sincerity. On the other hand,
his conquest of the things that would turn most people's heads, such
as fame or wealth, seemed to him of so little value that he could
hardly be called humble about them; he scorned them. He had the
greatest fame of any man then living. But he writes: "does some
bubble of fame torment you? Then fix your gaze on swift oblivion,
on the gulf of infinity this way and that, on the empty rattle of
plaudits and the undiscriminating fickleness of professed applause,
on the narrow range within which you are circumscribed. The whole
earth is but a point, your habitation but a tiny nook thereon . . ."
(4.3). Or was it wealth that was the magnet and source of pride?
For that too he cared little or nothing. He delighted in getting back
into the woolen tunic of the farmer; in Alexandria he walked the
streets in the clothes of the plain citizen; he asked his mother, who
was one of the wealthiest women in Rome, to give her fortune not
to him but to his sister. He was one of those for whom the forfeiture
of fame and wealth seemed hardly humility at all, since they were
not things he prized.

Anger and Resentment. The Stoic is the most military of moralists, in that he demands the most inflexible self-control, the most
iron courage in the face of peril, poverty, or pain. There is one emo-

tion for which the military man has been not so much admired as
indulged, namely anger or resentment, particularly if his honor is
involved; failure to feel and act on this emotion has often been read
as cowardice. It was with great difficulty that the practice of dueling
for offended pride or honor was finally put down; in England it
required the execution of the successful duelist and in America the
death of Alexander Hamilton to stop the practice. It is the more
surprising, therefore, to find that Marcus, himself a military man,
considered anger and resentment signs of weakness. "When any one
does you a wrong, set yourself at once to consider, what was the
point of view, good or bad, that led him wrong. As soon as you perceive it, you will be sorry for him, not surprised or angry" (7.26).
"In fits of anger remind yourself that true manliness is not passion,
but gentleness and courtesy, the more masculine as well as the more
human: this it is, and not irritation or discontentment, that implies
strength and nerve and manhood; the absence of passion gives the
measure of its power. Anger, like grief, is a mark of weakness; both
mean being wounded, and wincing" (11.18). Or more briefly: "Another's error—let it lie" (9.20).

Thus true courage lay in the control of anger and resentment,
not in giving them free rein. This was the result partly of Marcus's
determinism, partly of his conviction that the wrongdoer was acting
in ignorance of his own and others' good. He insisted that "before
the eye of god man should not ever cherish resentment or indigna-
tion. How can it be an evil for you, to follow the present authorisa-
tion of your own [rational] nature, and to accept the seasonable
course of Nature? Have you not been set here as an instrument for
the advantage of the universe?" (11.13.) It followed, again, that
punishment of a vindictive kind was wrong. Punishment of course
was necessary, but it must be inflicted only for the sake of deterrence
or reform.

The Self. Marcus constantly stressed the fact that the self was invincible, inaccessible, inviolable. And he went so far as to identify
the self with reason: "your true self—your understanding" (12.3).

When he said that anger and fear and laziness and drunkenness cannot touch the self, he did not mean to deny that these things may destroy men utterly. He meant that so long as this highest part of us retains its clearness of vision, so long as the reason which enables us to understand why men make such fools of themselves is doing its work, then things are not in the saddle and riding mankind; the self remains in command. Impulses are directed toward ends; thought can provide them with the proper ends or, by redirecting attention, deny them their ends until they wither away. Strength of will, as James would put it, lies in control of attention. Far more largely than we realize, the moulding power is intelligence; "for the motions of reason and mind are self-determinant, and refuse subordination to the motions of sense or impulse, both of which are animal in kind. The intellect claims primacy, and will not be brought into subjection; and justly so, for its function is to use all the rest" (7.55).[28]

Two Flaws

These are a few of the maxims with which the *Meditations* swarm. They do not, as we have said, make an ordered whole, though they lie within the larger framework of the Stoic system. Without subjecting this system to any formal examination, we can see two large flaws in it that stand out clearly in the light of modern knowledge.

First is its defective view of human nature, which is part of the nature to which the Stoics held we should conform. It is not true that man is a junction of two alien elements at war with each other, the animal and the human. The human rests on, continues, and crowns the animal nature. Man is more rightly conceived as a set of impulses, each one of them rooted in our animal past, but each endowed with a cognitive, an emotional, and a conative side. Self-realization is a legitimate aim, but it consists in developing these drives in the fullest and most harmonious way. The truly great of the world—the Leonardos, the Goethes, the Einsteins—are neither

Puritans nor sybarites; they are persons of powerful impulses directed to ends that their nature appoints. It is the business of reason to envisage and harmonize the ends of these passions and impulses, to encourage, not suppress them.

> Let us not always say
> "Spite of this flesh today
> I strove, made head, gained ground upon the whole!"
> As the bird wings and sings,
> Let us cry "All good things
> Are ours, nor soul helps flesh more, now, than flesh helps soul!"

Second, just as the Stoics misconceived the *human* nature that we must conform to, so they misconceived *cosmic* nature. "I am in harmony with all, that is a part of thy harmony, great Universe. . . . All is fruit for me, which thy seasons bear, O Nature!" (4.23). At this even the devoted Renan exclaims, "Ah, this is too much resignation, dear master!"[29] And surely he is right. What nature brings may be causally, even logically necessitated, but what is necessitated is not therefore good. Nature, seen in the large, certainly does not look like the product of perfect justice and goodness. The plague that Marcus's men brought back from the east and spread in Rome— was that a gift for which thanks are due to a benevolent nature? If nature can produce animals mighty as the elephant, which lives on plants, why does it also produce tigers, leopards, and crocodiles, which must tear other animals to pieces if they are to have breakfast? "In sober truth," says Mill in a masterly essay on Nature,

nearly all the things which men are hanged or imprisoned for doing to one another, are nature's every day performances. Killing, the most criminal act recognized by human laws, Nature does once to every being that lives; and in a large proportion of cases, after protracted tortures such as only the greatest monsters whom we read of ever purposely inflicted on their living fellow-creatures.[30]

If following nature means acting as nature does, rather than using her laws to defeat her indifference toward us and our ends, we are worshiping an illusion.

Marcus and the Christians

But probably the criticism most commonly brought against Marcus is not such incoherence of thought, but, strangely enough, a charge of gross cruelty. His attitude in matters religious was tolerant and in some ways so close to that of the Christians that one would expect some sign of sympathy with them. The fact is that there is not only no sign of such sympathy, but on the contrary clear evidence of his persecuting them. It was in his reign that Justin Martyr was put to death, that the aged Polycarp, Bishop of Smyrna, was burned at the stake, and that scores of Christians in Gaul and on the Danube were also executed. Is there any extenuation for such conduct?

It does not seem at first that there could be. Nevertheless historians have commonly dealt gently with Marcus for these tragedies, and when the circumstances are brought to light, his responsibility for them does wear a different aspect. During his reign the empire was swarming with religious sects, many of them fanatical, many of them hostile both to Roman religion and to Roman rule. The emperors and the Senate had worked out a policy toward such sects that was on the whole singularly tolerant; indeed the Romans accepted in their own pantheon many of the gods of their conquered peoples. Roman religion and theology were very elastic structures, and the attitudes of eminent men ranged all the way from the materialism of Lucretius to the pagan fundamentalism of Julian the Apostate. Marcus himself was tolerant of nearly everything but intolerance. Religion was part of the state; the emperor was at once secular head and the high priest of the Roman people. A rule established by Trajan asked of his subjects the same recognition of the Roman deities that the Romans had accorded to those of their provinces. If such recognition was refused, it was taken as a refusal to accept the Roman governance, and the recusant was found guilty of treason. This decree was followed by the succeeding emperors, including the Antonines. "The charge against Marcus Aurelius," says Henry Dwight Sedgwick, "is that he suffered the criminal law to take its course."[31]

Unfortunately the one thing that the Romans inflexibly insisted on was something the Christians would not, or could not, do. They refused to cast incense on pagan altars or do anything else that signified acceptance of the Roman deities. It might be thought that in virtue of all they had in common with Marcus, he could grant them exemption, and one can only believe that if he had known them for what they were, he would have found a way of doing so. But this he did not know. Apparently all the information that came to him, directly or indirectly, was adverse to them. Two of his old tutors, Rusticus and Fronto, became provincial governors, and both reported of the Christians most unfavorably. The reputation of the sect with the common people also worked against them. Their services were often held in private houses, which inflamed a pervasive Roman suspicion about conspiracies; they claimed in their meetings to be eating the flesh and drinking the blood of their god, which was easily misread by outsiders; they were rumored to consume the flesh of infants; and since some of their meetings were held at night, admittedly in an atmosphere of what they described as general love, rumors of sexual orgies began to float about them. Furthermore, they were largely Jews, and the Jews had long been troublesome subjects for the Romans; fifty years before Marcus's birth the Roman general Titus had thought it necessary to raze the Hebrew temple at Jerusalem. The Jews' unhappy role as scapegoats was already beginning When Marcus came home from the east in triumph and his soldiers brought with them a plague that destroyed a large part of the citizenry, the superstition-ridden people, needing to lodge the blame somewhere, fixed upon an obscure Eastern sect whose members refused service in the army and espoused such strange beliefs as that their leader, known to have been put to death, was still alive and would return to assume lordship over the whole earth.

The judges who served on the bench in the Christians' cases would have preferred to save the lives of the accused. When St. Paul was first brought before a Roman tribunal, the judge was Gallo, brother of the famous Seneca, who thought both the charges and the defense so absurd that he "drave them from the judgment seat" (Acts, 18:16). Festus, governor of Judaea, was reluctant to punish Paul and took his case to the court of King Agrippa, but when he heard Paul's explanation of his creed, he said: "Paul, thou art beside thyself; much learning doth make thee mad" (Acts, 26:24). Incidentally, in both these cases the accusations were brought not by Romans but by Jews, who naturally regarded the Christians as apostates; so the little community was surrounded by misapprehension and enmity. Both Tacitus and Pliny later served as Roman governors, and Suetonius as secretary to the emperor Hadrian; all in their official capacity observed the Christians; all had much the same impression of them; all reported that their belief was a "malignant," "mad," or "gross" superstition.[32]

When men as able as these sent in such unanimous reports, it was difficult for a distant emperor to do anything but what Marcus did. The Christians were given an opportunity not given to other offenders—they could go free if they repented. What distressed Marcus was that they so automatically refused to repent. "O for the soul ready, when the hour of dissolution comes," he exclaimed, "for extinction or dispersion or survival! But such readiness must proceed from inward conviction, not come of mere perversity like the Christians', but of a temper rational and grave . . ." (11.3). Such evidence as he had pointed to a spirit of group resistance to the official Roman obeisance to the gods, a spirit so inflexible as to be unmoved even by imminent martyrdom. But of course the tragedy remains that the man perhaps nearest to Christianity in the pagan world should have persecuted a group that he would have admired if he had understood them. He is a vivid illustration of his own teaching that a man may do wrong out of an ardent but uninstructed desire to do right.

Marcus the Invalid

In criticizing Marcus for this or any other shortcoming, it should be borne in mind that for much of his life he was something of an invalid. In his youth he was a vigorous horseman and ballplayer, and courted rough conditions; he even speaks lightly about finding a scorpion in his bed. But he was never physically strong, and his scorn of giving in to pain or weakness, combined with continual overwork, wreaked havoc on his health. There is more, no doubt, than fiction in Pater's reference to "one of those pitiless headaches, which since boyhood had been the 'thorn in his side,' challenging the pretensions of his philosophy to fortify one in humble endurances."[33] During much of his rule as emperor, Marcus suffered from pain in his chest and his stomach, the latter due probably to ulcers brought on by strain, and from a sleeplessness so constant that he had to fight off permanent low spirits.

Fortunately he had the greatest of living physicians, Galen, as his doctor. Cassius Dio records: "He ate very little food, and that always at night. He could not take anything in the daytime, except some of the medicine called *theriac*."[34] This was a medicine containing opium prescribed for him by Galen, which assuaged the pain and helped him to sleep; indeed he took it so often as to become dependent on it. Some historians have tried to find traces in the *Meditations* of his having become an addict like De Quincey, but their argument does not carry conviction. As the long campaign on the Danube dragged itself out, his longing for Italy increased. He confessed how hard it was to get up in the morning, and exhorted himself to face the new day like a Roman and a soldier. The book that has given so much consolation and strength to others was written by a man himself sorely overburdened.

His Place in History

What is it, in the end, that gives Marcus Aurelius and his book so lasting a radiance in human history? Not, certainly, the acuteness or originality of his thought; he would not have cut an impressive figure in a passage at arms with Socrates, and if set an examination on epistemology in a modern university, with its stress on linguistic nuances and the manipulation of symbols, he would have flunked flatly and serenely. Nor was he a great general or man of action like Caesar, whose effortless adequacy to every situation has made him unique. Neither as a thinker, then, nor as a man of action was Aurelius in or near the first rank.

His greatness lies in a simple fact: he made perhaps the noblest recorded effort to live by the light of reason. Reason for him meant two things: on the one hand the network of necessary linkages that held the world together, on the other hand philosophy, the practice of tracing those connections and bearing them in mind. To enter the tent of Marcus Aurelius is to see the commonplaces of life—its worries, its temptations to revenge, its impatience with stupidity, its complaint over the unfairness of fate, its petty prides, its ill-grounded fears, its ambitions for power, reputation, and wealth—against the background of human history and destiny as a whole. Most people, not excluding philosophers, hold high principles in private, which they tend to forget when they argue their bills with their plumbers or pronounce an opinion about the mayor or the mail service. Marcus lived his principles.

"What then can be his escort through life? One thing and one thing only, Philosophy" (2.17, Farquharson). "To be loyal to philosophy under whatsoever circumstances, and not join the babel of the silly and the ignorant, is a motto for all schools alike" (9.41). He attempted to treat things and people in practice as his philosophy revealed them to be. He had mastered the potent secret that anger, fear, and malice are responses to objects largely of our own making, that we can reconstruct these objects by understanding them, and that when they are so remoulded there is little or nothing left for the emotions to respond to, and they wither on the vine. Understand the man you hate, see him in the light of those causal laws that rule the world, and he becomes an object not of vengeance but of compassion. Be not puffed up: "A little while and your place will know you no more . . ." (12.21). "Spend your brief moment then according to nature's law, and serenely greet the journey's end, as an olive falls when it is ripe, blessing the branch that bare it and giving thanks to the tree which gave it life" (4.48).

Reason opened to Marcus Aurelius the freedom of a larger world where he felt emancipated from the pettiness and fickleness of his own impulsive life. "In the universe Asia and Europe are but corners; ocean a drop; Athos a grain; the span of time, a moment in eternity" (6.36). He tried not to live in two worlds, but to see them as one, to bring the breadth of his intellectual vision to bear on himself, on the people around him, and on the daily duties of a great office. If his place is unique in history, it is because he set himself a transcendent aim and came heroically near to reaching it.

JOHN STUART MILL

John Stuart Mill
Portrait by G. F. Watts, 1873   National Portrait Gallery, London

John Stuart Mill

Gladstone, who disagreed with Mill on nearly everything, described him nevertheless as "the saint of rationalism." The phrase was apt and it has stuck. Mill's influence has been out of all proportion to the acceptance he won for his views. The main thesis of his *Logic* has been abandoned; no one now accepts his theory of knowledge; to expose the inconsistencies of his ethics is a common pastime in philosophical classrooms; his economics is used to show how far rigorous reasoning can go wrong if it starts from wrong assumptions. Yet somehow the ghost of Mill will not down. His life after life rests not so much on his conclusions as on his quality of mind, a quality particularly appealing to youth. A young man picks up an essay by Mill—not improbably the *Liberty*—and begins reading. Here is evidently an old-fashioned writer and the start is slow. Heavy sentences half a page long, made heavier by their weight of abstract nouns—the youth has been expressly taught that this is not the way to write. But something makes him read on. A subdued eloquence in the rolling sentences, with their careful architecture, carries him along. The writer knows exactly what he wants to say, and it comes through with surprising clarity, precision, and force. The reader is held in spite of himself; and if he is like thousands before him, he will find that after an hour or two's exposure, he has been "hooked" by this unlikely, pedantic, Victorian mesmerist, whose spell remains though he is more than a century dead.

What is the character of this spell? It is, I think, that of an unmistakable dedication to reasonableness. This quality resolves itself in his case into a number of component qualities. In the first place, a love of truth is omnipresent in his work. Second, he maintains clarity firmly through the densest speculative thickets. Third, an exactitude of expression, without suffocating interest, suggests a statesman drafting a law. Fourth, with scrupulous, self-effacing fairness, he insists on dealing with opponents at their best and is quite ready to admit the difficulties in his own case. These are features that deserve dwelling on a little further.

Love of Truth

First, his love of truth. "Mill's insistence on the sacredness of truth," says Noel Annan, "had the force of a religious commandment; and it had an immense influence not only upon his rationalist followers but throughout the Victorian clerisy."[1] He was an intellectual if ever there was one. He had been brought up by a fanatically intellectualist father to think of the pursuit of truth as at once the noblest and the most delightful of all activities. He wrote of his father: "He never varied in rating intellectual enjoyments above all others, even in value as pleasures . . . ."[2] The most important thing about a man, James Mill held, was his beliefs; for if these were true and were carried out, they would make him a power for good, while if they were false, they would make him a curse, and the more of a curse the more conscientiously he practiced them. Not of course that the truth of a belief and its utility were the same thing; the two are profoundly different; and truth should be pursued for its own unique and priceless sake. William James dedicated his *Pragmatism* to John Stuart Mill with the suggestion that if he were living he would be the pragmatists' leader. Mill would have declined the compliment. For him understanding was its own justification, and he could have written with even more propriety than the Elizabethan Edward Dyer:

> My mind to me a kingdom is;
> Such present joys therein I find,
> That it excels all other bliss
> That earth affords or grows by kind . . . .

Even worse for him than the notion that we should seek truth merely for its utility would be the notion that its truth reduced to its utility. James seems to have assumed that because for Mill the rightness of an action lay in its utility, the truth of a belief must lie there too. Mill would have set him right.

Style of Thought

Second, there is the clearness of Mill's thinking and, in spite of too many long words in long sentences, of his writing. The most consistently clear writer in English is, I suppose, Macaulay, whose biographer Trevelyan says that he never wrote an obscure sentence in his life. And when, in the *Edinburgh Review,* Macaulay opened up his devastating batteries on the elder Mill, he taught a lesson to the younger Mill that took lasting effect. You cannot be clear to the many, Macaulay said, if you stay entirely among abstractions; you must touch earth repeatedly through instance and illustration. The elder Mill was an abstract and dry mind; the younger Mill was a stylist. Laymen can read Mill's *System of Logic* with ease who would be utterly baffled by the logics of Hegel and Bosanquet.

But the true source of Mill's clearness lay deeper. It was essentially the same as that of Descartes's clearness, namely his acquiring in youth a sure sense of when a problem was solved or anything truly explained. Here at least Mill's father helped. "Anything which could be found out by thinking I never was told, until I had exhausted my efforts to find it out for myself."[3] In his teens he formed a discussion club that met in the house of Grote the historian, chiefly to discuss economics. Through these discussions, he wrote,

I acquired, or very much strengthened, a mental habit to which I attribute all that I have ever done, or ever shall do, in speculation; that of never accepting half-solutions of difficulties as complete; never abandoning a puzzle, but again and again returning to it until it was cleared up; never allowing obscure corners of a subject to remain unexplored, because they did not appear important; never thinking that I perfectly understood any part of a subject until I understood the whole.[4]

His education was a continual struggle after clear understanding, and if he failed, he was apt to feel the sharp edge of his father's irritation. James Mill, he said, was the most impatient of men; John never forgot how this impatience exploded at his using the word "idea" without being able to say what he meant by it, and at his remarking that something was true in theory though not in practice. A high standard of clarity, achieved in any subject, he found could be carried over and used as an immanent criterion in economics and ethics, in metaphysics, politics, and literary criticism. Mill's standard of clearness, as it was for Descartes and really is for everyone else, was self-evidence. Unfortunately we differ in what we demand before a statement or an argument is accepted as evident. Mill's demands were stern, and that is why it is tonic to read him. "All things end in bafflement," said George Saintsbury, "but it is well not to be baffled too soon."

Precision

Third, Mill's precision. Clearness and precision usually go together, though one may be clear without being precise, as Shaw and Mencken often were, or precise without being clear, as so many sociologists and psychologists now are. Ideally, clearness is precision with due courtesy for one's audience. Precision itself has two forms, which again do not necessarily go together. One lies in the conformity of expression to the thought within; the other in its fidelity to the fact without. Cardinal Newman was a master in the first form, though he fell short in the second. Whitehead stands out in his fidelity to fact, while at times bumbling in giving shape to his ideas. Mill was conscientiously precise in both respects.

Fairness

Fourth and more important, there is Mill's fairness. He was always attempting to throttle prejudice in himself, and he disliked intensely arrogance, authority, or emotion, posing as insight. He refused to be deflected from the straight line he thought drawn by the evidence, even when, as on "the subjection of women," public opinion ran strongly against him. Harriet Taylor, who was discerning about him even if not impartial, wrote to him: "you would be the most remarkable man of your age if you had no other claim to be so than your perfect impartiality and your fixed love of justice."[5] Mill's godson, Bertrand Russell, who viewed him with more detachment, spoke to like effect: "His intellectual integrity was impeccable. When he engaged in controversy, he did so with the most minutely scrupulous fairness."[6]

It is some measure of Mill's fairness that he changed his mind so often. The value of consistency in a philosopher or politician is easily misconceived. To be sure, if he can be shown to be advancing two inconsistent beliefs at once, the criticism is decisive, for then he must be advocating something false. To a philosopher consistency is so important that Emerson's famous remark, "A foolish consistency is the hobgoblin of little minds," has often been held against him. After all, consistency is the best test of truth or untruth that we have. But inconsistency between beliefs held fifty years apart has a very different significance from that of beliefs held simultaneously; indeed if a man believes at seventy all that he believed at twenty, he is pretty certainly suffering from arrested development or intellectual sclerosis. One can make a plausible case for the charge that has been brought against Mill that he is the most inconsistent of philosophers. He changed his mind not only on minor points but on major ones in ethics, economics, psychology, religion, and politics. Where a fanatic who had once committed himself would cling to his position though the heavens fell, and a passive mind would veer like a weathervane with the winds of change, Mill did neither. He changed; he changed greatly; but in a way that left his fairness not only unimpugned but emphasized, since his changes were frank modifications of his old beliefs in the light of new evidence. Inconsistency in a system is a disaster; inconsistency in a man may be a witness at once to his integrity and his capacity for growth.

I have stressed the changes in Mill's beliefs as part of his reasonableness. But more significant for such reasonableness are his dominant beliefs themselves. I shall look at a few of those that are of especial interest because they remain live issues today. It is natural to take first his views on education, since he was the subject of one of the most remarkable educational experiments on record and thought and wrote about it later.

The Child Prodigy

When John was born, in 1806, his father was eking out a precarious living in London by writing occasional articles and reviews and lacked the means to send his children to good schools. His plan was first to teach his eldest son himself and then make him his deputy in teaching the younger children. As already remarked, James was an extreme intellectualist. His idea of progress was essentially Marx stood on his head, as Marx was essentially Hegel stood on his head. James Mill held that a people's beliefs determined their circumstances rather than the other way about, and that if they were given an elementary education, they would turn their faces toward the truth as the sunflower turns toward the sun. With true beliefs about morals and the proper ordering of society, their action would follow their thought to a new Jerusalem in England's green and pleasant land. John was to be raised as at once the exemplar and the propagandist of James's sweeping optimism.

With no loss of time and with heroic disregard of his own convenience, this "most impatient of men" sat the youngster down in the same room and at the same desk with himself, answering the child's questions as they arose. His demands on the boy and John's responses are described in the opening pages of Mill's *Autobiography* and have guaranteed the book an enduring and fascinated audience. John could not remember when he could not read Greek, which he began at three; Latin, as the poorer language, came later.

From my eighth to my twelfth year the Latin books which I remember reading were, the Bucolics of Virgil, and the first six books of the

Aeneid; all Horace except the Epodes; the Fables of Phaedrus; the first five books of Livy (to which from my love of the subject I voluntarily added, in my hours of leisure, the remainder of the first decade); all Sallust; a considerable part of Ovid's Metamorphoses; some plays of Terence; two or three books of Lucretius; several of the Orations of Cicero, and of his writings on oratory; also his letters to Atticus, my father taking the trouble to translate to me from the French the historical explanations in Mongault's notes. In Greek I read the Iliad and Odyssey through; one or two plays of Sophocles, Euripides, and Aristophanes, though by these I profited little; all Thucydides; the Hellenics of Xenophon; a great part of Demosthenes, Aeschines, and Lysias; Theocritus; Anacreon; part of the Anthology; a little of Dionysius; several books of Polybius; and lastly Aristotle's Rhetoric, which, as the first expressly scientific treatise on any moral or psychological subject which I had read, and containing many of the best observations of the ancients on human nature and life, my father made me study with peculiar care, and throw the matter of it into synoptic tables.[7]

All this was behind him at twelve. At thirteen, on walks, he was discussing with his father the *Prior* and *Posterior Analytics* of Aristotle and covering Plato *in extenso,* whose dialogues he could now read, he says, "as far as the language was concerned, with perfect ease." Also in his early teens he was put through a rigorous course of economics with the use of a new book by his father's friend Ricardo. James's aid gave out sooner in mathematics than in classics, but when it did, John carried on by his own momentum through analytic calculus. When he was eighteen, a new radical journal was started, the *Westminster Review,* designed to do battle with the conservative *Quarterly* and the Whig *Edinburgh* on their own high levels. Its first eighteen issues carried thirteen articles by Mill, dealing with history, political economy, and law.

What did Mill think in later years of this hothouse education? He never turned upon it with hatred, as some young prodigies later did upon theirs; John's criticism of his father was always muted, always qualified with admiration. But he did murmur that it was a little much to put the *Theaetetus* in the hands of a boy of seven; and his remark "I never was a boy" is called by W. L. Courtney "the most pathetic reproach that a son can ever address to his father on the management of his youthful years."[8] Play and playmates were practically unknown, and from ten or twelve on, his only fit companions were men of mature years.

Breakdown

At twenty he broke under the relentless pressure. When he seemed to be carrying everything before him, he suffered what he called "a crisis in my mental history." One day he asked himself:

"Suppose that all your objects in life were realized; that all the changes in institutions and opinions which you are looking forward to, could be completely effected at this very instant: would this be a great joy and happiness to you?" And an irrepressible self-consciousness distinctly answered, "No!" At this my heart sank within me: the whole foundation on which my life was constructed fell down. All my happiness was to have been found in the continual pursuit of this end. The end had ceased to charm, and how could there ever again be any interest in the means?
    I seemed to have nothing left to live for.[9]

For six months he continued his work, now as a clerk in the India office; those around him noticed nothing wrong; but inwardly he was haunted by the thought of suicide.

There have been many speculations as to the cause of Mill's breakdown. For his own explanation he fell back on his associationist psychology. According to its plausible teaching, what always moves our will is the desire to gain pleasure or to avoid pain. An essential part of education, therefore, should consist in the association of pleasure with the right things and the right actions. Much of this needed association nature takes care of for us; eating, drinking, sleeping, companionship bring their distinctive rewards so automatically and continuously that our pleasure in them becomes a fixture. But other activities need to have pleasure attached to them artificially by praise and reward, and pleasures so attached are less secure. The pleasures of the student or of the idealist devoted to distant ends are of this less secure kind. "The pains and pleasures thus forcibly associated with things," Mill pointed out, "are not connected with them by any natural tie; and it is therefore, I thought, essential to the durability of these associations, that they should have become so intense and inveterate as to be practically indissoluble, before the habitual exercise of the power of analysis had commenced."[10] You cannot feel as you normally do about the loveliness of a flower, or the beauty of a poem, or the power of a burst of eloquence, while engaged in dissecting it; "we murder to dissect." "To know that a feeling would make me happy if I had it," Mill continued, "did not give me the feeling. My education, I thought, had failed to create these feelings in sufficient strength to resist the dissolving influence of analysis, while the whole course of my intellectual cultivation had made precocious and premature analysis the inveterate habit of my mind."

To a modern psychologist, skeptical of associationism generally, this explanation is not convincing. For many years Mill had found his chief pleasure in analysis, and if his associationist theory was sound, he ought to have gained increasing pleasure in it instead of finding it suddenly empty of interest. There was more at work in the crisis than met even his own keen eye. The philosopher A. W. Levi thinks that the case cannot be dealt with short of a depth psychology that Mill could not have foreseen, and that what was really going on was a struggle between a repressed death wish directed against a father from whose dominance he saw no escape and a guilt that haunted him because of it; this struggle in his subconscious paralyzed his conscious behavior. This is an issue on which a layman may perhaps be excused for reserving judgment.

There is no doubt, however, that Mill was right in criticizing his education for its imbalance, for its almost exclusive stress on his intelligence to the neglect of his feelings. This imbalance was no accident on the part of his father, of whom he wrote: "For passionate emotions of all sorts, and for everything which has been said or written in exaltation of them, he professed the greatest contempt. He regarded them as a form of madness."[11] James avoided showing affection for his children, and Mill writes that his "older children neither loved him nor with any warmth of affection anyone else"[12] (a passage omitted from the published version of the *Autobiography*).

Mill's autobiography must be unique in containing no mention of a mother. But in this early draft of the book there do occur the words:

> a really warm hearted mother would in the first place have made my father a totally different being and in the second would have made the children grow up loving and being loved. But my mother with the very best intentions only knew how to pass her life in drudging for them. Whatever she could do for them she did and they liked her because she was kind to them but to make herself loved, looked up to, or even obeyed, required qualities which she unfortunately did not possess. I thus grew up in the absence of love and in the presence of fear . . . .

The result was a starvation of feeling that Mill only gradually cured by a self-imposed regimen of emotional education which began with the reading of Wordsworth. "Compared with the greatest poets," he remarked of Wordsworth, "he may be said to be the poet of un-poetical natures, possessed of quiet and contemplative tastes. But un-poetical natures are precisely those which require poetic cultivation. This cultivation Wordsworth is much more fitted to give, than poets who are intrinsically far more poets than he."[13] Mill recovered, but slowly and never totally. Carlyle complained of his talk as "wintry and sawdustish." And when he finally met someone who loved him totally, his own reaction was so extreme as to make him cut off his own family with an icy ostracism because they failed to see eye to eye with him about her.

Mill's Theory of Education

Though he suffered, and knew it, from his semimilitary intellectual boot training, he never turned his back on it; and when, toward the end of his life, the students of St. Andrews elected him their Lord Rector, he gave them a three-hour inaugural address which left them cheering, exhausted, and almost in despair about their own mental retardation. What they heard was a root-and-branch defense of liberal education by perhaps the most educated man in Britain, who held the discipline of even Oxford and Cambridge to be puerile, who had never had what he called the handicap of a college education, and who advocated a curriculum strikingly like his own.

Universities [he insisted] are not intended to teach the knowledge required to fit men for some special mode of gaining their livelihood. . . . What professional men should carry away with them from a University, is not professional knowledge, but that which should direct the use of their professional knowledge, and bring the light of general culture to illuminate the technicalities of a special pursuit. Men may be competent lawyers without general education, but it depends on general education to make them philosophic lawyers—who demand, and are capable of apprehending, principles, instead of merely cramming their memory with details. . . . Education makes a man a more intelligent shoemaker, if that be his occupation, but not by teaching him how to make shoes; it does so by the mental exercise it gives, and the habits it impresses."[14]

To the great question of his day, whether Oxford or Cambridge, the classics or the sciences should be the staple of education, he answered boldly, both. To make room for Greek and Latin he would exclude altogether the teaching of modern languages. "Universities do enough," he said, "to facilitate the study of modern languages, if they give a mastery over that ancient language which is the foundation of most of them, and the possession of which makes it easier to learn four or five of the Continental languages than it is to learn one of them without it."[15] And the classics should not be dallied with, as they commonly are in schools and colleges. "They should be carried as far as is sufficient to enable the pupil, in after life, to read the great works of ancient literature with ease."[16] He took a similarly rigorous view about mathematics and the physical sciences. But the science he esteemed most was logic, the science of thinking validly in any field. Education is designed to produce not encyclopedic minds, but thinking minds. "Logic is the great disperser of hazy and confused thinking: it clears up the fogs which hide from us our own ignorance, and make us believe that we understand a subject when we do not." It "forces us to think clearly, even when it cannot make us think correctly."[17] Mill went on to say that a proper liberal education should include physiology, psychology, philosophy, economics, and the fine arts. But the main aim of education was practical and reflective judgment, a mind trained to be critical everywhere in the use of evidence.

Some Assumptions of Mill

In stressing this aim I think Mill was right. But he was making some assumptions that, unless granted, much reduce his credibility.

He was assuming, perhaps most obviously, that other people were as able as he was. Strangely enough, he in fact believed this. He said that in memory and some other faculties he was below average, and that any healthy boy or girl in England could have accomplished what he did, given James Mill. One wonders what he would have made of intelligence tests, or of the view of Lewis Terman who, in the course of his study of young "geniuses," gave Mill, if I remember rightly, the highest of historically conjectured IQ's. His humility must have been in part a consequence of his extreme empiricism, which held that, with substantially the same possibilities, we are made what we are by nurture rather than nature, that is, by association made among our ideas in the course of our education.

It seems to me, though I cannot argue the matter here, that there is no good evidence either for Mill's doctrine of equality or for his empiricism. What is surely true is that most students could achieve enormously more than they do if our schools and colleges were less slack in their demands and their discipline than they are. If I may refer to my own limited experience, I spent a great deal of precious time on Greek and Latin in school and college and never came near Mill's standard of reading the classics with ease. If there was something deficient in myself, which was plain enough, there was also something deficient in the method of teaching and learning. To make one minor comment, I think students should be encouraged to use translations as aids to prevent constantly breaking the thread of thought through stopping to turn the pages of a dictionary. A. C. Benson, who taught at Eton, said that too many schoolboys carried away nothing from the study of Greek and Latin except the profound conviction that there were such languages. The classics should be taught more effectively or not taught at all.

Here comes the second assumption of Mill, that the classics have proved their right to educational priority. In his rectorial address he did, to be sure, give some evidence for this, enough perhaps to be persuasive for his own case. And I am sufficiently persuaded to admit to a special respect for critics who, like Eliot and Edmund Wilson, were classical scholars, and even for statesmen who were scholars, like Gladstone, Curzon, and Asquith. But what would happen if Mill's view were seriously applied to American education? There would certainly be a quick and general revolt. Such a priority would run afoul not only of the plain fact of unequal human endowment, but of the inexorable pressure of time. The advance of knowledge in the last century has changed roughly from an arithmetical to a geometrical progression, and the superiority of ancient literature to modern has been reversed, certainly in volume and probably in style. In the century of Freud and Einstein, or Russell and Shaw and the Jameses, it is a mere anachronism to devote most of one's education to what, for the schoolboy if not for the ripe classicist, seems like "the settling of *oun*'s place" and "the doctrine of the enclitic *de*." Oxford itself has abandoned its centuries-old Greek entrance requirement, and probably the most decisive vote cast against it was that of Gilbert Murray, Regius Professor of Greek.

Mill made a third questionable assumption: he thought that more could be crowded into a curriculum than any curriculum could hold. Any college dean presented with his list of requirements would resign in despair. To condense a thorough discipline in classics and mathematics together with a study of the basic physical, mental, and social sciences into about 120 academic hours would seem a fantastic impossibility.

But apart from these large subtractions for overoptimism, Mill's theory of education seems to me essentially sound. He admitted that thoroughness in one field could be profitably combined with limiting oneself to the main principles of others. Above all, in holding that the best product of education is the reasonable mind, in the sense of the mind best equipped to estimate evidence, he seems to me wholly right. One may perhaps agree with him also that the subject contributing most to this end is logic. What he meant by logic was, indeed, pretty remote from the symbolic logic that now holds the field, and I doubt whether he would have kept his dictum in the light of the change. Even if the attempted reduction by *Principia Mathematica* of logic to mathematics had succeeded, he would probably be unmoved, since he held that logic as he conceived it was a more useful tool than mathematics. Here, though I am not of Mill's persuasion in logic, I can only agree again. And I think the reading of his *Logic* is about as fine an exposure to lucid argumentation as one can find. I wish every university student might have his chance at it.

A System of Logic

But a book may have educational value far outweighing its ultimate soundness. Mill's *System of Logic,* though it is his greatest work, is a case in point. For if we turn now from education to logic and ask what he contributed to this field, the reluctant answer must be: nothing of first importance. His chapter on fallacies is admirable; his discussion of the ways of proving a causal connection, commonly called "Mill's methods," has become a classic; and he scatters illumination along the winding path of his two stout volumes. His book was an attempt, probably the best of all attempts, to write an empiricist logic. But an empiricist logic seems something very like a contradiction in terms. Logic is a study of reasoning, and reasoning is a seeing that one assertion follows from another. "Follows" means at its best *necessarily* follows. Now the empiricist has traditionally held that all our knowledge comes from sense experience. But the insight that *B* follows from *A,* that *A* necessitates *B,* cannot possibly come from sense experience. *A*'s necessitating *B* is not something that can be seen with the eye or heard with the ear, or tasted, felt, or smelt. Everyone believes that 7 and 5 not only do but must make 12 and no empiricist has succeeded in explaining that "must" away.

Both Mill's deductive and inductive logic broke down on this simple issue, and one need not become technical to see how. Take the simplest sort of syllogism "All men are mortal; Socrates is a man; therefore Socrates is mortal." Everyone agrees that the conclusion must be true if the premises are true. But can it be shown that they are true? There is no doubt about the second, "Socrates is a man." But what about the first, "All men are mortal"? That may be interpreted in two ways. It may be read first as saying that being a man entails dying, that the characteristics essential to man carry with them the characteristic of dying. If this is true, the syllogism is sound, for if the other qualities of being a man require the further quality of being mortal, then Socrates, who has these qualities, must have the further quality entailed by them. But of course that sort of necessity is precisely what an empiricist cannot admit, for it is not a sensible quality or relation.

So the empiricist must fall back on the other interpretation of his major premise. This takes "All men are mortal" as a statement about a class of individuals, Jones, Smith, Socrates, Brown, and so on. Now the only way an empiricist can show all of these are mortal is to go over them one by one. And here he is in a dilemma: if in counting heads to see that they are all mortal he includes Socrates, as of course he must, his argument becomes needless and begs the question, since he cannot know his major premise to be true without knowing already that his conclusion is true; indeed he is offering no argument at all. On the other hand, if he does not include Socrates in his count, his argument is broken-backed, for he cannot conclude from the fact that other men are mortal that Socrates is. On neither interpretation, therefore, does the syllogism prove anything. Caught by this dilemma, Mill maintained that the syllogism was really an argument from analogy, that because Socrates resembled other men in having certain qualities, he could be expected to resemble them also in others. Now the argument from analogy, though sometimes strong, never *proves* anything, since it does not claim to show that the resembling qualities necessitate the others. Mill had to admit that the central argument of traditional deductive logic was not in the strict sense reasoning at all.

It may be replied that in taking a major premise like "All men are mortal" Mill was giving the case away, since nobody pretends to see necessity in it. If he had taken instead a proposition that is plainly necessary, like one from mathematics, the conclusion would have followed absolutely. "Two straight lines do not enclose a space; this is a case of two straight lines; therefore this is a case in which they do not enclose a space." Most logicians would accept this without cavil. Mill's empiricism held him back. We certainly cannot gather from our limited experience that *all* such pairs of lines have this character, and where but to experience could Mill turn? If he admitted the proposition to be necessary, he was giving up empiricism, and if he did not, he was giving up deduction as proof. What he did, as he did so often, was to offer a compromise: mathematics was not certain, it only approached this asymptotically. Suppose, he argued, that two characteristics are presented to us together daily, and many times daily, with never an exception; will not this constant association between the two establish in our minds an unbreakable tie between them? Whenever we see the meeting of two straight lines on a square table, mat, or wall, the connection of two straight lines with their not enclosing a space has further confirmation; indeed it has been confirmed so constantly that we can no longer conceive their doing otherwise. Does this inability to conceive their divorce prove that their union is necessary? No, said Mill; it is only a psychological impossibility, naturally but confusedly taken as a logical one. The empiricist can thus account for the apparent necessity of mathematics without sacrificing his empiricism by admitting a real necessity.

I am not going to argue against this theory because the need for that has passed. Such an empiricism would leave us with the notion that it is only highly probable that two straight lines will not enclose a space, or two and two make four; and nobody now believes either, even among the empiricists. They admit that in logical and mathematical statements we have true necessity, but they add that this necessity links only our own ideas and reveals nothing of the outer world. Thus they end in skepticism. They believe in necessity, as Mill did not, but like the fabled dog, to save the shadowy bone of mental necessity, they drop the intelligibility of the world.

Induction

One would expect Mill to be more successful in dealing with inductive logic, and he was. He has not solved the problem of induction, but neither has anyone else; and as a critic remarked, he wrote clearly enough to be found out. What is the problem of induction? To put it at its simplest, it is this: scientific laws, by which for the present we shall mean causal laws, are supposed to be universally true. But they are not self-evident; they must be established by observation or experiment. That means that on the ground of relatively few cases, or perhaps of a single careful experiment, a universal law is taken to be established. Such establishment is actually accepted by science. Dr. Reed's few cases were accepted as decisive as to the cause of yellow fever; if in a single case the lead ball and the feather fall at the same rate in a vacuum, the law of accelerated fall is taken as holding for all cases. Now as an argument, this is scandalous. But to say that science generally is a scandal would be more scandalous still. How is science to escape the charge?

It does so by making a vast assumption, called the uniformity of nature. This means that the same cause always produces the same effect. If the earth's pull makes the ball and the feather fall at the same rate, it will act in the same way on all other masses unless in some way counteracted. Assume that nature acts thus uniformly, and the argument from a few cases, or even one, is impeccable; without that assumption it is worthless. Everything depends, then, on whether the assumption can be made out. Mill saw and stated the issue with his customary clearness. How did he deal with it?

He felt that he had to deal with it in the true empiricist manner. The principle of uniformity, he said, which allows you to argue from one or a few cases to all similar cases could itself be made out inductively. People have expected on the ground of a long experience that water would wet and fire burn; they have found these expectations verified, and they naturally argued that if they had succeeded in the past in arguing from past to future, they could safely continue to do so. Had they any right to do so? Mill thought they had. But surely he was mistaken. You can argue validly that if *A* causes *B*, it will in like circumstances do so tomorrow, because you are backed by the great assumption that nature always acts uniformly. But when that uniformity itself is in question, when you ask by what right you argue from past to future at all, you cannot settle *that* by arguing from past to future experience, for in doing so you are assuming the point at issue. Mill's empiricism broke down again.

My own inclination is to take the uniformity of nature as a necessary consequence of a necessary truth, namely the law of identity. But since most philosophers of science would shrink from this, I should be contented for the present with saying that uniformity is a postulate, that is, a proposition that cannot be proved either inductively or deductively but is progressively confirmed by experience. This is an unsatisfactory conclusion, since it leaves science hanging in the air, unable to establish logically any of its laws. That clear-eyed archempiricist Hume held that there is no more reason to believe that the sun will rise tomorrow than that it will not. Mill seems to have felt in his bones that this was absurd, and so no doubt do most of us, but the problem of induction does not lend itself to solution by feelings in the bones.

Mill's Ethics

To turn now to another field, it is probably by Mill's writings on ethics, slender as they are, that he is best known. In 1965 an editor of these writings, J. B. Schneewind, said that "In the last fifteen years there have been more essays dealing with the topic of 'Mill's Proof' [of his utilitarianism] than with any other single topic in the history of ethical thought . . . ."[18] These essays have shown, I think, that his moral philosophy is not to be dismissed by the sort of logic-chopping applied to him in many classrooms, even when this has the august support of G. E. Moore. To be sure, there are inconsistencies that lie on the surface for all to see, and these are due to a struggle between two opposite tendencies within him. In the end he achieved through compromise a sort of peace between these tendencies, but the verbal contradictions were never removed.

The struggle was between his early intellectual Benthamism and a maturing moral insight. Throughout Mill's youth, Bentham was the guide, philosopher, and friend of his father, and therefore of himself. Indeed when James Mill was laid up with gout, Bentham wrote to him asking the privilege, if the illness proved fatal, of becoming John's guardian. James replied:

I am not going to die, notwithstanding your zeal to come in for a legacy. However, if I were to die any time before this poor boy is a man, one of the things that would pinch me most sorely, would be, the being obliged to leave his mind unmade to the degree of excellence of which I hope to make it. But another thing is, that the only prospect which would lessen that pain, would be the leaving him in your hands. I therefore take your offer quite seriously . . . and then we may perhaps leave him a successor worthy of both of us.[19]

Bentham's neat, precise, and consistent theory of human nature and conduct proved irresistible to the young Mill, though it is clear from his famous essay on Bentham, written when he was thirty-two, that he was all too worthy a successor; he saw through and around the master with a clearness that was emancipated and disillusioning. For Bentham each man is a bee governed by the single interest of gathering honey in the form of his own pleasure or happiness. The great problem of the social reformer is how to make bees who are purely selfish act as if they were concerned about the happiness of others. Bentham proposed to do this by attaching "sanctions," as he called them, bonuses in the way of honey, to conduct that promoted "the greatest happiness of the greatest number" and pain to actions that hindered this; with much plausibility he recodified ethics and law in conformity with this ideal. John Mill, beginning as the most devoted of Benthamites, came to reject both the master's theory of human nature and the ethical system built upon it.

The Break with Bentham

First, he rejected the view that men are by nature egoists. Popular as the view has been among cynics, it can be given plausibility only by twisting human motives grotesquely, as when it is argued that the mother gets up in the night to comfort her crying infant only to relieve her own distress at his crying. Mill sees that in such distress there may be genuine sympathy, a concern for the happiness of others as well as for one's own; and that is not egoism. His chief hope for society lay in deepening and widening this sympathy by education and public opinion, in bringing men's concern for others to the point where they felt the happiness and misery of those around them almost as they felt their own, and acted accordingly. "As between [the agent's] own happiness and that of others," he wrote, "utilitarianism requires him to be as strictly impartial as a disinterested and benevolent spectator. In the golden rule of Jesus of Nazareth, we read the complete spirit of the ethics of utility. To do as you would be done by, and to love your neighbor as yourself, constitute the ideal perfection of utilitarian morality."[20] Bentham held that if men were to act altruistically, they must be shown that it is to their interest to do so; Mill held that they were capable of rationality to the point of self-sacrifice; they could and did on occasion forgo their own happiness for the greater happiness of others. The sacrifice of one's own greater happiness for the lesser happiness of another he thought irrational.

He went beyond Bentham in a second respect. Is it true, he asked, that pleasure is the only thing that gives value to an experience? Bentham's answer was a confident yes, and when it was pointed out

to him that in the work of a Michelangelo or a Beethoven, the speculative insight of a Plato or the prodigal self-giving of a Saint Francis,
there were other values than mere pleasure, he firmly denied it.
Amounts of pleasure being equal, pushpin (a popular game of the
time) was as good as poetry. This Mill could not stomach. In an
often quoted passage he asked himself the crucial question whether,
if the life of a well-fed pig could be shown to contain a greater
amount of pleasure than an equal period in the life of Socrates, he
would prefer the life of the pig. If pleasure is really the only thing
worth having, he ought to vote for the sty, but he confessed that he
would do no such thing. He tied himself into logical knots in trying
to make this answer consistent with hedonism, which it is not. He
said that some pleasures had a higher *quality* than others, which obviously would not do, since if, of two experiences that are equal in
the amount of their pleasure, one is rated above the other, it must be
something other than pleasure that tips the scale. He tried redemption by definition: "to desire any thing, except in proportion as the
idea of it is pleasant, is a physical and metaphysical impossibility."[21]
But the pleasantness of the desire for a thing is not the same, nor does
it vary with, the desirability of the thing desired. He admitted that
we love virtue and beauty and knowledge for their own sakes; and
when asked how he could say this while holding that only happiness
had value, replied in desperation that these goods were parts of happiness. They are no doubt parts of a happy experience, and parts that
condition the happiness, but to resolve them away into the feeling
side of the experience is not convincing analysis. By these and other
devices Mill tried to salvage hedonism. But hedonism is a preposter-
ous ethical theory, and Mill's mind kept breaking through its rickety
crate faster than he could repair it.

The Real Mill

Stanley Jevons said of Mill's mind that it was "essentially illogical,"[22]
and certainly these efforts to make an incredible theory credible do
not seem like the handiwork of a great logician. But I do not think

they report the true Mill. Beneath the logic-chopping, and even while he contradicts himself, one feels the push of an honest and able mind toward a more rational theory. In fact he had caught sight of this already in holding that the fundamental question of ethics is not "What is right?" but "What is good?" since if one can answer this latter question one can also answer the former, by saying that what is right is that which conduces to what is good. But then what *is* good? It is experience of some kind, for sunsets and music and even truth are not good except as experienced. But what makes an experience good?

Mill said that only such experience was good as was tinged with pleasure, and there again I think he was right. Take any experience that is universally held to be good in itself, and not merely as a means to something else—the experience, say, of poetry, or love, or understanding—and you find it positively toned, as Mill maintained. But when he added that we can and should value these things for their own sakes, he was admitting that we value them as ends, and not merely as means to pleasure, which on his avowed theory they ought to be. And when one puts the essay on utilitarianism together with the essay on liberty, with its insistence on each man's being himself up to the point where he restricts others from being themselves, I suspect we have in outline the ethics Mill was reaching for. The good society, he thought, is that in which each man gains the happiness that comes with realizing his own powers, that is, realizing them as fully as is consonant with giving the same privilege to others. That was the true reason why it was better to be a discontented Socrates than a contented pig: the magnificent sweep of the Socratic vision was in itself an almost incalculable good. Mill's theory, so amended in fragmentary admissions of his own, seems to me true.

Another thing should be said about his ethics: it is an ethics of reason, of the appeal to reason as the ultimate arbiter of both what is right and what is good. We must depend on our reason—on reasoning inductively and causally—to decide the best means to our ends, and that implies that in our complex modern society the intelligent and reflective person has a far better chance than others of finding what it is right to do. And what sort of insight is it that determines the *end* of conduct by judging as between the intrinsic goods that are open to us? Certainly not feeling, for feeling cannot judge. Mill believed that when he held knowledge to be better than ignorance, he was reporting a self-evident rational insight. And this implied that there was an objective truth to be found as to what good he ought to pursue at every moment, and by what means he should pursue it. Of course this is a flat rejection of all relativist ethics, and if it is correct, then Nietzsche, Sumner, and Westermarck, Russell, Ayer, and Benedict can only be mistaken. A sound morality demands and rests upon reasonableness. This, I venture to think, is the real Mill.

Harriet Taylor

His movement away from Benthamism would perhaps never have been made by himself. But he fell early under the influence of seers of a very different type: Coleridge, Carlyle, the Cambridge theologian F. D. Maurice, and John Sterling, of whom Carlyle wrote a masterly biography. Sterling was of all men, Mill said, the one he loved most. He could not have said "of all persons," for there was one person he loved more than Sterling and whose influence on him was greater than all of these others combined. I approach the love story of Mill and Harriet Taylor with hesitation because, like others who have studied it, I hardly know what to make of it; yet to ignore it is impossible. The bare facts are these. In 1830 Mill, aged 24, met Harriet Taylor, aged 23, at the house of a common friend. She had been married at 19 to John Taylor, 11 years her senior, who was a prosperous wholesale druggist. Taylor was a hearty, generous, outgoing man, much respected by his fellow Unitarians but without intellectual pretensions. Harriet did have such pretensions. She had written a little pleasing verse, was fond of reading and discussion, was interested in politics, and had emphatic views of her own, particularly on the rights of women. She met Mill at a time when she was chafing under her Victorian assignment of bearing children in rapid succession and brightening the corner where she was. In that corner she was fixed, apparently forever, with a husband whom she respected but regarded as her cultural inferior. For Mill the meeting was virtually a case of love at first sight. He was lonely and emotionally starved. As Carlyle put it many years later to Charles Eliot Norton: "that man, who, up to that time, had never so much as looked at a female creature, not even a cow, in the face, found himself opposite those great dark eyes, that were flashing unutterable things while he was discoursin' the utterable concernin' all sorts o' high topics."[23]

When John Taylor discovered the romance, he demanded that his wife see nothing more of Mill. The lovers tried to comply, but only briefly. Taylor suggested that his wife spend six months in Paris thinking the matter over, and perhaps her feelings would change. But Mill followed her there, and she soon returned to confess that she was more deeply involved than ever. At her desire, John Taylor established her at various places in the country where she could live apart from him, their two young sons being sent off to schools while the daughter, Helen, stayed with her mother. The affair became known and was the topic of much London gossip. Taylor did his magnanimous best to be patient and understanding. When this strange *ménage à trois* had dragged itself on for eighteen interminable years, John Taylor fell ill with cancer. Harriet, who was traveling with Mill on the continent, came home to nurse her husband through his last two months. This she did with genuine compassion, not unmixed, as her letters show, with self-pity. He left her his entire estate.

Mill and Harriet went on much as before, and two years later were quietly married at a country registrar's office. Only seven years of marriage were granted them, seven years of almost continuous illness for one or both. Mill soon developed consumption, and seems to have been given up by his doctor, who was also the Queen's physician, Sir James Clark. Fortunately the India House, where he now held a position which was roughly that of an undersecretary of state, gave him an eight-month leave. His method of meeting his malady was to go alone to the Continent, to take immense walks of fifteen or twenty miles a day in France, to mule-pack across Sicily, to explore Greece, which he knew well from his classical studies, from Thermopylae to Sparta, and if he saw a mountain, to climb it because it was there. This strenuous remedy, instead of killing him, cured him. Almost daily he sent voluminous letters to his wife, who was too ill to accompany him. During his travels he was always on the lookout for a retreat of tolerable climate where they could retire together, and in the end he found their El Dorado in Avignon in the south of France. Upon his retirement they set out for Avignon together. But Harriet had also contracted consumption, and she died in their hotel room almost immediately on their arrival. Mill buried her in the cemetery there. He bought a house nearby from which he could visit her grave daily, and set up to her memory a block of white Carrara marble imported at great expense from Italy. Fifteen years later he was laid there at her side.

Conflicting Estimates of Harriet

What is one to think of this consuming and enduring romance? Most of Mill's friends and contemporaries, the Carlyles for example, set Mill down as a dupe in the whole affair, and his wife as a faithless hussy. That the matter is not so simple has been shown by F. A. Hayek in his book *John Stuart Mill and Harriet Taylor,* and in the admirable life of Mill by Michael St. John Packe. It must be remembered that an affair which today would probably be settled by a quick divorce and the remarriage of both parties was seen very differently by the early Victorians, for whom that would have involved a standing public disgrace. It must be remembered too that if Mill's opinion of her were at all justified, the cooperation of these two was of real moment, not only for them but for the public. Mill was the most truthful of men; he observed and worked with Harriet closely for twenty-eight years; and his estimate of her was unequivocal and unvarying. That it should lean toward laudation in the dedication of his *Liberty* or in the long inscription on the marble at Avignon is not surprising; but the same opinion is set down over and over again in his diary, in his letters, and in his posthumous *Autobiography*. I will give one specimen of it from the latter:

> In general spiritual characteristics, as well as in temperament and orga-
> nisation, I have often compared her . . . to Shelley; but in thought and
> intellect, Shelley, so far as his powers were developed in his short life,
> was but a child compared with what she ultimately became. Alike in the
> highest regions of speculation and in the smaller practical concerns of
> daily life, her mind was the same perfect instrument, piercing to the very
> heart and marrow of the matter; always seizing the essential idea or
> principle. The same exactness and rapidity of operation, pervading as it
> did her sensitive as well as her mental faculties, would, with her gifts
> of feeling and imagination, have fitted her to be a consummate artist, as
> her fiery and tender soul and her vigorous eloquence would certainly have
> made her a great orator, and her profound knowledge of human nature
> and discernment and sagacity in practical life, would, in the times in
> which such a *carrière* was open to women, have made her eminent among
> the rulers of mankind. Her intellectual gifts did but minister to a moral
> character at once the noblest and the best balanced which I have ever met
> with in life.[24]

In the judgment that Harriet really was this paragon of moral, aesthetic, and intellectual power, Mill seems to have been in a minority of one. Jane Carlyle, at first swept off her feet by Harriet, soon changed her mind, and Carlyle himself, with the keenest of eyes for human quality, wrote to Sterling about Mill's involvement: "I have not seen any riddle of human life which I could so ill form a theory of."[25] Harriet's letters to Mill's family range from the affectionate to the acidulous, the shrewish, and the freezing; as a body they would not support a nomination to sainthood. That she did have intellectual ability there can be no reasonable doubt. Though she published nothing in prose herself except an article on the emancipation of women, an article probably revised by Mill, there remains an early manuscript of hers outlining the essential thesis of the essay on *Liberty* (it has been printed by Hayek);[26] and the best-known chapter of the *Principles of Political Economy,* entitled "The Probable Future of the Laboring Classes," was in Mill's words "entirely due to her." So were the increasing concessions to socialism made in the successive editions of that work until the last, when Mill after her death retreated a step or two. It is safe to say that in everything of importance he wrote after the *Political Economy,* she served as an adviser and a rigorous critic.

But when in his account of their collaboration he pictures himself as the amanuensis and Harriet as the thinker, when he writes to her, "I am but fit to be one wheel in an engine not the self-moving engine itself—a real majestic intellect, not to say moral nature, like yours, I can only look up to & admire,"[27] one feels uncomfortable. It recalls Goldwin Smith's remark that "Mill's hallucination as to his wife's genius deprived him of all authority whenever that came in . . . ."[28]

Probably no one will ever know the exact truth about this unique alliance. My guess would be as follows. Mill at twenty-four was ripe for inner revolution. He was a master logician and analyst; but logic and mathematics are the least humane because the most abstract of disciplines, and in making himself an intellectual machine he had broken under the strain. Having lost the power of normal feeling for others and enthusiasm for even the ends that make life worth living, he was groping his way toward "worlds not realized" of feeling and imagination. Suddenly he encountered a beautiful being who seemed to supply all his needs at once. His life had been, he said, loveless; here was someone who adored him. He had lived under the dominance of a sternly stoical and masculine father; here was someone who, with feminine tact, suggested without ordering, poured out her praise instead of holding it in pedagogical reserve, and read what he wrote with comprehension and enthusiasm. In the world of feeling, where he was a wistful stranger, she was gracefully at home; his causes were her causes, but with their human significance illumined and intensified by her warmth of imagination for the laboring and suffering men and women whom his intellectual radicalism was really designed to serve. She gave new vitality and allurement to the ends that in his own mind had become anemic phantoms, and she supplied him with a further potent end in her own approval of what he undertook. Her woman's intuition seized directly, and as it seemed to him by inspiration, points that he arrived at only by laborious ratiocination; and on one of his favorite issues, the subjection and emancipation of women, she could speak with an authority he could not rival.

But her contribution to their joint work was chiefly in the way of feeling, not of intellect, in spite of all Mill's protestations. She said of herself, "The desire to give & to receive feeling is almost the whole of my character."[29] And this was a larger part than he realized of his own repressed nature. Charles Eliot Norton, writing about him to Chauncey Wright, remarked on "the sentimental part of his intelligence, which is of immense force, and has only been kept in due subjection by his respect for his own reason."[30] It was Mill, not Harriet, who was the thinker and writer throughout. His biographer Packe makes a subtle point when he says of her: "She did not make him more romantic: rather she made him retire into his native rationalism, and justify the romantic standpoints which she gave him."[31]

A Janus-faced Affection

Whether Mill and Harriet Taylor were justified, even by the happiness and added power that their collaboration gave them, in wrecking the good John Taylor's family life is a question too complex for dogmatism. The relation between the sexes is an explosive subject, and whoever presumes to lay down the law has more valor than discretion. Sex is an instinct far older and deeper in our nature than even the faint beginnings of reflective thought, and numberless men with a reputation for rocklike reasonableness have been reduced to a fatuous adolescence under its power. But whatever we say of Mill on the main point, we cannot acquit him wholly. Self-effacing as he was, to the point of a rare kind of nobility, in his estimate of his wife, his glasses were so heavily tinted with rose whenever he looked in her direction that even subordinate matters connected with her were seen in a roseate light. Though he knew that he was acting in a way that most of his friends could not approve, he cut them off ruthlessly if he heard any rumors of criticism by them.

Still harder to accept is his attitude toward his own family. He had been living before his marriage with his mother and two unmarried sisters, who were devoted to him and proud of him. Harriet they had never met when he suddenly announced to them his impending marriage to her. For some reason or other they did not instantly call on her when the two returned to London. Apparently for this offense, Mill froze them out of his life and would have nothing to do with them; their letters to him pleading for a resumption of old affections received only formal and frigid replies, as did his mother in person when she came to his office at the India House to beg for reconciliation. He did call on her when she was dying, but six days before her death he wrote reminding her that she should appoint an executor of her will, preferably not himself, and that he was on medical advice leaving England for the Continent for a long stay. She did not see him again. To his brother George, whom he had not notified of his marriage, and who wrote a little plaintively to congratulate the pair, Mill replied in a letter beginning:

I have long ceased to be surprised at any want of good sense or good manners in what proceeds from you   you appear to be too thoughtless or too ignorant to be capable of either . . . . You profess to have taken great offence because you knew of our intended marriage "only at second hand." People generally hear of marriages at "second hand," I believe. If you mean that I did not write to you on the subject, I do not know any reason you had to expect that I should.[32]

Many years later he did relent and give assistance to one of the sisters, Mary, who was in distress. But no estimate of Mill as a reasonable man can overlook the fact that love in one direction can turn to flint in others.

Nor should it leave out a further curious fact. For the last fifteen years of his life, Mill's home was at Avignon with Harriet's daughter

Helen, who devoted herself to his care. She became a leader, though from a distance, in the English suffragette movement. "After Mill's death," says his biographer, "she became the jealous guardian of all his thoughts and relics. She grew priggish and overpowering; eventually, mean, suspicious, truculent and sometimes half beside herself with passion."[33] Thirty years after Mill's death, a niece of Helen found her still there, the house dilapidated and the garden overrun, her chief occupation picking up leaves and twigs. Yet Mill placed her along with Harriet on the same high pedestal. In a passage of the *Autobiography,* suppressed at first on the advice of Professor Bain, Mill wrote this:

Surely no one ever before was so fortunate, as, after such a loss as mine, to draw another prize in the lottery of life—another companion, stimulator, adviser, and instructor of the rarest quality. Whoever, either now or hereafter, may think of me and of the work I have done, must never forget that it is the product not of one intellect and conscience but of three, the least considerable of whom, and above all the least original, is the one whose name is attached to it.[34]

If it is difficult to believe that Mill had found one intellectual goddess before whom he could appropriately kneel, it is more difficult to believe that he had found two; and such a verbal shrine to the second only casts a shadow of doubt on his canonization of the first.

Having said all this, we must admit that, whatever their origin, there was a warmth, humanity, and moral urgency about Mill's later writing that we do not find in the earlier. One thinks of the essay *On Liberty,* on which he and his wife collaborated and which he published in 1859, the year after her death, and of *The Subjection of Women,* which was written in 1861 but not published till 1869. Since he probably owed his very interest in the subject of the latter book to his wife, we shall speak of that first.

The Subjection of Women

It seems strange that the women's movement has not made more use of *The Subjection of Women,* since it is one of the most convincing tracts ever devoted to the feminist cause. Perhaps the reasons are that the book is somewhat dated in matter and manner, that is, that the conditions against which it inveighed have been largely removed; and that it is written with the uncompromising abstractness of the logician rather than with the simplicity and verve of the popular advocate. Further, the "subjection" of women does not correspond to anything we know, particularly in America; the word suggests serfdom or slavery, which would inaccurately state the condition of most American women. But we must remember that during the last century the emancipation of women has advanced at an astonishing pace, partly by reason of Mill's powerful initiative. In 1869 the legal position of women in England was indeed subjection. The church required of a bride a vow of lifetime "obedience" to her husband. Everything she did was supposed to be done with his approval. Since the two were "one person in law," everything she owned, everything that she received by gift or inheritance, became his, though in this there was no reciprocity. Her children were by law his, not hers. She did not have the right to their guardianship, even after his death, unless he left a clause to that effect in his will. If she left him, nothing was hers to take with her, and he could compel her by law or force to return. Divorce was a public disgrace, and it required a special act of Parliament for divorced persons to remarry. Legal separation was possible only in cases of desertion or extreme cruelty, and was too expensive a process for any but the moneyed classes to afford. And "no amount of ill usage," said Mill, "without adultery superadded, will in England free a wife from her tormentor."[35]

British law about the family and the relations between the sexes was based on an ancient tradition in a country where tradition was notoriously strong. And that tradition was one of male power, of a sentiment almost universal among primitive peoples, that to the strong belongs the rule. By Mill's day, society's dependence on physical strength, in which men surpass women, had greatly changed, but women's position remained a relic of the primitive past. In the *Liberty* Mill argued that modern civilization has quite another basis; people have the right to exercise their powers as they choose up to a line beyond which it would conflict with the same right of someone else. This right belongs to persons as persons, and if it belongs to men as persons, it belongs equally to women.

We have remarked already that the relation between the sexes is a sensitive theme, and that the dogmatist about it is almost sure to make a fool of himself. Mill knew the dangers here, none better, and he was ready to call his generalizations conjectures, but he did venture upon a few nevertheless. He was convinced that apart from physical strength, women's capacities were the equal of men's, and in some respects superior. He speaks of "the more rapid insight into character, which is one of the admitted points of superiority in women over men," and their advantage in "intuitive perception," which means "a rapid and correct insight into practical fact." "With equality of experience and of general faculties, a woman usually sees much more than a man of what is immediately before her." Her interests are more commonly in things and people than in abstractions or in speculation. "A woman seldom runs wild after an abstraction." "The business of a woman's ordinary life is things in general, and can as little cease to go on as the world to go round." The result is that she has developed marked skill in shifting her attention fully and easily from one order of business to another. "And do we not find that the things in which men most excel women are those which require most plodding and long hammering at a single thought, while women do best what must be done rapidly?" His careful study of Indian history, in which there were many women rulers unknown to the West, confirmed him in thinking that "the natural capacity of women for government is very striking." When political accident has placed women in the seat of government, they have on the average, he found, done better than men. Yet places of political influence, the very places where women have proved themselves most unambiguously, were denied them under British law.

Mill knew the common objections to his position. For example, he had to admit that "No production in philosophy, science, or art, entitled to the first rank, has been the work of a woman." This sweeping indictment is an example of the dozens of charges of women's natural inferiority that he combatted. Now there are two reasons for an inferiority of performance: native endowment and the pressure of environment; in short, nature and nurture. Mill was a thoroughgoing believer in nurture. Just as he believed that any healthy boy or girl in England could, under such direction as had been given *him* by his father, have achieved all that he did, so he believed that the average woman, if granted the privileges and surrounded by the expectations and pressures of the average man, could accomplish all that he could. She was especially sensitive to the opinion of others because she had been taught to think that her success in life depended on her awaking the devotion of some man. The almost irresistible pressure of society pushed her toward domesticity. If she showed an interest in science or politics and wanted to make a profession of it, she was set down as queer and unfeminine, and the doors of all the best public schools and universities were closed in her face. In one profession, indeed, she had won a late entrance, the theater, and here her success rivaled the greatest of the men's. But public opinion about her intelligence, her endurance, her originality amounted to an unceasing battery upon her self-respect; her lack of confidence became her own worst enemy. Mill was not saying that the emancipation of women would bring Utopia; he did not know what it would bring, for it had never been tried. But he insisted that it was folly to prejudge the case against half the race. Whether women would or would not outshine men when admitted to the professions, they should have their chance to compete without shackles.

The Rising Wave of Success

The influence of Mill's reasonableness was felt not only through his books but also through a long course of actions, quiet at first, but increasingly conspicuous with the years. When he married Harriet Taylor, with her considerable inheritance, he set down formally in writing his disclaimer to any control over her person or her property. ". . . I absolutely disclaim and repudiate all pretension to have acquired any *rights* whatever by virtue of such marriage."[36] In his period in Parliament (1865-68), he soon caught the public eye. During a debate on the Reform Bill of 1867 he quietly rose and moved that the word "person" be substituted in the bill for the word "man." Many members were inclined to regard the motion with ribaldry, but Mill was in deadly earnest and would not be laughed down. He proceeded, says Packe, to give "a wise and reasoned discourse, appealing to expediency more often than to justice. He demolished all the obvious objections, that politics were not a woman's business, that women did not want to vote, that they preferred to wield the immense indirect power they had always had, or that they were already represented by the votes of their natural protectors."[37] And in spite of the refusal of many members to take the matter seriously, he got 73 votes, almost a third of the members in attendance. This was the first women's suffrage resolution ever introduced in the House of Commons.

Though he was defeated for reelection in 1868, he had broken the Parliamentary ice. A group of his fellow members agreed that a women's suffrage amendment should be introduced on May Day every year. In 1870 it was actually passed on the first reading by a majority of 30, and received 184 votes on a second reading. In 1871 it had 151 supporters, and in 1872, 143. Mill died in 1873. Packe terms it "an indication of his personal influence that, once he was dead, it took nearly fifty years and a world convulsion to bring enough opinion round, and that even then it was only achieved at the expense of riot, brutality, and martyrdom."[38]

In the session after Mill's defeat, and largely owing to his continuing influence, the House passed both the Married Women's Property Act and the National Education Act, which made education mandatory for girls as well as boys. Nine years after the *Subjection* appeared, Parliament granted to a woman the right of separation from a husband convicted of aggravated assault on her, and also the custody of her children under ten years old.

Mill worked heroically to organize women themselves for their own emancipation, but he confessed sadly that he was frustrated from the start by the unwillingness of outstanding women to come forward and commit themselves. Women of title were generally conservative, like their fathers and husbands, and shrank from any suspicion that they might be "radicals." Fortunately he found one fearless and attractive young woman of great ability, Lady Amberly, who was willing to campaign boldly for women's rights. She admired Mill's leadership so much that she invited him to serve as godfather to her little son. After some struggle with his religious scruples, Mill agreed and sent the infant a silver cup inscribed with his name, which happened to be Bertrand Russell. Able younger men too, like Lord Amberly, John Morley, Henry Fawcett, and Henry Sidgwick, rallied round Mill's banner. Though he thought the winning of the suffrage the most important point in the women's movement, their right to education was a corollary and necessity. "When Girton was founded," says his biographer Packe, "he drew up the first examination paper on Political Economy—and an extremely stiff one it was too. He also took an interest in the expansion of the women's college in Bedford Square. At his death he left the enormous sum of £6000, nearly half his total estate, to the cause of women's education."[39]

On Liberty: Its Thesis

Far more widely read than *The Subjection of Women* was the essay *On Liberty*. Mill himself said of it, "The 'Liberty' is likely to survive longer than anything else that I have written . . . ."[40] Noel Annan writes: "The Essay burnt itself into the consciousness of each succeeding generation of liberals: whatever else they discarded from mid-Victorian radicalism, they retained the Essay—it troubled the conscience of converted Marxists and mellowed the convictions of British socialists."[41] Asquith once described it as the charter of the British Liberal Party.

"The problem of freedom" has two very different meanings. The first is whether my choice to do this action rather than that is free in the sense of unconditioned or uncaused. This is the metaphysical question. Mill dealt with it in the *Logic,* coming out as a determinist. The other question is a political and ethical one: how far have I a right to think, speak, and act as I please? Mill held, correctly I think, that one can with perfect consistency deny that we have freedom in the first sense while defending the right to a high degree of freedom in the second; and he in fact did both.

His answer to the political problem is stated in his introduction to the essay *On Liberty*:

The object of this Essay is to assert one very simple principle, as entitled to govern absolutely the dealings of society with the individual in the way of compulsion and control . . . . That principle is, that the sole end for which mankind are warranted, individually or collectively, in interfering with the liberty of action of any of their number, is self-protection. That the only purpose for which power can be rightfully exercised over any member of a civilized community, against his will, is to prevent harm to others. His own good, either physical or moral, is not a sufficient warrant. He cannot rightfully be compelled to do or forbear because it will be better for him to do so, because it will make him happier, because, in the opinions of others, to do so would be wise, or even right. These are good reasons for remonstrating with him, or reasoning with him, or persuading him, or entreating him, but not for compelling him, or visiting him with any evil in case he do otherwise. To justify that, the conduct from which it is desired to deter him, must be calculated to produce evil to some one else. The only part of the conduct of any one, for which he is amenable to society, is that which concerns others. In the part which merely concerns himself, his independence is, of right, absolute. Over himself, over his own body and mind, the individual is sovereign.[42]

Many or most of us would accept this teaching without demur, and wonder why it should have aroused so much resentment. Is it anything more than a statement of the major premise of the American Civil Liberties Union? Has it not been espoused and even exceeded by justices of our Supreme Court, for example Hugo Black? On such questions some brief comments may be made. First, in most parts of the world, the doctrine would, even now, be regarded as radical if not revolutionary. It would be rejected by all the Communist governments, by most of those of the so-called Third World, and by some even of the "free world." Second, the liberty Mill was contending for went far beyond politics. He was as much concerned about coercion by public opinion as about coercion by law, partly no doubt because he had felt it so keenly himself as a result of his unconventional life. Third, the *Liberty* is far more than a legal brief. It is a remarkable piece of literature, combining in Mill's unique fashion precision of statement with an eloquent compassion for those everywhere who are oppressed.

Freedom of Thought

For his crucial example in the essay, Mill takes freedom of thought and speech. The argument he offers for it is surprisingly simple. A belief that is threatened may be either true or false, and he holds that in either case the attempt to suppress it does more harm than good.

Suppose that the belief is false. There would seem to be nothing sinister in rooting out an intellectual weed. But the assumption here, says Mill, is that those in power are infallible judges of weeds and flowers, able to proscribe doctrines as false in advance of their free discussion. Do governments have such discernment? It must be remembered that new truth is usually arrived at precisely by the minds that question established opinion; and government and public opinion have shown extreme obtuseness in recognizing truth in the mouths of dissidents, whom in numberless cases they have silenced and persecuted. Socrates was the best and wisest man who up to that time had appeared in the world; the Athenian public was the best instructed that had ever been called on to pass judgment, and that enlightened public put Socrates to death. Four centuries later in the only case, Mill says, which after that of Socrates would not be an anticlimax, the best man whom Judaea had produced was put to death with the approval of the leaders of his people. Probably the noblest ruler who has ever headed a state was Marcus Aurelius, and yet with his consent Christians were thrown to wild beasts in Roman arenas. If men such as Socrates and Christ could be put to death as impious malefactors, what teacher or teaching can be called safe? If the wisest of rulers can permit the persecution of the best of men, what government can be trusted to decide for us what to think? Dr. Johnson suggested that persecution was, after all, a useful winnower; truth would successfully run its gauntlet, while error would falter and fail. This prompted Mill to open up the combined batteries of his learning and his scorn:

> History teems with instances of truth put down by persecution. If not suppressed for ever, it may be thrown back for centuries. To speak only of religious opinions: the Reformation broke out at least twenty times before Luther, and was put down. Arnold of Brescia was put down. Fra Dolcino was put down. Savonarola was put down. The Albigeois were put down. The Vaudois were put down. The Lollards were put down. The Hussites were put down. Even after the era of Luther, wherever persecution was persisted in, it was successful. In Spain, Italy, Flanders, the Austrian empire, Protestantism was rooted out; and, most likely, would have been so in England had Queen Mary lived, or Queen Elizabeth died.[43]

It was a devastating barrage, and the ghost of Dr. Johnson, for once overwhelmed, was left fleeing in confusion down the alleys off Fleet Street. It cannot be said that these are old and extreme cases that have had no later parallels; Hitler, Stalin, Idi Amin, and many others have arisen to give Mill's argument a ghastly corroboration.

The contention, then, that a government is justified in putting down false opinion is unacceptable because no government is qualified to say with certainty what *is* false. Now take the other supposition, namely that the doctrine in question is true. It is natural enough to say that truth should be preserved at all costs, and that objectors to it should be made to hold their peace. But Mill would have none of this either. He might have taken the same line as before and argued that public opinion is no more safe a judge of truth than of falsity, but he took another and more novel course. As often with him, he chose to argue the case in his opponent's strongest field. Here it was that of religious truth and more particularly of Christian ethics. Many regarded the New Testament teaching on conduct as revealed, and therefore beyond legitimate questioning. But though a belief that is never questioned may maintain itself in words, Mill replies, in time it will be only in words. If not critically thought about, it will lose all vitality and wither away into a mechanical ritual.

All Christians believe that the blessed are the poor and humble, and those who are ill-used by the world; that it is easier for a camel to pass through the eye of a needle than for a rich man to enter the kingdom of heaven; that they should judge not, lest they be judged; that they should swear not at all; that they should love their neighbour as themselves; that if one take their cloak, they should give him their coat also; that they should take no thought for the morrow; that if they would be perfect, they should sell all that they have and give it to the poor. They are not insincere when they say that they believe these things. They do believe them, as people believe what they have always heard lauded and never discussed. . . . Had it been thus [with the early Christians], Christianity never would have expanded from an obscure sect of the despised Hebrews into the religion of the Roman empire. When their enemies said, "See how these Christians love one another" (a remark not likely to be made by anybody now), they assuredly had a much livelier feeling of the meaning of their creed than they have ever had since.[44]

Mill deplores "the deep slumber of a decided belief," and holds that no one understands even his own belief wholly until he has explored its grounds and implications. Since most men are too sluggish to do that, it is important that public criticism should do it for them. For only when seen to be self-maintaining will any belief remain alive, responsible, or secure.

The Importance of Being Oneself

What Mill was pleading for was not so much freedom itself as for the kind of minds he thought freedom would encourage. While no admirer of the opinion of plain people, he was a determined defender of their rights, an antidemocratic defender of democracy. He was not an admirer of the nobility either, and when the princess

Alice, accompanied by the crown princess of Prussia, expressed a wish to come and see him at Avignon, he was not interested enough to receive them. But while he did not attach much value to English opinion at any social level, he had an almost unlimited faith in what, with freedom and education, that opinion might become. Freedom for all to act and think as their own powers enabled them, education to elicit and stimulate those powers, with the resultant diversity of minds—these were the real goals of the essay *On Liberty*. Mill gave two cheers for democracy, for it alone could generate a responsible people. He feared it because the tyranny of the majority was able to flatten individuality as a steamroller does clods in a field. Speaking for the England of his time, he wrote:

> . . . the individual or the family do not ask themselves—what do I prefer? or, what would suit my character and disposition? or, what would allow the best and highest in me to have fair play, and enable it to grow and thrive? They ask themselves, what is suitable to my position? what is usually done by persons of my station and pecuniary circumstances? . . . I do not mean that they choose what is customary, in preference to what suits their own inclination. It does not occur to them to have any inclination, except for what is customary. . . . they like in crowds; they exercise choice only among things commonly done: peculiarity of taste, eccentricity of conduct, are shunned equally with crimes: until by dint of not following their own nature, they have no nature to follow. . . .[45]

Thus for Mill the great danger of democracy is self-defeat. Public opinion demands conformity; conformity destroys individuality; and if individuality is destroyed, the men of character and genius that democracy requires for its leadership are destroyed with it. Mill's *Liberty* was the clarion call to English youth that Emerson's "Self-Reliance" was to young Americans.

Has the essay stood up under more than a century of examination? One hopes that it still moves and convinces its thousands in our colleges, but its influence may be due in some measure to an ambiguity that lies at its heart and allows both the individualist and the socialist to claim it for his own. You can in effect, Mill says, draw a line around the individual. Within that line lie the thoughts, words, and deeds that affect only himself; and within that circle the state must keep its hands off. But moving from within across the line are the acts that affect others, and here the state has a right to regulate. Can any such line be drawn? Does not everything we say or do affect the lives of others? Whether I speak carelessly or correctly, whether I am habitually punctual or late, whether my dress and person are clean or filthy, whether I spend my time reading Mill or the comics, makes a difference to society. Mill often talks as if they did not, and holds therefore that the choice should be left to me. But socialists can surely argue that by Mill's standard society may resort to pressure in all such cases. One can imagine a Communist claiming that the state is following Mill to the letter by interfering only when a man's conduct affects others and only in the interest of the general happiness; that when it fixes a boy's profession or silences a dissident, it is only acting where others are affected and only acting for the public good. This is a logical inference, and yet at odds with all Mill stood for. What it shows is that you cannot draw with any sharpness the line he tried to draw.

The main difference between individualist and socialist is not as to the end, which equally is the good of society as a whole. The difference is in the means by which that good is to be sought. Mill thought that it is best attained in a civilized country by giving the individual his head. Lenin and Mao held that is is best attained by the opposite course, by putting all men on treadmills thoughtfully constructed by the state. To most of us in the "free world" Mill seems clearly right. But in the world at large he is still fighting in a minority on the defensive. Strangely enough, his most formidable enemy was a shabby man whom he not improbably passed without notice on the London streets or in the British Museum, a man too obscure to call for mention in any of his thousands of pages. As regards what Mill meant by liberty, Marx has now darkened the sky over much of the world.

The Politician

It is as a writer that Mill is now remembered, but in the brief term he served in Parliament for the distinguished constituency of Westminster, he gave an admirable example, as we have seen, of the rational man in politics. He did not believe in long and expensive campaigns, refused to engage in one, and took to the hustings for only a week before the election. At one working-class rally a heckler rose and asked whether he did or did not say in print that the English working class were generally liars. He replied in two words, "I did." Whereupon, to his astonishment, he was greeted with a storm of applause. Here at least was a politician who would not hedge. He was elected by a creditable margin. In Parliament he maintained, though often in a small minority, the views advocated in his writings. He was an adroit debater, given perhaps to overfine distinctions which were not much lightened by humor. But on one occasion Sir John Pakington taunted him with having called the Conservative party "the stupid party." He replied:

I never meant to say that the Conservatives are generally stupid. I meant to say that stupid people are generally Conservative. I believe that is so obviously and universally admitted a principle that I hardly think any gentleman will deny it. . . . There is so much dense, solid force in sheer stupidity, that any body of able men with that force pressing behind them may ensure victory in many a struggle . . . .[46]

Mill spoke for more freedom and more peasant proprietorship in Ireland, for the prosecution of Governor Eyre for his brutal treatment of blacks in Jamaica, and for the extension of the English suffrage to the poorer classes as well as to women. As a Parliamentary speaker he was not as effective as he deserved to be; his attempts to get everything exactly right made him slow and hesitant: Gladstone said he spoke like a statue, and Disraeli that he spoke like a finishing governess. But his known integrity and ability gave his voice weight, and though he was not reelected, Gladstone summed up Parliamentary feeling in saying, "He did us all good."

Religion

I will but glance at one more field of Mill's multifarious interests, religion. He said that perhaps alone among Englishmen he was brought up with no religious views at all. His father avoided discussion of the subject. But on two occasions Mill became seriously involved in such discussion. The first came when he was writing his main metaphysical work, *An Examination of Sir William Hamilton's Philosophy*. Hamilton, a very learned professor at Edinburgh, was a follower of Kant, who held that human reason was applicable only to the objects of our own perception and could tell us nothing about the ultimate nature of things, or therefore about God. This doctrine was borrowed by Dean Mansel of St. Paul's, whose inference from it was that the proper approach to Deity was not through reason but through a simple faith in scriptural revelation. His book on *The Limits of Religious Thought* took substantially the line of Kierkegaard and Karl Barth that "God is wholly other" than man's reason or conscience can understand. He may order Samuel to destroy the Amorites, man, woman, and suckling child, but faith tells us nevertheless that he is perfectly good, and that by such faith only can we be saved.

This was too much for Mill. In his essay on *Nature* he pointed out, as had one of his favorite poets, Tennyson, that nature was "red in tooth and claw with ravine," a state of things which an omnipotent creator could have avoided, and therefore must have desired.

when I am told that I must believe this, and at the same time call this being by the names which express and affirm the highest human morality, I say in plain terms that I will not. Whatever power such a being may have over me, there is one thing which he shall not do: he shall not compel me to worship him. I will call no being good, who is not what I mean when I apply that epithet to my fellow-creatures; and if such a being can sentence me to hell for not so calling him, to hell I will go.[47]

There was, and is, no convincing answer to Mill on this point, and his stand, according to McTaggart, marked an epoch in theological controversy. Mill virtually killed Mansel as a theological force. This was perhaps a pity, for Kierkegaard and Brunner, Barth and Niebuhr, who later revived so much of his theory, seem to have known nothing of him, though as a writer, scholar, and logician he stood above any of them. In answering Mansel, Mill was *a fortiori* answering them all.

Mill's other excursion into theology came to light only after his death, with the appearance of his essay on *Theism*. This came as a shock to agnostic followers, who had accounted him their leader. He did not reverse his earlier views; he still held it inconsistent to call God at once omnipotent and morally good. Yet the amount of apparent purposiveness in nature seemed to him also inconsistent with its government merely by the laws of physics. So he admitted as a hypothesis that at least did not collide with fact the notion of a God who was good but limited in power and struggling like his creatures to mould a nature that was itself indifferent. Again, since he was too sane a mind to be taken in by behaviorism, and the connection between mind and body was obscure, he conceded that there was a bare possibility of consciousness surviving bodily death.

He was increasingly puzzled as to the proper attitude to take toward Christ. The more he studied Jesus, the profounder he seemed, not in intellect indeed, but in moral insight, and Mill hardly knew how to explain him by the sort of "ethology" or sociology of character that he had sought with high hopes to develop in his *Logic*. So he admitted that "it remains a possibility that Christ actually was what he supposed himself to be—not God, for he never made the smallest pretension to that character and would probably have thought such a pretension as blasphemous as it seemed to the men who condemned him—but a man charged with a special, express, and unique commission from God to lead mankind to truth and virtue . . . ."[48] This marks Mill's closest approach to Christianity, and again it is ambiguous. One can hardly believe that he meant to accept a breach in natural law, but this language leaves it moot.

Reasonableness

What such ambiguity shows, as W. L. Courtney remarked, is the passionate attempt Mill made to be fair to all sides of a case. He wanted to know why thoughtful Christians believed as they did and how they felt; and in this he largely succeeded. ". . . Goethe's de-

vice, 'many-sidedness'," he wrote, "was one which I would most willingly . . . have taken for mine."[49] It was noted that in Parliament
he sometimes stated the case of an opponent, before refuting it, more
strongly than the opponent had himself. This practice exemplified
his theory of what understanding a belief meant. He admitted that
in mathematics

all the argument is on one side. There are no objections, and no answers
to objections. But on every subject on which difference of opinion is
possible, the truth depends on a balance to be struck between two sets of
conflicting reasons. . . . when we turn to subjects infinitely more complicated, to morals, religion, politics, social relations, and the business of life,
three-fourths of the arguments for every disputed opinion consist in dis-
pelling the appearances which favour some opinion different from it. . . .
He who knows only his own side of the case, knows little of that.[50]

He was equally emphatic on the ethics of controversy:

In general, opinions contrary to those commonly received can only obtain
a hearing by studied moderation of language, and the most cautious
avoidance of unnecessary offence, from which they hardly ever deviate
even in a slight degree without losing ground . . . opinion ought, in
every instance, to determine its verdict by the circumstances of the individual case; condemning every one   in whose mode of advocacy either
want of candour, or malignity, bigotry, or intolerance of feeling manifest
themselves; but not inferring these vices from the side which a person
takes, though it be the contrary side of the question to our own; and giving merited honour to every one, whatever opinion he may hold, who has
calmness to see and honesty to state what his opponents and their opinions
really are, exaggerating nothing to their discredit, keeping nothing back
which tells, or can be supposed to tell, in their favour. This is the real
morality of public discussion . . . .[51]

Mill was of course not a rationalist in the philosophic sense, and
it is exceptionally easy to find inconsistencies, even on major issues,
in his teaching. Why, then, has he had so enormous an influence?
Largely, I think, because in argumentative practice he lived up as
few men have done to the high preaching we have just been listening
to. His very ambiguities and inconsistencies are the result of his in-

sistent effort to see all sides of the question. It is no wonder that fanatics, visionaries, even prophets like Carlyle should look at him askance. "As if," Carlyle wrote to his brother on reading the *Liberty,* "it were a sin to control, or coerce into better methods, human swine in any way . . . *Ach Gott im Himmel!*"[52] Here the difference appears between two ultimate assumptions about humankind. At bottom Carlyle seems to have believed that, though some men were heroes, most men were swine, made to be herded by the heroes; and therefore he could not be a democrat. Neither was Mill a democrat if that meant accepting majorities as safe guides. But he believed that most men had the essentials in them, that they really wanted to know the truth and do the right, and that they would, if given a chance, move toward these things as moths to the light.

F. A. Hayek's verdict on Mill seems to me fair:

he will again be recognized as one of the really great figures of his period, a great moral figure perhaps more than a great thinker, and one in whom even his purely intellectual achievements are mainly due to his profound conviction of the supreme moral value of unrelenting intellectual effort. Not by temperament but out of a deeply ingrained sense that this was his duty did Mill grow to be the "Saint of Rationalism" . . . .[53]

ERNEST RENAN

Ernest Renan
After Léon Bonnat, 1892
From Renan, *Souvenirs d'enfance et de jeunesse*
(Paris: Nelson and Calmann-Lévy, n.d.)

Ernest Renan

Next to romantic love, religion is the area of human life where reason is most easily swept away. Against faith, reason has little chance with the great majority. This is clear enough from the most general statistics. Millions of Christians believe in the Trinity; millions of Moslems deny it. They cannot both be right: reason has failed in one case or the other. The Zoroastrians believe that the world is governed by two deities—one good, one bad. Buddha and Confucius manage to dispense with the idea of a personal god altogether, the one accepting an all-embracing deity into which we are at last absorbed, the other dispensing with theology almost wholly and substituting a manual of human conduct. Now truth is one consistent whole. And if it is reason that gives us truth, it can hardly have been reason that tells us that God is one and two and three, that he is a person and not a person, that he is both good and bad.

What did in fact dictate these contradictions is not an easy question. That a struggling, half-formed reason had some part in it must be admitted. Religion is not philosophy, but neither does it exclude this; it is an attempt by the whole man to adjust himself to what he takes to be ultimately true and good. His creed is the convergent result of many causes. His imagination about first and last things, his helplessness and insecurity in a world he did not make, his habits of conformity to the culture about him, the suggestion of his own religion that belief is a duty and disbelief a sin, the teaching that faith is "another dimension" which offers another road to truth—these influences are much more powerful in moulding men's creeds than any independent exercise of their intellect.

German "Higher Criticism"

To look at Christianity in this way, to treat it like other religions as a natural human development, with the strengths and weaknesses of other human enterprises, was a late achievement in the West. It was hardly possible before Descartes unintentionally, and Hobbes and Voltaire deliberately, applied to religion the critical standards they applied to physics and history. They were all anathematized for it. But the Reformation had let loose a free play of intellect that was bound to grow wherever it was not held down. So it is not an accident that the acme of religious self-criticism should have been reached in the land of the great heretic, Luther. Its beginning, in the full modern sense, was made by a suave and innocent-seeming Hamburg banker, Hermann Reimarus, who spent his spare time studying Oriental languages and writing a secular account of the Gospels so searching in its skepticism that, foreseeing the obloquy it would bring on himself and his family, he did not even try to publish it. Fortunately his daughter sent portions of it to Lessing, who recognized their value and had them printed anonymously under the name of "the Wolfenbüttel Fragments." There followed a spate of German works whose massive scholarship and decisiveness for theology deserve comparison with that unique outburst of German music in the eighteenth and nineteenth centuries which seemed to Whitehead so inexplicable.

The peak of this higher criticism was achieved in 1835 with the *Leben Jesu* of David Friedrich Strauss, a graduate of Tübingen still in his twenties. It was a majestic work of combined scholarship and philosophy which has not been equaled in its field before or since. A century and a half later Strauss remains the man who has to be dealt with by any orthodox Christian scholar. Why, then, in selecting a man to stand for rationality in religion, do we pass Strauss over and turn to Renan? The answer is that religion is so largely a matter of imagination and mystical feeling, of human sympathy and moral idealism, that only one who can enter into these things fully can write of it as it is. Renan had these things. Too often German criticism did not.

Certainly the logical force with which Strauss shattered the supernatural carapace that had surrounded Jesus through the centuries was formidable. But no biography written primarily to shatter can do its subject full justice. And the fugitive figure who was left when the Germans had done their work was so attenuated that there was little to say of him except that he existed, and some doubted even that. Renan, who was as skeptical of the supernatural as Strauss, wrote with love and reverence rather than hate, and brought Jesus to vivid historical life. Without deserting scholarship, of which he was a master, he saw shining between the fragmented lines of the Gospels a wholly human but unique and benignant presence, and described it with an eloquence worthy of the subject.

Vie de Jésus

Renan's *Vie de Jésus* appeared in June 1863. Though written by an unlikely source of best sellers, a teacher of Hebrew, it became at once the talk of Paris, surpassing in popularity any novel of the time. Edition after edition was printed, only to be exhausted in eight or ten days. By November it had appeared in Dutch, German, and Italian translations, and a version in English was under way. France's weightiest critic, Sainte-Beuve, hailed it as a masterpiece. For the thirteenth edition the text was for the first time seriously revised, but meanwhile Renan had vastly increased the circle of its readers by issuing a cheap edition at 1 franc 25 centimes, in the interest, he said, of the poor, whom he called the true disciples of Jesus. But the book made its appeal to every level of cultivation. Joseph Henry Allen, the church historian, has described it as "the one great literary monument of a century of New Testament criticism."[1] John Haynes Holmes, who wrote the introduction to an American edition of 1927, says: "It ranks with Darwin's *Origin of Species* and Marx's *Das Kapital* as a work which changed forever the currents of the world's thought and life."[2]

Strange Child

It is the author of this book and his ways of thinking about religion that will be considered in this essay.

No one would guess from Renan's beginning what he was to become. There was no intellectual distinction and little of ordinary education in his family tree. He was born in the village of Tréguier on the coast of Brittany in 1823. Born prematurely, he hung for a while between life and death; but a local "witch," having thrown his tiny shirt into a holy well and observed that it floated rather than sank, announced that the fairies loved him and that he would live. His mother was reassured. She was herself "a little lively gypsy of a woman, black as a prune from Agen, and with Gascon blood in her,"[3] as well as a sunny disposition and a lively wit. The boy's father was a gentle, impractical, dreamy man, who eked out an irregular living by means of his fishing smack, which he plied up and down the stormy Breton coast. One day when his son was five the crew came in without him; he had leaped or fallen into the sea; no one knew which. The mother, with the help of several older children, managed to keep their home in Tréguier, and there Ernest Renan lived for his first fifteen years.

There was nothing notable about Tréguier except that it was an ancient center of religion. Its town and port were negligible, but its streets ran upward and converged on a high hill crowned by a Gothic cathedral whose spire and bells dominated the countryside. In its long shadow lay schools and convents where the teaching remained, like itself, unchanged from the Middle Ages. To one of these Catholic schools young Ernest Renan trudged daily. He was a strange boy in both body and mind. He had a great head, an ill-managed body, and short legs that carried him somewhat unsteadily all his life. For sports he had neither skill nor interest, and partly for this reason was regarded by his fellow pupils as something of a sissy. And there were other reasons for looking askance at him. He actually enjoyed school. He liked and admired his teachers, whom he took as voices of a venerable wisdom. He liked to go up into the cathedral alone and sit there quietly, musing and dreaming by himself. This proneness to dreamy abstraction he often laid in later years to his Celtic blood. At any rate, the stories of saints and angels, of witches and demons, with which the countryside abounded and of which his mother carried in her head an inexhaustible store, he had no difficulty in taking as fact. Some of these stories he told in the delightful book of his old age, *Souvenirs d'enfance et de jeunesse.*

This book, the *Souvenirs,* is so charged with Renan's special qualities that one is tempted to translate a bit of its untranslatable prose. Here is its opening paragraph:

> One of the most widely spread legends of Brittany is that of the reputed town of Is, which, at a time unknown, had been swallowed up by the sea. The site of this fabulous city is pointed out at various places on the coast, and fishermen tell strange tales about it. On stormy days, they say, one may see in the trough of the waves the steeple tops of its churches; on days of calm one hears the sound of bells rising from the abyss and caroling the hymn of the day. It often comes over me that I have at the bottom of my heart a town of Is, which goes on ringing its insistent bells and summoning to the sacred offices the faithful who no longer hear them. Sometimes I stop and cup my ear for these tremulous tones which seem to reach me from infinite depths like voices from another world. Especially with the coming of old age, it has been a pleasure in the repose of summer to recall these far-off echoes of an Atlantis that has vanished.[4]

These sentences suggest the history of Renan. It is a history of struggle between incompatible worlds, the world of his happy and unquestioning youth and the world of disillusionment of France's greatest scholar. The bells of Tréguier kept ringing in the deeper levels of his being; the idealism of the church, its moral rigor, the beauty and dignity of its ancient ritual, haunted him always, even when his name had become a symbol, the world over, for modern skepticism. What was singular about Renan was that the two loves continued side by side to the end. The enthusiasm with which he embraced the new had no room for bitterness about the old.

During his years at Tréguier there was no intimation of what was to follow. He was so faithful and promising a devotee that there could be no doubt of his destination—he would become a priest among his Breton neighbors and spend his life baptizing, marrying, and burying them. Finishing at the top of his class and winning every prize open to him, he was considered by the priests who were his teachers as their finest offering to the Virgin and the Christian cause.

The Move to Paris

The next step in his career seemed to justify their hopes. He was discovered by Abbé Dupanloup, who was the energetic head of the Catholic Seminary of Saint-Nicholas-du-Chardonnet in Paris, and was attempting to make it into a training school for young aristocrats and intellectuals. He was scanning the horizon for youths of social distinction, scholarly brilliance, or both. An assistant brought to his attention the record of this youth in an obscure Breton village, and, as Renan wrote,

In a minute my fate was decided. "Bring him," said the imperious superior. I was fifteen and a half years old, not yet at the age for reflection. I was on vacation at a friend's house in a village not far from Tréguier. On the fourth of September, in the afternoon, a messenger searched me out. I remember my return home as if it were yesterday. There were three miles to cover on foot across the countryside. The pious reverberations of the evening Angelus answered each other from parish to parish, filling the air with something calm, sweet, and melancholy, the essence of the life I was about to leave forever. The next day I set out for Paris; on the seventh, I saw around me things as new to me as if I had been abruptly dropped down in France from Tahiti or Timbuctoo.[5]

Saint Nicholas was an elite school of about two hundred boys preparing for the priesthood. At its head was a man who had achieved fame in the church by securing the deathbed repentance of Prince de Talleyrand, and was destined to become a distinguished bishop. Dupanloup ran his school as if he were the commanding general of a military academy. His domination of the place was so complete that punishments were unnecessary; a word from him and any straggler from the regiment fell back into line. If this word did not suffice, a polite letter came from the commander's office pointing out that there seemed to be some incompatibility between the seminary and the boy, who would be good enough to pack up at once and leave. In his lonely room, surrounded by sophisticated young Parisians, the awkward peasant lad was miserable. He could not sleep. He considered throwing himself out of the window to the city street below. His best friend in the class shut himself up in his room and died of what appeared to be sheer homesickness. Renan was perhaps saved by an odd circumstance. He wrote a letter to his mother, filled with an affection so forlorn, passionate, and eloquent that the priest who censored the mail took note of it and passed it on to the head. At the evening assembly of that day, Dupanloup mentioned it as a piece of masterly writing, and between the austere headmaster and the odd newcomer there developed both friendship and respect. This was not quite an accident. Dupanloup also had a widowed mother for whom he had a boundless affection, so he understood the letter and its writer as most others could not.

Renan's three years at Saint Nicholas were nevertheless not happy. Neither science nor philosophy appeared in the seminary's curriculum, and he was hungry for both. The studies were wholly literary and religious, and for a person as well versed in the classics as Renan already was, to spend years on the refinements of Virgilian style and the details of ecclesiastical history gave him the sense of tramping a treadmill. The seminary lacked, as he wrote later, the very "idea of a critical research into truth." He was a young man of precocious critical intellect which was left to whir furiously in cutting chaff. And since the teaching was all on one side, there was nothing to arouse or support questioning; the names of Voltaire, Rousseau, and Diderot were discreetly unmentioned, and though the school was in Paris, it remained a fortress before whose walls the winds of contemporary literature and theory seemed to die away in discouragement.

After three years of this regimented life, the students made a momentous choice. Those whose call to the priesthood had become in-audible went their several ways; those in whom it still rang clear were graduated to Saint Sulpice, the most renowned of training schools for the French church. Renan's teachers knew that his book-ishness, solitariness, and absentmindedness would add up to a queer figure as a parish priest, but they knew also that the church had need of scholars, and that here they had a good one. He was urged to go on to Saint Sulpice, and he went. Many visitors to Paris will remem-ber plodding along on some little street off the Boulevard St. Ger-main and suddenly coming out on a magnificent square almost filled by a vast basilica, its corners adorned with statues of Massillon, Féne-lon, and other great clerics of the French past. On one side of this square is a row of buildings which are the headquarters of the Sul-pician order. Of this order Renan was to be a member for the next four years. But according to its rigorous schedule the first two of these years had to be devoted to philosophy, the final two to a crown-ing exposure to the direct light from on high that came with theol-ogy. Renan was herded off with the other young philosophers to a rural retreat at Issy, in the suburbs of the city, where the palace of Marguerite de Valois, first wife of Henry IV, had been turned over to the order.

Issy and Philosophy

At Issy he gained for the first time what he had so long wanted, not rhetorical defenses of doctrines whose truth was guaranteed already but objective searches after truth, made with no prior commitments except to the evidence. As usual, he loved and admired his teachers, of whom he has left a gallery of etchings in the *Souvenirs,* but his education at Issy was chiefly self-education. He read furiously and continuously. For the whole of his two years there he did not once take the time to walk back into the city. In the large garden he had a favorite stone bench, and there his teachers and fellow students would see him, even on cold winter days, bundled up in layers of

well-worn clothes, happily lost in the arguments of some philosopher. He wanted to see with his own eyes. From Descartes and his
even more admired Malebranche, "the finest dreamer, the most implacable logician who ever existed,"[6] he learned that one could
achieve a clearness that amounted to certainty. "My regular reading,"
he wrote, "was Pascal, Malebranche, Euler, Locke, Leibniz, Descartes, Reid, Dugald Stewart."[7] The odd presence in this list of Euler
should be noticed, for Renan took mathematics as the ideal of intelligibility and proof. He was already reading English, as the appearance of these three assorted British writers attests. That Leibniz
is included does not show that he was reading German, for Leibniz
wrote in both German and French; but he was learning German
and would soon be reveling in Kant and Hegel.

Reading philosophy is innocent enough; philosophizing is something else, and, as Emerson pointed out, is a dangerous business.
Descartes founded modern philosophy by insisting that the supreme
court in the life of thought is the "clear and distinct perception" of
one's own mind. He set out to doubt everything that he could not
thus see to be true. He found that he could doubt everything—everything, that is, except the fact of his own consciousness, the fact, for
example, that he was doubting. If he did that, he was doing the
doubting that he was supposed to be doubting about. To admit that
one was doing something and at the same time to doubt that one
was doing it was inconsistent; and what was inconsistent could not
be true. How did one know that? It seemed indeed self-evident. And
if this were questioned, one could argue: Either this or nothing. If
both sides of a contradiction can be true, then one cannot know that
anything is true, for whatever one said would admit along with it
its own denial. In consistency, then, the rationalist had an absolute
test which every claim to truth must pass.

But how did all this sit with the young philosopher's theology?
The Sulpicians were rigorous, traditional Catholics, holding that the
entire Old and New Testaments, as approved at Trent, were true.
But no one who knew his Bible as Renan did could fail to note that

Scripture fell short of consistency at many points. For example, the stories of the birth of Christ, the coming of the Magi, the Resurrection, the conversion of Paul, all contained flat and undeniable contradictions. They must be accepted nevertheless. There were thus two standards of truth, the secular and the religious. What was ruled out as impossible by secular reason, revelation might require one to believe as truth without defect.

Outwardly Renan was faithful in all his observances, in accordance with what he called "the most essential of Catholic virtues, docility."[8] Inwardly, a struggle was going on for the integrity of his mind. He could not reach consistency by making an anthology of Scripture, or by taking it upon himself to reinterpret the sacred text. "At Saint Sulpice no attenuation of Scriptural dogmas was permitted," he writes; "the Fathers, the councils, and the doctors of the church appeared as the sources of Christianity."[9] But over and over again, as he sat reading these doctors' pronouncements, he seemed to hear a quiet voice saying, "Cela n'est pas vrai. Cela n'est pas vrai." For a time he set the voice down to diabolical obsession, but that was too great a concession to the system that was in question. He took his problem to his professors, who assured him that his troubles were adolescent rashes that he would soon outgrow. One of his advisers indeed did not. M. Gottofrey, who taught metaphysics, though believing the whole discipline to be a farce, was a passionate devotee with a keen sense for incipient heresy. Of his classes with him Renan writes:

My argumentations in Latin, given with a firm and emphatic air, astonished and disquieted him. Sometimes I had too much reason on my side; sometimes I brought into plain light what I found faulty in arguments offered as valid. One day when my objections had been pushed vigorously, and when, in view of the feebleness of the replies, smiles spread in the classroom, he put a stop to the discussion. That evening he took me aside. He pointed out to me eloquently what was anti-Christian in the commitment to reason and the harm that rationalism did to faith. In strange agitation, he reproached me with my passion for study. Research! What good was that? Everything essential for us is known. Science saves no souls. And, his excitement rising more and more, he said to me with a deeply felt emphasis: "You are not a Christian."[10]

Renan was shocked, and in the chapel wept tears of contrition at the feet of the Virgin. But looking back on this incident thirty-five years later, he admitted that Gottofrey was right, and wished that he had seen as clearly himself as did his keen-eyed teacher. If he had left the church then and there, and turned to science, he thought he might have achieved something in it; and he added that he had reached independently some of the conclusions of his honored contemporary across the Channel, Darwin.

Saint Sulpice and Theology

When, after two years at Issy, the time came for him to transfer to the great theological seminary of Saint Sulpice in Paris, he hesitated. Heart and head were divided. He loved the church; he admired his teachers; he found continual delight in books and study and contemplation. He knew that he was something of a misfit, that he was socially timid, physically unprepossessing, hopeless as a man of action. But priests, he added to himself, need not be parish priests; they could also be professors, and the ideal life for him he thought to be that of the scholar in a seminary, preferably with few students, and given over to the pursuit of truth. Furthermore, like many other lonely minds with few friends, he was deeply affectionate, and was sure that his defection from the church would leave his mother heartbroken. On the other hand, it was becoming painfully plain to him that the philosophers at Issy had done their work and that many of the historical "facts" and theological dogmas laid down in Scripture he could no longer say he believed. And doubt or disbelief, even on minor dogmas, was regarded by the Sulpicians of the 1840s as intolerable, for the creed was a single seamless whole, so that one could not pick and choose among its dogmas, as many "liberals" are doing today. To reject one was to reject all. Renan's letters to his mother are not free from deception either of her or of himself. Again consulting his advisers, he was assured that this too would pass, and with a troubled spirit he submitted, accepted the tonsure, which was the first formal step to the priesthood, and in October 1843 entered the seminary of Saint Sulpice. Theology, he hoped, would resolve the doubts that philosophy had insinuated.

What happened was just the opposite. The study of Scripture in its original languages turned doubt into flat disbelief. Renan was not a genius in philosophy; he was a genius in language, and he fell at once under the influence of Le Hir, who, besides being perhaps the best Hebrew scholar in Europe, was a fellow Breton and took the brilliant young man under his wing. Renan learned Hebrew in order to read the Old Testament, and he mastered the language with such swift ease that in his second year he was teaching it. In that year he was also allowed to take classes at the Sorbonne under the Orientalist Quatremère, who taught him the secular method of studying religious texts. He read the book of Isaiah, and saw that there was not one Isaiah, as the church had taught, but two. He read the book of Daniel, whose prophecies were accepted by the church as inspired, and concluded that it was too unreliable to have a place in Scripture at all. He read the Pentateuch, which was accepted by the church as written by Moses, though Moses could hardly have written the account of his own death. It was thus not the metaphysical difficulties of two worlds of truth that finally settled the balance; it was rather the drip, drip on the soil of his mind of hundreds of these incidents of contradiction, of the historically incredible, of parallels with pagan religion, that wore his creed away by their attrition.

Defection

Renan completed his full course at Saint Sulpice, and the next step was ordination. That step he never took. He could not live in two worlds at once without feeling a hypocrite in both; at last he had to choose. In October 1845 he doffed his clerical garb, bought some cheap civilian clothes, and moved into a boardinghouse for pupils of the Lycée Henri Quatre, where, in return for helping students with their lessons for two hours every evening, he was given board, lodging, and laundry. Here he remained for three and a half years. His time was mostly his own, and he used it for an almost feverish productivity. He attended courses, given gratis, at the Sorbonne and the Collège de France, won his baccalaureate and *licence,* mastered Sanskrit, and wrote a history and comparative grammar of the Semitic languages, for which he received the Volney Prize of 1,200 francs. He followed this in two years with a book on the Greek language in the West from the fifth to the fourteenth centuries, which won him a prize of 2,000 francs. He entered the competitive test for the *agrégé* in philosophy and came out number one. He submitted two theses for the doctorate, one in Latin, the other in French, the latter being the first draft of his book on Averroës, the Arabic commentator on Aristotle. Since it was not the sort of work that publishers welcome, he paid for its publication himself. It fell under the eye of the omnivorous John Morley, who wrote in his diary: "Began Renan's *Averroës.* There is such a mixture of scholar and writer as no longer exists to my knowledge. And what a mixture it is, when the world is so lucky as to find it."[11] Since few scholars were qualified to examine him in this field, a board of examiners was collected consisting of the most distinguished professors in France, and Renan's name as a scholar began to be known. He could easily have secured a post in a *lycée,* but he decided to bide his time till a chair at the Sorbonne or the Collège de France was empty. Though he was charmingly modest toward other scholars, he knew his powers and did not hold them cheaply. Half intoxicated with the prospects that his new freedom of thought opened to him, he completed in four or five months a large volume on *The Future of Science.* He asked an opinion on it from his friend Augustin Thierry, who thought it immature, so he put it away in a drawer of his desk. There it waited for nearly forty years, when at last he published it with the introduction that, by then at least, it needed.

This *Avenir de la science* is the nearest thing to a rounded philosophy that Renan offers us. Nature is all, and law is king. The rule of law is nowhere broken, and those breaches of it that are so constantly reported in our own and the other scriptures are works of the imagination, trying to explain in anthropomorphic terms what the writers had too little science to understand. There is no supernature behind the scenes, breaking in at odd times and for unintelligible reasons. Not that the beliefs in such events are priestly impostures; they are the natural and honest results of an attempt to make sense of things by a reason groping for grounds and calling in imagination to help where it fails. All religions, on their dogmatic side, are attempts of this kind to interpret a universe that produces men in profusion and as carelessly destroys them. These attempts are partly to explain, partly to buoy up man's feeble spirits in facing a universe before which he is helpless.

In modern science and philosophy reason is coming of age. Its business is to distinguish myth from fact, the work of fear and desire from that of thought, the values of beauty and duty from that of truth. And of all the values, truth stands first. Renan occasionally startles us by assuming that religion too puts truth first, that in fighting *against* religious tradition he is fighting *for* true religion, and that in arguing for the humanity of Jesus he has Jesus as his ally. Revelations are many; reason is one; and should not religion pursue in all honesty the ultimate truth? The revelation of mature reason is the only revelation; "to know," he wrote, "is to be initiated into God." However that may be, he knew his own aim. In his early years he wanted for his epitaph the verse from Genesis: "I have fought the fights of God and have prevailed";[12] in later years he preferred the simple words that did finally appear on his tomb, "Veritatem dilexi," my delight has been in truth.

Italy

In 1849 the young man had an adventure that left him glad he had not rushed into print. The Ministry of Education sent him on a mission to Italy to report for French scholars on its manuscript collections, particularly those in Arabic and Syrian. The mission was a great success. He visited most of the larger cities of Italy, explored at will the libraries of the Vatican, Monte Cassino, Venice, and Florence, brought to light an unpublished writing by Abelard, found to his delight an Arabic text of Averroës, had a conversation with Pope Pius IX, whom he found amiable but narrow, visited Naples, whose religion revolted him with its crude saint worship and sensuality, and spent five splendid months in Rome. The old city overwhelmed him. Not a very observant person, he had his eyes opened to beauty. "Would you believe it . . . ," he wrote to his friend Berthelot,

> I am entirely changed. I am no longer French, I no longer criticize . . . .
> You know that with me religious impressions are very strong, and, as a
> consequence of my education, they mingle in indefinable proportions with
> the most mysterious instincts of our nature. . . . I had not understood
> what a popular religion really is, a religion accepted by the people naïvely
> and without criticism; I had not understood a people incessantly creative
> in religion, taking the dogmas of it in a living and true way. . . . I have
> found in this people, in its faith, in its civilization, an incomparable lofti-
> ness, poetry, and ideality. . . . Our idealism is abstract, severe, without
> images; that of this people is plastic, turned to form, invincibly led to
> translation and expression. You cannot walk a quarter of an hour in Rome
> without being struck with the prodigious fecundity of images. Every-
> where paintings, statues, churches, monasteries; nothing commonplace,
> nothing vulgar, the ideal penetrating everywhere. If you enter a
> church, you find a painting of Raphael, Domenico, Albani, a Madonna
> of Pietro da Cortona, a statue of Michael Angelo.[13]

In the light of this experience, Renan came back feeling that his *Future of Science* was too intellectualistic, too much a gospel of salvation by disinfectants available only to an elite. He played seriously with the idea of making the noncognitive element in religion the essential one, and identifying it with the sense of beauty. These Italian peasants knew nothing about the truths and deceptions of dogma, but they lived in a world of beauty that bathed them nevertheless in a continued sunshine of noble images, figures of power and dignity, and that idealization of the human form and spirit which belongs to the true artist.

Palestine

Valuable as this Italian visit was in mellowing and enriching Renan's view of religion, his next commission was more productive still. In 1860 a massacre of Christians in Lebanon led to the occupation of the country by French troops; and the French government, eager to exploit its new acquisition, sent Renan to direct excavations in the Biblical lands, leaving him much freedom to say where and how. He was liberally helped by the French soldiers, who did not have too much to do, and by Lebanese eager to earn pocket money; and he did unearth a few antiquities that were sent home to French museums. But what chiefly came from his expedition was his book, the *Vie de Jésus*. It was not so much the record of his journeys as the report of an imaginative inspiration that came to him as he followed the steps of the figure who fascinated him above all others in history. He followed these steps from Bethany to Jerusalem and the Mount of Olives, trudged up and down the shores of Jordan and the Sea of Galilee, talked with the people, supped with them and stayed in their houses, and tried to catch the Oriental ways of thinking and feeling. He had none of the apparatus of scholarship with him, much of the time only his Bible and Josephus. He had spent many years studying the New Testament, but that is a book of fragments in which the story is told in different orders, with differing facts, and with interpretations of the main character so various as to drive scholars to despair. The remorseless Strauss had gone through every detail of the Gospels with a magnifying glass, a scalpel, a steely freedom from any distorting reverence, and an erudition almost past belief. When his massive *Leben Jesu* had been completed, and turned into French by Littré and into English by George Eliot, the Gospels seemed to such scholars as Matthew Arnold to have been blown into a thousand pieces. It is clear today, it was clear to Renan, that no scholarship would ever put those pieces together again. The old picture of Jesus became a picture puzzle, with the pieces scattered and many of them missing, and with the pattern that might have unified them lost forever.

Strauss's approach was logical. What was Jesus' attitude toward divorce if he prohibited it unconditionally in Mark and Luke, and admitted it for adultery in Matthew? How could the Magi have been guided by a star that stood over a particular house in a particular town, when it stands over half the earth? In contrast, Renan's approach was imaginative and psychological. Here was a spirit of such extraordinary drawing power that millions had bowed before him as no less than Deity. What was inside that mind of his? How did he think of himself? How did he feel about his fellows? What were the aims that alienated him from his own people and brought him to so early a tragedy? There, in what is called the Holy Land, Renan lay in his tent on his stomach, scribbling furiously to catch the vision before it vanished. He was thirty-seven, and at the summit of his power. What he brought home with him was a manuscript described variously as a masterpiece of historical romance, of blasphemy, of negation, of creative insight, and of literary genius. But note that common to all these descriptions is the term "masterpiece."

What was it that made this book unique? It was the combination in one credible narrative of two attiudes that, until he wrote, seemed to cancel each other out. On the one hand was a complete skepticism as to the existence of a supernatural world. On the other hand was a profound reverence and adoration for the person of Jesus. The result was that it had something gratifying for everybody. Agnostic scientists and philosophers read it with delight, for it brought the weight of an authoritative scholarship to bear on their side. Devout Christians could read it with an almost equal pleasure because, in spite of its questioning of dogma, it painted a picture of the Master that was compellingly attractive. More important still, many persons whose minds were divided, suspicious of religion though drawn by its moral idealism, found here a tenable position. The extent of

Renan's achievement will be clearer if we say something about each side of his synthesis.

Miracles

He was met at the outset by the problem of miracles. Should the life that he was to record begin with the announcement to Mary by the angel Gabriel of a birth with no human father, and a star-guided visit by wise men from the East? Or was it the natural birth of a son to a Jewish carpenter and his wife? He could not begin without deciding the philosophy in accordance with which the book was to be written. In the life as told in the Gospels, the natural and supernatural threads are woven together so closely that they move from one to the other without a break. But Renan had thought this problem through as he listened to his masters at Saint Sulpice. He did not dismiss miracles a priori.[14] He held with Hume that the only way men could know whether a stone would sink or float in water was to drop it and see. There was nothing, then, in the report of a birth by a virgin that could be ruled out as impossible. But was it probable? Today every biologist would scout such a report as a fable. On investigation it would always conceal a natural event whose conditions, given honest testimony, could be precisely known. The scientific mind rejects the very notion of a miracle as superstition. What medical man, if a new disease appeared, would discourage inquiry into it on the ground that it might have no natural cause at all? No respected man of science would take such a view, and if he did, he would quickly forfeit such respect as he had.

Is this prejudice on the part of the scientific community? Renan was clear that it was not. Does this mean that under no conditions would a scientist accept supernatural interposition? No again, says Renan, for that would be dogmatism on the other side. Suppose a man were to appear in a Paris hospital claiming the power to raise the dead, and suppose a corpse was present whose vital functions, as attested by a team of competent physicians, had ceased four days ago, as in the case of Lazarus, so that general decomposition had set in.

Suppose, further, that by a wave of his hand the visitor restored all the normal functions again, and the dead man leaped up fresh and healthy. Would the physicians refuse belief that the supernatural had intervened? Renan did not think they would,[15] though they might well invite a repetition in other cases to avoid possible deception. But this sort of event does not occur.

To the question, then, of the reality of miracles, Renan's answer is simple:

miracles only occur when people believe in them. The supernatural is the creation of faith. . . . The credulity of the witness is the condition of a miracle. No miracle is produced before those who are able or permitted to discuss and criticize it. To this there is not a single exception. Cicero, with his usual good sense and penetration, asks: "Since when has this secret force disappeared; has it not been since men have become less credulous?"[16]

What we have here is a form of Mill's argument from concomitant variations. When miracles are generally believed in, they are common; as the belief in them declines, so do they. "It must be remembered that all antiquity, with the exception of the great scientific schools of Greece and their Roman disciples, accepted miracles; and that Jesus not only believed in them but had not the least idea of a natural order governed by fixed laws."[17] Indeed miracle is a modern conception that developed along with the notion of natural law. Before such laws were recognized as universal, there were no clear lines between events that were merely astonishing because exceptional, events that were unexplained through the ignorance of the time, and events that were inexplicable because they had no natural causes at all. Today the reign of law has become so thoroughly established that a historian who believed an exceptional event to be an accident or a miracle would be put down by his peers as a booby. Even in accepting Heisenberg's indeterminacy, they show small inclination to connect it with supernatural interposition.

In the course of his discussions of miracles, Renan introduces many fortifying considerations, though in the casual way of a musing man of letters rather than in that of a philosopher marshaling an argument. "A miracle . . . far from being a proof of divine power, would be rather an avowal of weakness, since the divinity would be correcting by it his first plan, thus showing its insufficiency."[18] Again, it was common practice to exalt a candidate for high religious honors by endowing him with miracles:

when it was sought to establish the cult of Apollonius of Tyana . . . it was not thought possible to succeed in this except by inventing a vast cycle of miracles. . . . Jesus had, therefore, to choose between these two alternatives—either to renounce his vision, or to become a thaumaturge. . . . One of his most deeply rooted opinions was that by faith and prayer man had full power over nature."[19]

There is no need to attribute deception to him in claiming this power. Again: "The types of the Gospel miracles, in fact, do not present great variety; they are repetitions of each other and seem built on a very small number of models, accommodated to the taste of the country."[20] Some of these, classed as psychological, may well have occurred as reported; the influence on a disturbed mind by another that is calm, fearless, and loving has often proved curative. The movement of this class of abnormal cures or any considerable part of it to the moral field just so far reduces the problem of miracles.

Once more, some of the miracles are expressly reported as fulfillments of prophecy. It must be remembered that all the Gospels were written a generation or more after the death of Jesus by persons concerned to show him as superhuman. His fulfillment of prophecy was one of the most persuasive ways of showing this. And the prophecies were generally so vague that the task was not of great difficulty. "No Jewish work of the time," says Renan, "gives a series of prophecies drawing up exactly what the Messiah should accomplish. Many Messianic allusions reported by the evangelists are so subtle, so indirect, that one cannot believe they all responded to a generally admitted doctrine."[21] To the vagueness of the prophecies must be added that their fulfillments, as actually reported, are full of contradictions, as one would expect of recollections written long after the events and in order to prove a point. Scholars cannot, of course, accept contradictions; if logic goes, all thought and discourse go with it. Can responsible writers of history accept sporadic intrusions from another world? No historian, says Renan, would do it now, even when the means of reporting are immeasurably improved. Why should we do it for events taking place many centuries ago among persons to whom fixed law was unknown, and inconsistently recorded at second- or thirdhand long afterward by persons of tendentious motive?

Renan, like Strauss, was trying to write scientific history. And "no just notion of the true nature of history is possible," Strauss wrote, "without a perception of the inviolability of the chain of finite causes, and of the impossibility of miracles."[22] Constantine may have thought he saw in the sky, as the battle reached its crisis, a cross with the words, "In hoc signo vinces." The belief that he saw the sign may have occurred and may in fact have turned the tide. But if some force intervened from outside nature to determine the outcome of the battle, if the earth did really cease to revolve while Joshua completed his slaughter of the Amorites, if a normal human body did walk on water as if it were solid ground, then history in the ordinary sense has become impossible. Common causality may at any moment be suspended, and explanations based on it cannot be relied upon. If miracles occur, the fact that history would have to be rewritten in the light of them does not prove them false, granted. But let it be remembered that if we follow the evidence there is a great mass of miracles attending the lives of Mohammedan and Christian saints that are as well attested as those of the Gospels. And to accept these en masse would render history, as Gibbon and Renan wrote it, an unsortable congeries of normal explanations and irruptions from on high.

The Rational and the Supernatural

But after all, it may be said, the rejection of miracles does not commit us to rejecting the whole supernatural realm along with them. One may decline to accept the walking on the water or the raising of Lazarus without abandoning the teaching of the church on the second coming, on heaven and hell, on the incarnation, on the Trinity, on the atonement, and on its attendant plan of salvation. Many thoughtful moderns have found peace of mind in such a compromise. Not Renan. The two networks of belief were too closely intermeshed to be severed at our convenience. What, for example, are we to make of the dogmas of the second coming and of heaven and hell? The explicit and repeated teaching of the Gospels is that Christ is to come in clouds of glory in his own generation to separate eternally the sheep from the goats. His prediction proved untrue. He thought he was the expected Messiah of the Jews. It turned out that he was not. Incidentally, we must not impute to him the claim to be Deity, omniscient and omnipotent, nor was this claimed for him by the synoptics, which represent him as doing what even omniscience could not do, namely growing in knowledge. The claim to Deity was rather that of John, the latest and least reliable of the evangelists, who was commending him to the more educated by the use of Greek concepts of which Jesus knew nothing.

Now if Jesus was fallible about the Messiahship and his destiny, was he infallible in theology? For that matter, what was his theology? It was clearly not that of John, and since he was not given to metaphysical theorizing, it will probably never be known. But the part of it that has proved central in Christian thought is the atonement, the doctrine that he was the second Adam. Just as the first Adam had disobeyed his Creator and "brought sin into the world and all our woe," so the second had brought the possibility of salvation by his perfect submission and sinlessness. By his sinless life and sacrificial death he made it possible for an angry Deity to extend clemency to some at least of his creatures. Unfortunately these selected persons were relatively few. The mass of mankind remained subject to terrible punishment, not only for the immense and mounting corruption they had been inheriting since Adam, but for their own persisting disbelief and disobedience. Jesus himself seems never to have taught this doctrine, wtih its intellectual and moral incoherence and its enthronement of injustice at the heart of Christian faith; it was imposed on him by Paul and the church fathers. The judgment of these men, when faced by a conflict between reason and revelation, was too often the fanatical cry of Tertullian, *"Credo quia absurdum est."*

Renan, confronting the incredibility of miracles, and catching with the practiced eye of the Orientalist the continuity of the miracle stories and the theological stories, came to a momentous decision. He could not accept the miraculous without abandoning science; he could not abandon science without abandoning rationality. Nor could he accept the tangled web of theology which was draped over the miraculous without abandoning logic; and he could not abandon logic without abandoning his rationality again. That he would not and could not do. It would be to give up the quest of truth itself. He had reached the crossroads, and must take one road or the other. To live in a world of supernature, a world of angels and demons, a world where most men were to be condemned for the sins of their ancestors, and where causal law was suspended continually by incursions from a changeable Deity, was impossible unless one embraced a new standard of truth, at variance with that of reason. One must be ready to say of the same proposition that it was false for reason but true in religion. This Renan could not say. And to him it seemed clear that the choice was "All or nothing, supernaturalism absolute or rationalism without reservation."[20] And without reservation he cast his lot with the rationalists.

This implies that the *Vie de Jésus* is not a life of Jesus the Christ at all. The Christmas heraldry with which he is introduced to the world by Saint Luke, his identity with Godhead as pronounced by Saint John, the transcendental machinery of redemption with which he was invested by Saint Paul, were all stripped away. What was left? Nothing was left but a human being living in the cultural aridity of a remote corner of the empire. To most readers of the New Testament, this would leave the book eviscerated of everything that made it religiously important.

The Uniqueness of the Human Jesus

If it did not do so for Renan, it was by reason of the character of the human being that remained. For him Jesus, though not divine, was unique, and in a uniquely important way. He is the only man who has taken love as the glory of the human spirit, and lived and died in loyalty to that conviction. Renan, who was a connoisseur of religions, believed that here was a new religion, the ultimate religion, indeed the only tenable religion. It meant a transformation of man's mind, a radical change in the quality and scope of his affections, an inward revolution that would sweep away what seemed to be insuperable barriers of class, sex, nation, and race. "Jesus," said Renan, "founded religion in human history, as Socrates did philosophy, and Aristotle science."[24] He had no taste for the dogmas of the theologians. "God, thought of simply as Father, was the whole theology of Jesus." "Jesus did not have visions," Renan added; "God does not speak to him as to someone outside himself; God is in him; he feels himself to be with God, and he draws from his own heart what he says of his Father. He lives in the bosom of God by communication at every moment . . . ."[25] In the first sentence of his essay on "The Critical Historians of Jesus," Renan writes: "They say that Angelico of Fiesole never painted the heads of the Virgin or the Christ except on his knees; it would be well for criticism to imitate his example, and only after having adored them, to face the radiance of certain figures before which the ages have bent low."[26] The religion of Jesus was "a pure religion, without forms, without temple, and without priest; it was the moral judgment of the world, delegated to the conscience of the just man, and to the arm of the people."[27] "He is the only man before whom I bow."[28]

These and a hundred other passages make it clear that in spite of Renan's alienation from Christian belief Jesus remained for him a figure to be reverenced, followed, and loved. But on his own assumptions, was there any justification for such attitudes? Are they not directed upon a figure who never existed? Jesus is adored as the founder of the one true religion. But that founder clearly believed in angels and demons, in the speedy coming of the kingdom, in a Father who was real and heard our prayers and sometimes in consequence changed his mind. These convictions lay at the heart of Jesus' religion, and Renan accepted none of them. How could he exalt as the founder of true religion one who would have insisted that what had been left to him was no religion at all?

Objections and the Reply

To this question I doubt whether Renan had a wholly adequate answer. But as the author of perhaps the most credible plan yet offered for preserving the position of Jesus in a world of science, he deserves to be heard in reply. The reply, I think, would have taken two quite different lines.

First he would have pointed out that Jesus was an Oriental, and that the Oriental and Western minds work differently, particularly in matters political and religious. The Western mind recognizes a sharp division between the activities of the head and those of the heart, and is suspicious of infringements of feeling upon belief. Slogans, sentimentality, the endless association in advertising of crude or even harmful products with beauty or strength, are seductive but they are not evidence, and the man of some education takes pride in remaining unmoved by them. In this respect Renan was a thoroughly Westernized mind; for him the passion with which a belief was held had no bearing whatever on its truth.

The East has never been quite content with this sharp division. In the traditional Indian philosophy it is hard to detect when the voice of reason ends and the voice of mystical aspiration begins, and the two voices are often blended into an attractive but dangerous harmony. In the voice of the Hebrew prophets, "Woe unto you, Tyre and Sidon," "Woe unto you, scribes and Pharisees," the object may take its form from the emotional repulsion. "The literal truth is not greatly prized by the Oriental; he sees everything through the medium of his ideas, his interests, and his passions."[29] In saying that Jesus was an Oriental, Renan was thus saying that too often his head followed his heart. If Jesus had a mystical sense of "something far more deeply interfused," if, like many poets, he felt least alone when most alone, he was doing what mystics have done since their tribe began, namely projecting a real object that complemented the feeling and justified it. Jesus talked with his Father as if He were in the same room. Sometimes he was answered, sometimes not, and at one tragic moment toward the end he seems to have lost his faith that any answering presence was there at all. Now it was Renan's belief, to put it baldly, that the Father, as Jesus conceived him, had never been there, and that this "magnified non-natural man," as Arnold called him, was partly the creature of the religion that Jesus inherited, partly the projection of his own loving and imaginative mind.

If this seems to attribute to Jesus a monstrous and impossible error, Renan would remind us, first, that he did make mistakes, and second, that this was a mistake of an eminently natural kind. That he was not beyond errors is easily shown if one takes the thankless trouble of looking for them. He shared the expectations of his people of a coming Messiah, and believed that these expectations were fulfilled in him. We have seen that he looked forward to an early judgment, which never came. He misread the character of Judas. Schweitzer even says: "Jesus shared the Jewish racial exclusiveness wholly and unreservedly."[30] The dogma of errorlessness is thus impossible to sustain. And what error could be more natural or more general than that of finding in and through nature an animating spirit like the only one we directly know, our own? Tylor thought that all religion, and Frazer that all science, had its root in animism. Feuerbach thought, and surely rightly, that man tends to create God in his own image. Evelyn Underhill thought, and again rightly, that what the great religious mystics found revealed in their visions was a God fulfilling the preconceptions that they brought with them in their own religion: thus the Moslem Sufis found a wholly unitary

Deity; St. Theresa claimed it had been revealed to her how God could be three in one; and George Fox found a Deity that looked with stern disfavor on dancing, music, and Shakespeare. Renan would have said that Jesus' immense elevation above these mystics in stature did not preclude his sharing with them this all but inevitable proclivity.

The Religion of a Rationalist

To the charge, then, that Renan was venerating a figure from which he had excised all that tradition had taken as worth venerating, he would have pleaded guilty, but with such mitigating circumstances as to remove the sting from the charge. But to this he would have added a second answer in which no pleas in mitigation were needed. It involved his naturalistic theory of religion. He was a thoroughgoing evolutionist regarding both body and mind. He believed that consciousness, having evolved from matter, had gone on evolving toward levels on which reason could take control and direct men's actions toward ends deliberately chosen. These ends were not dictated by any authority from outside this ascending movement; they were appointed by forces within it—partly by the potentialities of the growing mind itself, partly by their anticipated fulfillments, deliberately chosen as ends. These fulfillments formed the great intrinsic goods of life—the experience of love and friendship, the enjoyment of beauty, the doing of justice, the glow of a healthy body, the sweep of an enlightened and comprehensive mind. In the ordered exercise of these faculties lay the only true spiritual life. The agent that compared and weighed these goods and made the choice among them was reason. The spiritual life was the rational life. To make it anything else, to make it depend, for example, on a supernatural order on whose very nature and very existence the religions of the world disagree, seemed to Renan a cruel straitjacketing of what was best and highest in man. It was forcing him back into the monastery at a moment when the possibilities of the free spirit were just looming into sight. True religion is the pursuit of the ideal life, not for oneself alone but for all men, the endeavor to bring to all the fullest possible fruition of the powers with which nature had endowed them.

Renan took the bold step of saying that in substance this was the religion of Jesus himself. The announced intention of Jesus, of course, was to introduce the kingdom of heaven. But what did he mean by that? His biographers give two quite different accounts of it, between which one can only say that he wavered. One was the account in which he was to come in clouds of glory, backed by irresistible angelic hosts, to judge the quick and the dead, and to set up on earth a kingdom of the saved. This dream was continuous with the old Jewish dreams of the conquering Messiah and the dramatic celestial events that would herald his advent. Renan, following Strauss, put down this whole fabric as mythology. The advent stories were disproved by multiple contradictions with themselves and with known facts, while the eschatological parts were falsified by history.

But alongside this mythical conception of the kingdom, Jesus entertained another, as different from it almost as day from night. It was that of an inner kingdom, a kingdom that had its only existence in men's minds. Jesus was an Israelite who shared many of the hopes and delusions of his people, but it is also true, Renan insists, that he "was no longer a Jew. He was revolutionary in the highest degree; he called all men to a religion founded on the sole character of their being children of God."[31] And being a child of God was not a matter of obeying rules or offering sacrifices or visiting the temple or being a success in the world. Jesus cared for none of these things. What he thought important, and alone important, was renewing the inward man. He turned the popular scale of values upside down. The quality of one's spirit was the only thing that counted; it even determined whether or not one was a member of the kingdom. Renan tells the story of Jesus meeting at the well with the Samaritan woman, and his asking her for a drink. She was astonished, for the Jews had no dealings with Samaritans. She expected a rebuke, and by way of anticipating it, said, "our fathers worshipped in this mountain; and ye say that in Jerusalem is the place where one ought to worship. Jesus saith unto her, Woman, believe me, the hour cometh when ye shall neither in this mountain, nor yet at Jerusalem, worship the Father . . . but when the true worshippers shall worship the Father in spirit and in truth . . . ." Renan seizes upon this simple passage as the cue for one of his bursts of solemn eloquence.

The day when he uttered these words he was truly the son of God. He spoke for the first time the word on which will rest the structure of the enduring religion. He founded for all times and all lands the pure worship, that which all elevated souls will practice till the end of time. Not only was his religion, on that day, the best religion of humanity, it was the absolute religion; and if other planets have inhabitants endowed with reason and morality, their religion cannot differ from that which Jesus proclaimed by the well of Jacob. Man has not been able to maintain this religion, for one attains the ideal only transiently. This saying of Jesus has been a light in a dark night . . . . But the light will become full day, and after having run through all the cycles of errors, man will return to these words as the immortal expression of his faith and hope.[32]

Whether Jesus would have accepted this interpretation of his words—a family of children without a Father, a kingdom of heaven where heaven was a fiction, a kingdom of God in the absence of God— seems highly questionable. It illustrates what Henry Cadbury has called in the title of one of his books, "the perils of modernizing Jesus." Nevertheless Renan would have stuck to his interpretation and held that in introducing a "worship in spirit and in truth" Jesus was going further than perhaps he knew. He had broken with the traditions of his people, broken with the law and the prophets; was he not moving toward an attitude quite unshackled to dogma, in which spirit and truth were all? It would be absurd to plant in his mind retrospectively the erudition of Strauss and Frazer and Freud, but if he had known what they knew about the fabricating and reifying of fantasy, would he have continued to embrace the cosmology he inherited, with its loving but vengeful Deity atop a hierarchy of angels and demons, with heaven and hell in the offing?

Renan's conjecture would be No; Jesus' allegiance to truth would have made it impossible.

But whatever he might have said, what we must say ourselves is clear. Greatness and goodness of spirit are not anchored in any theological creed. Knowledge, love, friendship, justice, beauty are not the conclusions of syllogisms with speculative major premises. They are experiences that make life worth living. The more we have of them, the richer life will be, whether our creed contains thirty-nine articles or a thousand or none. It was this pursuit of the known goods of the human spirit, this quest for a grail that man would never wholly capture, that Renan attributed to Jesus and accepted as the universal religion.

Was it really a religion at all? Many of course denied this, and insisted that it was only ethical idealism wearing the mask of religion. Renan met these attacks serenely; he had been where his attackers were; he understood them and had much sympathy with them. But he seldom replied. He was not much interested in the semantical question. Perhaps it was true that he was reconceiving religion when he substituted the Good for God as the ultimate object of men's devotion, but if so, it was because he was trying to conceive religion in a way that would preserve its ardor while dropping its superstition. And by insistently taking his own line, he went far toward establishing two points of the first importance.

The Ethics of the Intellect

One is that the intellectual life has its own ethics, whose overriding rule is to follow the evidence where it leads. With the results of his historical researches before him, Renan could not live with himself if he continued to profess his old beliefs; he had found contradictions abounding in a text supposed to be revealed and errorless. This was so clear to him, he said, that he would stake his eternal future upon it. It was also clear to him that many of those who did believe were doing so for the wrong reasons—because, like Newman, they avoided exposure to the strongest evidence against them, or because, like Keble, they repressed their doubts by "main force," or because, like Pascal, they thought that if there was a chance in a million that the doctrine of eternal punishment was true, belief was the course of prudence. All this seemed to Renan intellectual dishonesty. The honor of the scholar rested on one stringent demand: Equate your assent to what the known and relevant facts require. This stress on intellectual honor proved a remarkable liberating force, for it not only removed the moral stigma from sincere doubt but reversed the moral status of many believers and many skeptics. The debate was made the more lively by other events of the time. The conversion of Newman to Catholicism coincided almost exactly with that of Renan in the other direction; Darwin's *Origin of Species* of 1859 raised a storm over religion and science which cleared the way for the *Vie de Jésus* of four years later; and Tennyson's *In Memoriam* of 1850 had struggled with the same issue in memorable verse:

> There lives more faith in honest doubt,
> Believe me, than in half the creeds.

Morality Not Based on Theology

Second, as already intimated, Renan helped to sever the powerful cable that had hitherto bound morality to religion. In the past, if one wanted examples of good men or women, one turned first to exemplars of the Christian faith, to Saint Francis or Saint Ignatius, to John Wesley or John Woolman. And no one could deny that their religious belief had affected these noble lives decisively. But when Renan heard it said that belief was a necessary condition of living a noble life, and therefore that a stroke at orthodoxy was an attempt to undermine morality, he denied it roundly. Here he was surely right. Socrates never heard of Christianity, but "Sancte Socrates, ora pro nobis," Erasmus once exclaimed. Marcus Aurelius misunderstood the Christians and even persecuted them, but in Renan's masterly account of him he comes through as perhaps the best man

who ever sat on a throne. Renan's own time was prolific of examples
to whom he could have pointed with effect. Just across the Channel
from him were J. S. Mill, "the saint of rationalism," T. H. Huxley,
John Morley, Leslie Stephen, and Henry Sidgwick, none of whom
was able to accept Christian belief. The best kind of goodness is not
that which looks forward to some posthumous reward or that which
is accepted on authority, but that which seeks the good because it is
clearly seen to be good. Indeed Renan, against his protests, could
himself be cited as a case in point, for his life was a signal example
of his own teaching. So far as his character was concerned, the loss
of his old belief, instead of being an explosion and a catastrophe,
was like the dropping of a pin. He was warmhearted, kindly, affectionate, honorable, and hard-working both before and after his conversion. He changed his habit but not his habits. He saw no reason
why he should.

A Sketch of Renan's *Life*

A biography of Jesus that left out the supernatural seemed to most
believers in the nineteenth century, and would seem to most in the
twentieth, an impossibility. Renan showed that this was not so, and
we shall, in the briefest way, sketch the life that he presented. Jesus
was born, he says, not in Bethlehem, as tradition has it, but in Nazareth, a town with a reputation that led men to say, "Can any good
thing come out of Nazareth?" His parents, brothers, and sisters
were artisans of this town, and he was apprenticed in carpentry. His
language was a Syrian dialect mixed with Hebrew. He probably
knew no Greek, and he seems never to have been in touch with any
form of Greek culture. Though Nazareth was a somewhat squalid
town, the Galilean countryside around it was full of beauty, and he
loved walking through its flowery fields. Our knowledge of the first
thirty years of his life is almost zero, but we can infer that he was
an imaginative youth, steeped in the poetry of the Psalms, and that
he read the books of Daniel and probably Enoch with a full belief

in their prophecies of a coming Messiah who would save his people and give them the rulership of mankind. "He knew only Judaism; his mind preserved that fresh innocence which is always weakened by an extended and varied culture."[33] Science in the modern sense being unknown to him, he saw no sharp line between the natural and the supernatural; past and future interventions by the hand of God were matters of course.

Now if an ethically sensitive and imaginative mind is brought up exclusively on the Psalms and the prophets, he is bound to develop a distinctive inward life. To Jesus the Twenty-third Psalm was fact as well as poetry; God was not a remotely enthroned Deity, but a presence with whom he could commune and take counsel, in whom he could find comfort and solace and strength, whose will he could know directly if he listened without self-will. He felt that some of the prophets had caught the divine will more faithfully than others. If the world really was coming speedily to an end, was there any point in preparing plans for one's own or the nation's prosperity, in laying up treasure, in founding a family, in any sort of worldly distinction? Surely not. If outward things were so soon to be overthrown, there was nothing of any importance except the sort of person that the great Judge found one to be. So cleanse the inside of the cup; the outside did not matter. And what did this cleansing mean? Purity of heart. But what did that mean? It meant freedom from malice and hatred and selfishness and pride and envy. And how were these evils to be overcome? The secret of power over them lay in love. That had been said before of the love of family, friend, and nation. But it had never been said before with such passionate and infectious conviction, or with such complete overleaping by love of all barriers, whether of class, nation, sex, color, or wealth.

It is clear that Jesus did not know from the beginning either his own power or his own message. Partly by way of finding out, he went to visit a strange hermit in the desert called John the Baptist, some of whose convictions he shared, but whose teaching was more narrow and negative, consisting chiefly in the exhortation to repent, for the kingdom was at hand. John at once recognized in Jesus a fellow spirit, but a greater than he, and this gave the young evangelist more confidence. He formed a working center of twelve friends who were devoted to him personally and believed his teachings, and these he sent out along the Galilean highways and byways, telling his Gospel or good news. They were all manual workers but one, who was a petty tax collector.

None of them really understood him, and his two favorites, Peter and John, who reported his work, misrepresented him. Peter, on whose recollections of him the book of Mark is largely based, was overimpressed by his supposed powers as a thaumaturge, believing that he could still a storm at sea, transfer devils from men to swine, and conjure up food at will, that he could heal the sick and even raise the dead; and Mark correspondingly stresses these legends about him. John seems to have delayed writing his sketch of the Master till he was an old man, and then wrote a life that was largely a theological apologetic, devoted to convincing readers of Greek by the use of their own speculative ideas that Jesus was the Logos, the incarnation on earth of the godhead itself. All the Gospels were written long after the death of Jesus, and all are compilations of fragmentary memories and stories still circulating about him. They seldom told the same story in the same way; they were as innocent of historical as of scientific standards. Jesus is, indeed, mentioned by two historians of a higher class, Josephus and Tacitus, but neither takes him seriously. In choosing a group of barely literate friends to carry his message to the world, the founder of Christianity paid a heavy price in the communication of himself to the world, though of course he might have replied: "Why record me for posterity if there is to be no posterity?"

Probably the closest we come to the actual man is in one of the two main sources of the book of Matthew. These sources are the book of Mark and the lost book of "Q," as the Germans call it, standing for *Quelle* or source. This was a collection of the sayings of Jesus gathered by an unknown author. Matthew strung many of these sayings together in the priceless Sermon on the Mount, which is the fullest statement we have of the original Christian teaching. It begins characteristically with a shower of blessings on the meek and the merciful, the pure in heart and the peacemakers, those who hunger and thirst after the good life, and those who are maltreated because they do. Men are not only to give up harming others but also being angry with them, not only adultery but also lust; they are not to resist attack but to overcome it with kindness and good will. They need take little care for food or dress or creature comforts or the future; God will take care of his own. There is frank recognition that most men will not accept such teaching, but also the plain addendum that if they do not they are in eternal peril.

Jesus made his headquarters at the little town of Capernaum on the shore of the Sea of Galilee, where he lived in the household of the brothers Peter and Andrew. Among the humble people of the Galilean towns his message of love and peace found a ready response, especially from women; with women and children he seems to have felt an affinity, though never of a questionable kind. As his influence increased, he came gradually to the conviction that he *was* the Messiah foretold by the prophets, but also that he must be a messiah of revolution. Like other devout Jews, he made it a practice to visit frequently the sacred shrine at Jerusalem, the Temple, which was then being reconstructed on a grandiose scale. His visit in the year 31 was a turning point, for it made plain to him that any reconciliation between his own ideal of Judaism and that of the Temple was impossible. He and his little band of Galileans were held in contempt by the doctors and legalists who swarmed in its porches and were stubbornly deaf to his message. He in turn found their disputations trivial, their pride in rigid conformity to Mosaic rule repellent, their sale and slaughter of animals for sacrifice cruel, and their formalism, self-seeking, and worldliness unendurable. Their emphasis was on an outward conformity to the law; his was on a purity of motive that could be trusted to make its own law.

About a year and a half later Jesus visited Jerusalem again for a period of several months. He and his disciples preached their doctrine now with increasingly sharp warnings about their hearers' indifference in view of an impending judgment; but the response of the hardened and sect-ridden Jerusalemese was very unlike that of the simple peasants of Galilee. To most of them he was just another of the religious fanatics of whom the capital was full. But when, shortly before the feast of the Passover, his followers organized a triumphal entry into the city, proclaiming him King of the Jews, the chief priests thought it time to act. By order of the high priest, Caiaphas, he was brought before the Sanhedrim for trial. There was no difficulty in producing evidence against him. Had he not said that he could destroy the Temple and rebuild it in three days? He admitted having said so. Had he not proclaimed himself the Messiah? Yes, that too he admitted. Indeed he declined to offer any formal defense; he knew perfectly well that in both teaching and action he had defied the Mosaic law. In earlier days the Sanhedrim would have declared him guilty of profanation, and he would have been taken out immediately and stoned to death. But under current Roman rule the Sanhedrim could not execute a death sentence without the consent of the Roman governor. Jesus was therefore escorted to the office of Pontius Pilate, who interviewed him privately, and announced to the anger of the waiting mob that he had found no fault in him. The mob set up a howl of "Crucify him!" Pilate was embarrassed and taken aback. It was the Roman custom to let the local laws take their course unless that course outraged completely the Roman sense of justice. He proposed that another prisoner be turned over instead; the mob was not appeased. He proposed that the prisoner be scourged, hoping that this might be thought sufficient. It was not. The spokesmen of the mob then pointed out to him that Jesus, in calling himself King of the Jews, was violating Roman as well as Jewish law, and that he was therefore insulting the Emperor Tiberius himself, the suggestion being that a report to Tiberius would do the governor no good. This was too much for Pilate, and he reluctantly gave in.

Crucifixion was a Roman punishment devised for slaves and others who did not deserve the honor of being put to death by the Roman sword. It was fiendish beyond description and often kept the victim in agony for three or four days before he died. In this case it was mercifully over in three hours. The body was claimed by a rich friend, Joseph of Arimathea, and placed in an empty rock tomb which he owned. There, for Renan, the tragic story ends. The resurrection, the strange appearances after death, the ascension, are all, like the events that heralded Jesus' birth, the products of a later mythology.

Renan's "Dilemma"

It is more than a hundred years since Renan wrote the *Life,* and the controversy it tried to settle still goes on. To quote an eminent apologist of our time, C. S. Lewis;

"You must make your choice. Either this man was, and is, the Son of God: or else a madman or something worse. You can shut Him up for a fool, you can spit at Him and kill Him as a demon; or you can fall at His feet and call Him Lord and God. But don't let us come with any patronising nonsense about His being a great human teacher. He hasn't left that open to us. He didn't intend to."[84]

There is the dilemma, starkly stated, which millions still feel. Renan thought he had found a way between the horns. Lewis did not. Both were able and honest men. What are we to say?

For one thing, the two sides are not on a par. A "dilemma" is a logical argument in which you attempt to show an opponent that his position commits him to one or other of two equally objectionable propositions. But what we have at stake here is not really two propositions. The rationalist indeed has a proposition, namely that nature is one whole whose events are governed by natural laws. The alternative to this, as Mr. Lewis offers it, is: "you can fall at His feet and call Him Lord and God." But that is not so much a proposition as an act, an attitude, a Kierkegaardian commitment, a Pascalian insistence that "the heart has its reasons that the reason knows not of." It is true that the object of the attitude, "Lord and God," implies propositions, though what precisely they state would not be easy to discover. In any case, such elements of belief as may be present are drawn less from reasons than from experiences of another kind. Many persons, when they read the Gospels, seem to feel the presence of a more than human wisdom, goodness, and power, a sense to which the antique beauty of the King James Bible no doubt contributes. Many others have had experiences of intense and exalted mystical feeling which leave them with a certitude regarded as superior to any that might be gained by reasoning. It would be foolish to bemean the importance of these experiences, for often they have changed in an instant the course of a life. But they do not seem to be experiences of a cognitive kind at all. One cannot prove or disprove a feeling, though there may be plenty of reasons for distrusting it, however exalted, when offered as ground for a belief. Mystical experiences are often admitted to be ineffable. Moreover they have been used, as we have seen already, to support the most diverse and even incompatible conclusions; and there have been mystical experiences not of the goodness but of the intense evil at work in the world.

But let us not dismiss the mystical "insight" summarily. For the sake of fuller understanding, let us grant that it discloses a supernatural character in the Jesus of the Gospels, and ask what such a disclosure involves, for its implications are far-reaching. It implies through the miracles the breakage of laws in all the major sciences—in physics by the walking on the water, in chemistry by making wine of water, in astronomy by the darkness over the whole earth, in biology by the revitalizing of a decaying corpse, in psychology by demon possession. Why should miracles have been confined to so short a period in so small a spot on the earth, and recorded with such inconsistencies as to make acceptance of them difficult? And as asked already, why is it that, if they continue, they seem to dwindle as knowledge improves?

It may be said that if Jesus was Deity he was omnipotent, omniscient, and morally perfect, and such a being we have no right to question. But if we follow the inspired record, he was none of these things. We are told that in a certain town, when the mood of the people was hostile, he could do little; if so, he was not omnipotent. He made errors in small things and in great; he thought that David wrote Psalm 110 (Mark 12:36), which critics think impossible, and that the end of the present world would come in his generation, which it did not; thus he was not omniscient. He announced: "whosoever shall say, Thou fool, shall be in danger of hell fire" (Matt. 5:22), but on at least two occasions he used the forbidden phrase himself (Matt. 23:17; Luke 24:25). More important, though his teaching was offered as laying down at least guidelines for the good life, he ignored almost wholly two values that the modern world, following Greece, regards as among the most precious of all, knowledge and beauty. His moral teaching, lofty as it was, fell conspicuously short of perfection.

Nor did his conduct conform wholly with his teaching. His language to his enemies the Pharisees was not the language of love, even the love of enemies. Renan says of it: "Socrates and Molière only touched the skin. He carried fire and rage to the very marrow."[35] Again, as to the claim made for him of identity with God, we have the testimony, or rather the significant absence of testimony, of Jesus himself. As Renan reminds us: "That Jesus never dreamed of presenting himself as the very incarnation of God, there is no manner of doubt. Such an idea was profoundly alien to the Jewish mind; there is no trace of it in the first three Gospels; it is suggested only in certain passages of the Gospel of John, which can least be accepted as echoing the thought of Jesus."[36]

We have been developing some implications of the view held by C. S. Lewis and other opponents of Renan that the only right attitude toward Jesus is one of worshipful acceptance of him as "Lord and God." There is another implication that cannot be passed over. Jesus taught that the world is governed by a God of love who is concerned about the good of all his creatures. How this is to be rendered consistent with the teaching that he will consign many or most of them to eternal torture I do not know. But passing that by, do the facts of man's world and history lend support to such a view? Does the world of present knowledge look like a world created by such a Deity? For an objective observer, it is hard to see how this question can be answered by anything but a bleak negation. So far as we know, we are alone in the universe on a small satellite of a dying sun, surrounded by billions of stars, the vast majority of which are incapable of supporting human life at all. The prospect for our earth is that it will in time become a black cinder without light, heat, or therefore life. And even the nature of our own planet seems utterly indifferent to values. We are told that the Deity who made and governs it is concerned about the fall of a sparrow. Why then does he create animals who cannot live without tearing others in pieces for their daily food? A Deity who we are assured is full of love and mercy somehow produces the Kallikak family, children with incurable cancer, mongoloids with no hope of living normal human lives, volcanoes that bury cities, epidemics that decimate populations, hurricanes that destroy everything in their paths. Of course there are theological explanations for these evils and all others. They are due to man's perverse use of free will, or they are necessary for his education, or they contribute to some good unseen but accepted on faith, or they will themselves be seen as good if placed in a wider context. These arguments may do credit to the hearts but certainly not to the heads of the theologians who proffer them. The problem of evil is the despair of an honest theism. In sum, the good Mr. Lewis's prescription of falling at the feet of Jesus as Lord and God is more than a commitment of the will. If carried through, it involves a whole cosmology, and that cosmology conflicts with fact at innumerable points.

Rationalism as Inevitable

Renan saw and felt to the full how attractive this cosmology was if only one could forget its multiple inconsistencies with itself and with fact. But of course he could not forget them. His first loyalty was to reason, since he could not abandon that without abandoning truth itself. So he threw himself at the feet of reason, resolved to follow its mandates wherever they led. But he could not follow them while retaining two conflicting standards of truth, reason and revelation. That they do conflict he was now perfectly clear. He was clear, too, that in choosing the cosmology of science as interpreted by reflection he was not making a Kierkegaardian commitment or "leap of faith"; he was appealing to the immanent standard that nature has implanted in the minds of all men, a standard they must follow if they think at all. It is often said by the fideist that the man who appeals to logic is using faith as much as the devotee, only he is using faith in logic rather than faith in revelation. But the two "faiths" are utterly different. Faith in revelation may be accepted or rejected; faith in logic, if that means anything, *must* be accepted and *cannot* be rejected. We accept logic because we have to. We cannot deny the law of contradiction, for example, if we try. Denying it would mean that both sides of a contradiction could be true, in which case our denial of it would permit of its still being true.

In deciding for rationalism Renan was as genuinely embracing a system with far-flung implications as if he had elected supernaturalism. And to say that the scientific world view provides a solid and errorless base would be itself a bit of mythology. Science is full of gaps and riddles; biology does not know how life began, nor astronomy how the universe began; physicists quarrel about what complementarity and the uncertainty principle mean; and mathematics has its unsolved paradoxes. And beyond all we know there stretches an infinity of mystery. Reflective scientists would agree with Newton that we have only picked up a few pebbles on the shore of knowledge. All of this must be admitted. But it is true also that the world of common sense and science forms an organized whole of thought which is the indispensable base of any exploration beyond it. It is what we appeal to in distinguishing astrology from astronomy, alchemy from chemistry, charlatanry from sense. This comprehensive and orderly system is the test of truth that we actually use and the best we can hope to have.

The Problem of the Historical Jesus

But it is idle to say that in accepting this system Renan's troubles were over. Where in this new world of his was he to find a place for the figure of Jesus? Was he a mere man? To this, of course, Renan answered Yes. But his answer, far from denigrating Jesus, was given with so profound a reverence that many who had been neutral to the faith now felt that they could be Christians. The trouble with other great critics such as Strauss, whose *Leben Jesu* was more scholarly than Renan's, is that the figure of Jesus almost disappears in a mist of uncertainty and contradiction. The strength of Renan is his positiveness. Drawing freely on the imagination of a devout, poetic, and eloquent Celt, he painted a portrait of Jesus that is at once naturalistic, magnetic, and credible.

Renan's Jesus, though "a mere man," stands at the summit of humanity. The last sentence of the *Life* runs: "whatever may be the unexpected phenomena of the future, Jesus will not be surpassed. . . . All the ages will proclaim that, among the sons of men, there is none born who is greater than Jesus." At times Renan explicitly refers to him as divine. But here he was using the term in his own sense. For him the divine was not something descended from above but something achieved from below. Evolution was for him a teleological movement in which man slowly realized his potential and approximated to the ideal. God was sometimes thought of as the process itself, sometimes as the ideal that lay at the end of the process; when Renan spoke of Jesus as divine, he was presumably calling him the fullest approximation man had made to the ideal immanent in all his striving. While many theologians would consider this appraisal as degrading, there are moralists who would account it as too high, in view, for example, of the limited sympathy of Jesus for such values as those of the Greeks. What value would he attach to the life of Einstein, or to the Metropolitan Museum of Art, or to the

Olympic Games? Renan would probably reply that Jesus made no pronouncement about these things because he had never been exposed to them and so had no occasion to pass judgment on them, but that his judgment would have been sound if offered. He alone has succeeded in living exclusively for the ideal. ". . . Jesus has founded the absolute religion. . . . His symbols are not fixed dogmas, but images susceptible of indefinite interpretations. We should search in vain for one theological proposition in the Gospel."[37] Renan was perhaps too fond of these striking and sweeping judgments, but he is suggesting something here that even the critical modern moralist may accept. If Jesus' law of love can be read as concern for the largest good, it would be accepted by many moralists as the ultimate law of conduct.

Renan's exaltation of Jesus in spite of his own defection from the church was no mere indulgence of a fancy. It was a necessity of his case. What he was trying to do was to paint the portrait of a figure that could plausibly be recognized as the *fons et origo* of the religion of the West; and considering the history of that religion, considering the able minds and large spirits that it had convinced, considering that it had made a conquest of the most advanced civilizations of the world, a mere Saint Peter or a mere Saint Paul would not serve. Here Renan had a harder task than his theological opponents. If you start with the notion that the world consists of two layers, one of nature, the other of a supernature that everywhere hovers over it, and that from time to time flashes of miraculous lightning pass from the upper to the lower, you have a marvelous recourse when in historical difficulty. When there are gaps in your natural explanations of recorded events, the gaps need not remain unfilled, for there is always the possibility that in the current of human events an almighty finger has intervened. Such a recourse was not open to Renan. Even for the origin of Christianity he had forsworn it. But he must offer some credible substitute. Behind the mists and riddles of the four Gospels there was some powerful and luminous personal presence. What was it like?

Renan's Jesus, as we have said, is unique. If we had to name an approximation to him, it would probably be Saint Francis. He was certainly remote from Socrates, who conquered by the adroitness of his intellect. He was not a Chrysostom, who swept men away by his eloquence. Still less, of course, was he a Caesar with his supreme mastery of force and guile. Renan's Jesus has been called a charmer, and this, though inadequate, is true. He won his early followers by the sheer attractiveness of a simple, single-minded life on the highest level. At its center was a transparently selfless love for others, and particularly for the rags and tatters of society, the down-at-heel, the sick, the exploited, the prostitutes, the hopeless. We catch an echo of him in the irresistible Saint Francis, who, if he saw a leper, would run and embrace him as a prized lost brother. You can hardly remain an enemy or even indifferent to a man who you know loves you, who never loses his temper with you, who always forgives, who takes habitual delight in finding what you need and giving it to you. The strongest deterrents to happiness are states of mind: malice, envy, jealousy, selfishness, hatred, greed. Jesus abjured these attitudes in thought and act. He therefore carried with him an atmosphere of invincible peace and radiancy. It was highly contagious and in itself curative to many ills of the spirit. He was without fear not only because his own attitude was so disarming, but because he felt himself surrounded and enfolded by a Deity who felt toward him as *he* felt toward others. This was not for him a conclusion, but an immediate, vivid presence. He loved children and thought we should all be better if we could keep, as we grow older, their joy in life, their trust, and their openness to what is new.

The Charge of Betrayal

In spite of Renan's reverence for Jesus, his actual estimate of him could only be considered by orthodox Christians as a betrayal, and while his book was met with a chorus of applause on one side, there was a roar of disapproval on the other. One searching criticism came from Richard William Church in a series of articles in the British

Guardian. Church was the man whom Gladstone plucked from the obscure rectory of Whatley in Somerset and made Dean of Saint Paul's. Besides being a distinguished cleric, he was one of the finest writers of the Victorian period. Against Renan's *Vie* he made two particularly damaging criticisms. First was the inadequacy of the figure Renan portrayed to account for the growth of Christianity; second was the necessity of saying that the highest of human characters was also a fraud. As for the first:

History has seen strange hypotheses; but of all extravagant notions, the one that the world has been conquered by what was originally an idyllic gypsying party is the most grotesque. That these *"petits comités de bonnes gens,"* though influenced by a great example and wakened out of their "delicious pastoral" by a heroic death, should have been able to make an impression on Judaean faith, Greek intellect, and Roman civilisation, and to give an impulse to mankind which has lasted to this day, is surely one of the most incredible hypotheses ever accepted, under the desperate necessity of avoiding an unwelcome alternative.[38]

What Dean Church is saying is that only if Jesus was *really* Deity incarnate, only if the miracles *really* occurred, only if his body *really* rose and left the tomb empty, could the growth of the Christian church be explained. But whether or not these things were real, would not the same effects have been produced if the disciples and Saint Paul and the church fathers *believed* them to be real? Strauss and Renan produced effective evidence to show that our present records, compiled a generation or more after the events described, were largely legendary; and if they are right, it was the vigorous evangelism and organizing power of the early Christians that advanced the faith through the next few centuries. That such committed belief could produce social and political change on a large scale was shown in the seventh and eighth centuries when the followers of Mohammed hurtled like a thunderbolt across the north of Africa and up through Spain into the middle of France before the jehad was halted at Poitiers. As for the expansion of Christianity in the Roman Empire, the historical reasons for it have been presented

persuasively by Gibbon, whose famous fifteenth chapter is devoted
to them. The causes of the success, he finds, were the zeal of the
early Christians, inherited from their Jewish predecessors, the doctrine of immortality, which held out so much more hope than the
dreary pagan teaching, the firmly held tradition that the church
alone wielded miraculous powers, the genuine virtues of the Christians in a sink of Roman corruption, and finally the rapid consolida-
tion of the church into a powerful Catholic hierarchy of pope,
bishops, and priests. These causes can no doubt be extended by
present-day historians. The upshot of the long research is to cast a
large doubt over Dean Church's argument that Christian history is
inexplicable except through a supernatural origin.

What of his other allegation, that Renan's Jesus must have been
a charlatan? "It is undeniable," the Dean writes,

that our Lord professed to work miracles. They were not merely attributed
to Him by those who came after Him. If we accept in any degree the
Gospel account, He not only wrought miracles, but claimed to do so; and
M. Renan admits it—that is, he admits that the highest, purest, most
Divine person ever seen on earth (for all this he declares in the most un-
qualified terms) stooped to the arts of Simon Magus or Apollonius of
Tyana. . . . Moreover, He was so almost of necessity; for M. Renan holds
that without the support of an alleged supernatural character and power,
His work must have perished. . . . "He had to choose between these two
alternatives, either renouncing his mission or becoming a thaumaturge."[39]

Renan anticipated this grave objection and replied to it in advance.

History is impossible unless one admits frankly that sincerity must be
estimated in different ways. Everything great is the achievement of the
people, but one cannot lead the people without lending oneself to their
ideas. The philosopher who, knowing this, isolates himself and entrenches
himself in his nobility is genuinely praiseworthy. But he who takes
humanity along with its illusions and tries to work upon it and with it is
not to be condemned. . . . It is easy for us, feeble as we are, to call this
deception, and, proud in our timid honor, to treat with disdain the heroes
who have fought the battle of life under other conditions. When we shall
have done with our scruples about what they did with their deceits, we
shall have the right to take a high line with them.[40]

This leaves one uneasy. It sounds like the admission of deceit in Jesus combined with a rather defiant apology for it; and many may take the defense of a morally perfect being as itself an impertinence. But this response is not wholly convincing. Jesus did not claim perfection ("None is good but one, that is, God"), and some of his acts must be admitted to be inconsistent either with others or with clearly perceived standards of our own. His acceptance of an everlasting hell and his invective against the Pharisees are hard to reconcile with his gospel of love, and some of his parables, like that of the buried treasure or the equal payment for an hour's work and a day's, are hard to reconcile with our sense of justice. Unhappily, therefore, deceit cannot simply be ruled out on grounds that we are here dealing with perfection. But need deception be imputed at all? Jesus was aware of a unique power over men; he was convinced that this was due to a divine presence that he was also sure he felt; and in what we know of the relation of body and mind there is nothing to forbid the suggestion that such power or such convictions can actually cure certain mental disorders. So far his claim to perform miracles may have been made with complete sincerity. But his alleged walking on the water, his stilling of a storm at sea, his raising of the dead are events of a very different order. There is no plausible way of bringing them under natural law. We must either admit them to be intrusions of the supernatural into the natural world or else fall back on the theory of Strauss that they were the mythical embellishments of later biographers, reporting sincerely but uncritically what they presumed to have happened. Such a theory would relieve all parties from the painful charge of deliberate deceit; and if one takes into account the readiness of these reporters to accept the miraculous, and the interval between the events and their recording, it is perhaps the most believable theory we have.

Henriette

Renan's *Vie de Jésus,* though much the most famous and influential of his writings, was only the first installment of a work in seven volumes on *The Origins of Christianity*. Before we leave this first great success, we must mention another person who was almost a coauthor of the book, and whose relation to Renan was unique, his sister Henriette. She inherited the withdrawn and melancholy disposition of their father rather than the lively and forthgoing disposition of their mother. Her features were not attractive and were marred by a birthmark. She was twelve years older than Ernest, and when the child appeared, she seemed to have found her vocation, namely to devote herself to his care. Five years later, when the father was lost at sea, leaving the family burdened with deprivation and debt, she worked hard to keep the home together. Fortunately she had an able mind, and she ventured to open a small school of her own, but it failed. When she went out to walk or shop, one was apt, if one observed closely, to see a small boy with big and tousled head shyly peering out from under her cloak. He later wrote of her: "She attached herself to me with the whole strength of her tender and timid heart, athirst for love. I still remember my baby tyrannies; she never chafed at them. Dressed to go out to some girlish party, she would come to kiss me good-bye, and I would cling to her frock, beseech her to turn back, not to leave me! And she would turn round, take off her best gown and sit at home with me."[41]

When he was twelve and she was twenty-four, she felt that more money must somehow be earned if the home was to be cleared of debt and the boy educated as he should be. She bravely went to Paris, and found a lowly post in a girls' school, where she worked for sixteen hours a day. Her ability and conscientiousness soon brought her a better post, though she longed to be back with the family in Tréguier. Instead, when a more remunerative offer came from a Polish aristocratic family to return with them to Poland as tutor and retainer, she accepted it and spent some bitter winters in Polish exile.

Through a voluminous interchange of letters, she followed every move of Ernest as he went to Saint Nicholas, to Issy, and to Saint Sulpice; and about every move he consulted her anxiously. Mean-

while, through her own quiet reading and thinking, she had reached
an intellectual position close to his own. She hoped he would not become a priest, because she wanted him to keep his intellectual independence, though she tried not to influence his decision. When he
left the church and went into lodgings in Paris, she managed to
send him from her savings 1,500 francs, a considerable sum for
those days, and though he used little of the money, it gave him a
new security. By 1850 she had paid her father's debts, was ill, and
wanted to come back to France. Ernest went to Berlin to meet her
and bring her to Paris. The boy she had left was now a rising man
of letters; the sister he had regained looked tired, ill, and old. The
two took a small apartment near the Val-de-Grâce.

Our solitude [Renan wrote] was absolute. She had no social ties and
hardly sought to form any. . . . Her respect for my work was all-govern-
ing. I have seen her sitting for hours by my side of an evening, scarcely
breathing for fear of interrupting me; she only wanted to see me . . . .
Thanks to her rigorous economy, and with singularly limited resources,
she made me a home in which nothing was ever lacking and which had
an austere charm of its own. Our thoughts were so perfectly in unison
that we scarcely needed to communicate them. Our general views of God
and the world were identical. In the theories I was developing in that
time, there was not a nuance too delicate for her understanding.[42]

This idyllic life lasted about six years. Henriette had once suggested to Ernest that he should marry, but without much thought
of what that would mean to her. When he did fall in love with
Cornélie Scheffer, the charming niece of the painter Ary Scheffer,
panic descended on the small household. He wrote:

We passed through every storm of which love is capable. When she told
me that, in proposing my marriage, she had only wished to test what I
meant to her, and declared that the moment of my union with another
would be that of her departure, I felt death in my heart. . . .
Finally the day arrived when I felt obliged to break out of this cruel
agony. Forced to choose between two affections, I sacrificed everything to
the older one, to the one which looked most like a duty. I told Miss Scheffer that I would see her no more, unless my sister's heart ceased to bleed.

It was evening; I came back to tell my sister what I had done. A strong revulsion took place in her heart; to have prevented a union that I wished, and that she highly appreciated, awoke in her a cruel remorse. Early the next morning she hurried to the Scheffers'; she spent long hours with my fiancée; they wept together; they parted happy and friends. In short, after as before my marriage we had everything in common. It was her economy that made our new household possible. Without her I could not have borne my new duties. My confidence in her goodness was, indeed, so great that the naïveté of my conduct did not strike me until much later. . . . The birth of my little [son] Ary wiped away the last trace of her tears.[43]

In our studies of reasonable men, we have so far found that rationality was most likely to falter in its dealings with the other sex. Renan can hardly be acquitted of such faltering. What he was asking of his sister and his fiancée was something that would impose a severe strain on anyone, and it says much for the large-mindedness of Henriette and still more perhaps of Cornélie that the plan worked as well as it did.

The ménage à trois was maintained for several years. In 1860 an opportunity arose for Henriette to work again with Ernest alone. He had given two important lectures before the Academy of Inscriptions on Phoenician history, in the course of which he predicted that if excavations were made at Byblos significant records of this history would be found. Hortense Cornu, a childhood playmate of the emperor Louis Napoleon, attended his lectures regularly, and she passed on this prediction of his to the emperor with the comment that Renan himself would make a good director of such excavations. The emperor, eager for repute as a supporter of French arts and sciences, in 1860 authorized an expedition, with large freedom of choice in its work, a ship and generous funds at its disposal, and with Renan at its head. Renan set out, with Henriette at his side, and conducted excavations at Byblos, Tyre, Sidon, and other places, from which he was able to send back tons of ancient artifacts to the museums of Paris.

The pair spent about a year in the Near East, but undoubtedly the high point of it was a period of thirty-four days when they struck down into Galilee, followed the very road taken by Jesus on his way to Jerusalem, and visited Bethany, Capernaum, and many other places with names familiar from the Gospels. Returning to Ghazir in Lebanon in July 1861, the two took a small house, and in spite of their exhaustion Renan threw himself into the writing of his *Vie de Jésus*.

When reading the Gospels in Galilee, the personality of the great founder had affected me powerfully. In the midst of the greatest conceivable peace I wrote, with the aid of the Gospels and Josephus, a *Life of Jesus* . . . . From morning to evening I was intoxicated with the ideas that unrolled before me. With them I went to sleep, and the first rays of the sun rising from behind the mountain gave them back to me clearer and more vivid than the evening before. . . . Page by page as I wrote, Henriette copied it. "This book," she said, "I shall love . . . ." Her joy was complete, and these moments were without doubt the sweetest of her life. Our intellectual and moral communion had never been so intimate.[44]

As the book, written at great speed, neared completion, he wrote to his friend Berthelot on September 12: "I truly believe that in this work the reader will have before his eyes living beings, and not those pale, lifeless phantoms of Jesus, Mary, Peter, etc., which have passed into the state of abstractions and mere types. . . . Have I succeeded? You will judge."[45]

For Henriette, it was not all rhapsody. She did everything for him—tied his tie, kept his accounts, watched over his eating, copied his scripts, mothered him, scolded him, and relieved him of concern for physical wants. But he was so lost in his work that he had no time for anything else. She wrote sadly to Berthelot: ". . . he is so absorbed by the work of his mission, so preoccupied with what it has already given him or what it promises, that I truly do not know if he is aware of my presence."[46] She knew, however, that this was rather the engrossment of the scholar than lack of affection, and Renan's apologies when he realized that he had offended were deep and disarming.

Early in September, still working on the book, the two went to the port of Amschit to supervise a shipment of sarcophagi. Henriette came down with a fever, but went on copying manuscript till she was in a daze. Ernest too contracted the disease, and no adequate medical service was available for either. He went into delirium, and as he began to come out of it, he was told that his sister had died two days before. She was buried in a rock tomb offered by a native friend. Ernest abandoned further work, and as soon as he was able returned to Paris. He wrote a beautiful little book entitled *Ma Soeur Henriette,* which he confined to a hundred copies, to be distributed to friends; he could not bear the thought of making a profit out of such a book; and it was to her that he dedicated the *Life* that they jointly produced. Henriette would long ago have been forgotten except for one lasting monument which she largely fashioned with her own hands. That monument was Ernest Renan.

An Obstinate Officialdom

Henriette never saw the famous book in print. Nor did she share his delight when his ambition of many years was realized in 1862: he was appointed professor of Hebrew at the Collège de France. It had long been obvious that he was the man for the post, but the minister of public instruction, knowing this to be true, deliberately put off for five years any request for nominations to the vacant chair. Finally both the Academy of Inscriptions and the faculty of the Collège de France sent in nominations of their own, both asking the appointment of Renan. The minister could no longer delay. In January 1862 Renan was appointed by imperial decree. It was the first time anyone but a faithful Catholic had been appointed, and in the statement he submitted of how he understood his duties he reserved "the right to treat freely from the standpoint of the historian, literary man, philosopher, and scholar, all religious questions brought up by the subject of the course."[47] This the minister deleted in his own statement of the conditions. Nevertheless Renan announced the place and time of his inaugural lecture. There would be trouble, he knew. The Catholics were outraged, because the professor of Hebrew was traditionally an interpreter of the Bible as well as a tutor in language. The radical students of the Latin Quarter, though acquiescent in his skepticism, were annoyed that he should have accepted office under the emperor. When the time came, he found the lecture room thronged and a crowd outside that required the police to control them. His friend Hippolyte Taine was there and wrote: "For three-quarters of an hour there was a storm of vociferations, savage howls and laughter. . . . Renan entered; amidst a thunder of cheers, howls and waving of hats. A few hisses were immediately covered by another round of applause; for twenty minutes he could not say a word, but attempted by useless gestures to obtain silence."[48] When at last he succeeded, the hearers were rewarded with an eloquent and, for the most part, uncontroversial address. But it did contain these significant words:

Since I shall bring into my teaching no dogmatism, since I shall always limit myself to an appeal to your reason, to setting before you what I consider most probable, leaving you perfect liberty of judgment, who can complain? Only those who believe themselves to have a monopoly of the truth. But they must renounce being the masters of the world. In our days, Galileo would not kneel to beg pardon for having discovered the truth.[49]

That made it clear that only one authority would be recognized in Renan's classroom, and it was neither that of the minister of instruction nor that of any church, but that of reason, conceived as the universal and objective means to truth. This would seem inoffensive enough, but it did not satisfy the French government, over which the church still held a powerful influence. Four days later, Renan's course was suspended by imperial decree. Renan wrote to his English friend Grant Duff: "The suspension was ordered on account of the reclamations [protests] of certain cardinals, which were almost threatening, and after most insistent efforts with the Empress by several bishops."[50] He refused to resign the chair and continued teaching the course to a few students in his own house. Then the government cut off the emolument of the chair itself. Some seven years later he was nominated again by both the august bodies that had done so before. He was appointed to the chair once more, and this time held it until his death. France's best critic, Sainte-Beuve, said to him even before the end was known: "You won for us the right of discussion in this matter, hitherto forbidden." Renan's triumph in this long struggle was a landmark in the history of French freedom of thought.

Ornament of French Literature

With the publication of the earlier volumes of his *Origins of Christianity,* Renan's place as scholar and writer was secure. He was elected president of the Academy of Inscriptions and Belles Lettres, and in 1878 he received the highest accolade that French writers can achieve, election to the French Academy. The Academy had been founded by Cardinal Richelieu, and in his address of acceptance Renan wondered what the great churchman would have thought of the admission of such a man as he. But he held the new Academy, though now catholic with a small "c," to be far better than the old, and early in his two-hour acceptance speech he sounded the note of harmony. "To bring men together is almost to reconcile them; it is at least to render the human spirit the most signal of services, since the pacific work of civilization results from contradictory elements, maintained face to face, obliged to tolerate one another, and leading on to mutual comprehension and almost to love."[51] His benignity toward his critics, whom he seldom answered, was unhappily not reciprocated. Though he had been a member, his old teacher Dupanloup, now bishop of Orléans, was not there; he had written his own life of Christ to help annul the influence of Renan's book, and had resigned his seat in the Academy to protest the election of Littré, who compiled the famous dictionary but had shown so evil a spirit as to have translated Strauss into French.

A figure of controversy all his life, Renan in his later years became a widely acclaimed ornament of French scholarship and literature. The seventh and final volume on early Christianity carried the story through the age of Marcus Aurelius, who was one of his heroes. A five-volume *History of Israel* was the pleasant work of his declining years, though he saw only three of the volumes published. He achieved what in early days was the height of his ambition; he became official head of the Collège de France. With indifferent success he tried his hand at philosophic drama, and with brilliant success at translations of *Ecclesiastes, The Song of Songs,* and *Job,* the latter being, oddly enough, the first of his books to be placed on the church's *Index.* He died on October 2, 1892.

Renan As an Intellect

We have touched on the high points of a remarkable life. But looking at Renan now more narrowly and personally, we ask, What sort of man was he? Since we are nominating him for a high place among reasonable men, it is natural to look first at his mind, in the sense of his intelligence. On this we have a round pronouncement from Émile Faguet, no mean judge of minds. In his *History of the French Language and Literature* he says. "Renan can be described in a single word which is happily not a formula: he was the most intelligent man of the nineteenth century";[52] and Taine, the author of a well-known work on intelligence, had prophesied when Renan was only thirty-five, "he will be one of the great men of this century."[53] Renan would himself have given the first place in this respect to Hegel. And it is true that Renan lacked the power of a systematic philosopher to follow a line of thought through all its implications till it embraced everything in its network. He was like Emerson in his reliance on brilliant intuitions, finely phrased but offered as self-evident. Taine writes of a discussion he had with Renan, Berthelot also being present:

He is, above everything, a passionate, nervous man, beset by his own ideas. He walked up and down my room as if he were in a cage, with the jerky tones and gestures of Invention in full ebullition. There is a great difference between him and Berthelot, who is as quiet as a patient, labouring ox . . . . It is the contrast between Inspiration and Meditation. . . .

Renan is perfectly incapable of precise formulae; he does not go from one precise truth to another, but feels his way as he goes. He has *impressions,* a word which expresses the whole thing. Philosophy and generalizations are but the echoes of things within him; he has no system, but only glimmerings and sensations.[54]

The result was that he was not a consistent thinker; and he was inclined, again like Emerson, to be rather defiant about it. "Woe to him who does not contradict himself at least once a day,"[55] he used to remark. And again:

The first step of one who wants to think is to harden himself in the face of contradictions, leaving to the future the task of reconciling them. The man who is logical in his system of life is certainly a narrow mind. For I defy him, in the actual state of the human mind, to bring into harmony all the components of human nature. If he wants a system all of a piece, he will be reduced to denying and excluding.[56]

George Saintsbury thought that his inconsistency invaded his standard of criticism itself, and classed him with "people who, as Scherer (not exactly a bigot) said of Renan, accept and reject parts of the same document, possessing exactly the same claims to acceptance or grounds for rejection, according to their own convenience or choice."[57] But it must be remembered that some of his inconsistencies were the result of his openness of mind. In his early work, for example, he placed the Gospel of John on the same level of reliability as the Synoptics; he later gave this up in face of the opposite view of a majority of higher critics. In earlier editions of the *Life,* he suggested that Jesus may have connived in some deception about the raising of Lazarus, which again he abandoned in later editions. These are not so much inconsistencies as changes of mind in conformity with more evidence. Some have taken the great crisis of his life, the transition from Rome to rationalism, as itself an irrational Kierkegaardian leap. There is no ground for this imputation.

It is true that at a certain time he could accept miracles by the score, and that at the outset of the *Life of Jesus* he could say without argument that miracles never occurred. But this was no arbitrary leap. A new generalization, even when uttered as an aphorism, may issue from a new system of thought. James showed that even a conversion that seems sudden may be the outcome of a long subconscious struggle between two opposing systems. When Renan was a youth, exposed only to orthodox influences, his thought revolved wholly in the old circle of interchange between God and man, God breaking through the natural order to stay the sun in its course or to raise the dead to life, and man changing God's mind by his fervid importunity. In the course of a few years this inherited universe had become for him a set of cloud castles, disintegrating in the winds of science. When he compared the world of the Eastern religions with their pageants of gods and goddesses, with their countless miracles supporting conflicting orthodoxies; when he found in the New Testament itself incessant variations in the reporting of the same events (he speaks of six or seven conflicting accounts of the resurrection),[58] the voice of his logical conscience, as we have noted, kept protesting, "But this is not true." And when he compared this world with that of modern science, incomplete, to be sure, in every direction, but unified and advancing under its increasingly verified postulate of causality, he could not remain where he was. It was as if an iceberg had slowly turned over and with curious quietness come to rest with its subaqueous (in this case its rational) side up. We sometimes forget that many persons who are outstanding for the rationality of their judgment spend little time in conscious reasoning. (For a discussion of the office of the subconscious in reasoning, see my *Nature of Thought,* volume 2, chapter 24.)

For all this, Renan loved the work of brooding thought; he seems to have been made for it. "To Renan," says his biographer Mott, "every moment stolen from intellectual pursuits was a moment wasted."[59] It is true that his mind did not have the magnificent unity of Gibbon's, who launched himself early on an enterprise that employed all his powers, completed it in an incomparable manner, and then died; Renan scattered himself far more widely. Still, he too was preoccupied his life long with one large central enterprise—the early development of Western religion. The seven volumes of the *Origines* alone took twenty of the central years of his life. With his main quest always calling him, he did not try or claim to keep abreast of current literature. "Before mere physical suffering," says Madame Darmesteter, "he was ever serene as an image of Buddha. Enforced idleness was a sorer burden, and sometimes he would half complain that in his childhood he had never learned to play."[60] But he found delight enough in his devotion to truth. The same friend quotes him as saying that he had "a lively taste for the universe."[61] He would have been a vigorous antipragmatist for he thought that in science and philosophy an aim at anything but truth perverted the inquiry. In his early notebooks there is an exclamatory entry: "It is the useful that I abhor. Blasphemy to submit science to *anything useful!*"[62] And at the end of his life appeared an article entitled "Examination of Philosophic Conscience," which began: "The first duty of a sincere man is not to influence his own opinions, but to let reality reflect itself within him as in the camera obscura of the photographer, and to be present only as a spectator of the inward conflicts of ideas in the depth of his consciousness."[63]

His Warmth of Spirit

All this sounds as if Renan were an intellectualist; but has there ever been an intellectualist Celt? He quotes at his own expense the remark of "that great observer Challemel-Lacour," that he thought like a man, felt like a woman, and acted like a child.[64] But he could never have written as he did without a vivid imagination and an exceptionally warm heart. It was that warmth of heart which made him cling to the figure of Jesus, even when the aura of the supernatural had been stripped away. Indeed at times his heart almost rebelled against his intelligence. "There are moments," he wrote to

Abbé Cognat, "when I think I will amputate my reason, and live
only for the mystic life. Except my judgment, except the faculty
which weighs and criticises, the Catholic Church responds to every
function of my soul. I must therefore sacrifice either the Church or
my judgment . . . ."[65] The remarkable thing about Renan is that
he sacrificed neither. He satisfied his intellect by sweeping from his
mind the whole dogmatic side of Christianity; he satisfied his heart
by keeping to the end a passionate love of the founder. In his way
he was in love with love. Schweitzer has written:

> There is no historical task which so reveals a man's true self as the writ-
> ing of a Life of Jesus. No vital force comes into the figure unless a man
> breathes into it all the hate or all the love of which he is capable. The
> stronger the love, or the stronger the hate, the more life-like the figure
> which is produced. For hate as well as love can write a Life of Jesus, and
> the greatest of them are written with hate: that of Reimarus, the Wolfen-
> büttel Fragmentist, and that of David Friedrich Strauss.[66]

"But love," said Renan, "is possible without faith. . . . Jesus cannot
belong solely to those who call themselves his disciples. He is the
common honor of all who share a human heart. His glory does not
consist in being relegated out of history; we render him a truer
worship in showing that history as a whole is incomprehensible
without him."[67] Renan strove after his conversion to rationalism, as
before, to make his life an *imitatio Christi*. A biographer who read
most of his available writing remarked: "It is impossible to find in
his published works a single expression of personal hatred."[68] Those
who make religious belief the condition of goodness commonly say
that where such goodness appears in the absence of belief it is the
deposit of an earlier religious training. Renan would admit that
there was some truth in this in his own case; and his reverence for
his Catholic teachers vied with that of Marcus Aurelius for his
pagan ones. But it was a veneration for their goodness rather than
their intelligence. And his genial and affectionate disposition must
have been a gift, in no small measure, of nature and the Fates.

However he came by it, Renan carried about with him a sunniness and kindliness of temper that conferred on him a unique charm. The critical Goncourt jotted down in his journal after a visit to him: "The man, always more charming and more affectionately polished as one comes to know him better. He is a type in his unfortunate physique of moral grace; in this apostle of doubt, there is the lofty and intelligent amiability of a priest of science."[69] He combined intellectual sophistication with moral simplicity, honor, and loyalty; for example when his friend Ollivier suggested that he present himself as a candidate for the Academy, he replied that he should be glad to do so if it did not involve his opposing Monseigneur Dupanloup, to whom he owed too much to want to deprive him of a possible distinction. This attitude, as we have seen, was hardly reciprocated by its beneficiary.

Renan was said to know everyone worth knowing in Paris, and was a popular guest. His mind did not run to small talk, and when the conversation did, he could be disconcertingly silent, lost in thoughts of his own; then he would suddenly become aware that someone had said something, and with smiling benignance exclaim, "How true that is!" When he did participate, it was in that pure French which he so fastidiously wrote and which Frenchmen so admire. Dr. William Barry has said of him that he was "Caliban to look upon, but Ariel when he opened his lips."[70]

A Happy Man

Part of his popularity rose from his being so obviously a happy man. In his youth he had wanted above all to be a researcher and writer, and throughout his maturity he was able to be both. "How often," he wrote,

in my poor room amid my books, have I tasted the fullness of happiness and defied the whole world to procure for any one purer joys than those I found in the calm and disinterested exercise of my own thought! How often, dropping my pen and abandoning myself to the thousand sentiments whose mingling produces an instant elevation of the whole being, I have said to heaven: Only give me life, I will take care of the rest.[71]

He was never rich, for most of his writings were not of the kind that make best sellers, and he knew the meaning of sheer privation; but this does not seem to have troubled him much, for he attached small importance to owning things. "Like the patriarch of Assisi," he said half playfully, "I have passed through the world without any serious attachment to it, as a mere tenant, if I may say so. Both of us, without having anything of our own, have found ourselves rich. God gave us the usufruct of the universe, and we have been content to enjoy without possession."[72]

When one considers that Renan was the object of aversion and obloquy to great numbers of his contemporaries, who greeted with anger any attempt to honor him, this persisting unruffled serenity becomes all the more surprising. It was largely the product, I think, of his inwardness and detachment. When, as a result of his thought and research, he saw clearly that something was true, he saw with equal clearness that there was no point in being enraged with opponents who lacked his access to the evidence. Here his Christian ethic permeated his feeling. To meet anger with anger was a waste of spirit. He was writing in his twenties: "The insults of a blackguard touch his like, but do not reach us. Thus those whose inward excellence has made them susceptible, irritable, and jealous for an outward dignity in proportion to their worth have not yet risen above a certain level nor understood the true royalty of men of mind."[73] A cheerfulness based on such self-respect was not easily shaken. The closing lines of his *Souvenirs* were characteristic:

The existence that has been granted me without my asking it has been a blessing to me. If it were offered to me again, I would gratefully accept it anew. . . . Unless my last years hold in reserve for me some extremely cruel sufferings, I shall have, in bidding adieu to life, only thanks to give to the cause of all good for the charming promenade through reality that it has permitted me to take.[74]

Unhappily his last years did bring cruel sufferings. We have heard him described as physically a Caliban. That was untrue; but it cannot be denied that in his case body and mind were ill-matched. His arms and legs were both too short, and he always had some difficulty in walking. As a boy he could never play the games that other boys delighted in; he sat on a bench instead, and read a book or mused. In his middle years, living a sedentary life, he developed a girth that placed an undue strain on his heart, and he seemed ten years older than he was. He lived, working continually and cheerfully, until he was sixty-nine, but in his last years he suffered a physical martyrdom under the joint battering of neuralgia, gout, rheumatism, and weakening of the heart. Only an inveterately cheerful soul, fortified by philosophy, could have borne it with his serenity.

"But surely," it may be said, "his philosophy was not of the sort that would fortify anyone." And so far as serenity of mind depends on belief in a personal God presiding over nature and human life, and guaranteeing to those who trust in him an eternity of happiness, the critic is right. Renan believed that what he knew of nature and history was utterly inconsistent with governance by such a Deity, and that the evidence for the dependence of mind on body was so strong as to make the persistence of personality improbable in the extreme.

But if one attacks Renan for these conclusions, one should do so with certain facts in mind. First, on both these conclusions a larger proportion of philosophers and scientists would agree with him today than a century ago. Second, in estimating the effect of these beliefs on the happiness of thoughtful men, we must take into account their implications. The God that Renan abandoned was one who condemned the great majority of the race to an afterlife to which extinction would be a welcome alternative. Even for those who were somehow certain of salvation, such a thought could hardly be an occasion for happiness, though the great Aquinas found one of the satisfactions of heaven to lie in the sight of the damned below. Third, it is not only what is believed, but how and why it is believed, that affects the contentment of the believer. Renan held that as a thinker it was his duty to follow the evidence; and this he tried to do, even when it threatened to jeopardize his future. In thus following his conscience he consoled himself at times, to the astonishment of opponents, by reflecting that at least he had Jesus on his side. And one wonders whether Renan, with all his obviously sincere negations, was not a happier man than Newman, who, for example, having opposed infallibility before 1870, had to believe it after Rome had spoken. Finally, Renan's philosophy extended far beyond the region of dogma. It was largely an eclectic wisdom of life collected as a bee collects honey, by roaming widely among the flowers of the human species, Socrates, Marcus Aurelius, Francis of Assisi, his beloved Augustin Thierry, and many others. Fortunately honor, kindliness, courage, self-respect, public concern, all of which bear on happiness, are not the monopoly of any faith.

The Philosopher

As for Renan's philosophy in the professional's sense, it must be admitted to be unsystematic and imprecise. Probably in most histories of philosophy he would not appear at all, even in the index. He was convinced, with one of his heroes, Spinoza, that nature was one interknit whole, with no supernature floating above it. This nature was everywhere animate, but so far as we know, conscious only at one point, namely the planet earth. There were two ultimate mysteries for Renan—how nature produced consciousness, and whether as a whole it had any goals or purposes; and about both he thought it futile to speculate. Certainly nature as we know it is indifferent to human values; it kills off Shelleys and Schuberts at thirty and allows many of the baser sort to flourish. Together with its product, man, it is governed in every detail by causal law, but in this Renan found nothing inconsistent with purposive evolution or with the gradual taking over by human reason of the causes, physical and psychical, that determine its destiny. Man can fashion himself and his environment in accordance with his own ends. What are these ends? They are the intrinsic goods of experience that all men want, whether they think about them explicitly or not—such values as truth, beauty, pleasure, a clear conscience, love. Renan was not a hedonist; he thought all these values self-evidently good, and their pursuit therefore self-evidently right and a duty. He would, I think, have said with Hegel that in conduct whatever was right was rational, and that whatever was rational was right.

For metaphysics, traditionally held to be the central field of philosophy, Renan had little use. "I lost early in life," he says, "all confidence in the sort of abstract metaphysics which claims to be a science over and above the other sciences and to solve by itself the highest problems of humanity. Positive science remained for me the sole source of truth."[75] But by "science" he meant something much broader than natural science; for him it was the application of reason in any special field. History was science; indeed Henri Peyre has said that "history, in Renan's terms, became the true philosophy."[76] Such history was not merely the recording of events but also their explanation and interpretation, the kind of history he tried to write in *The Origins of Christianity*. "Aristotle has truly said," he remarked in *The Gospels*, " 'There is no science except of what is general.' History itself, history properly speaking, history exposed to the light of day and founded upon documents, does it escape this necessity? Certainly not; we do not know exactly the details of anything. That which is of moment is the general lines, the great resultant facts which remain true even though all the details may be erroneous."[77] Science in this comprehensive sense, the rendering intelligible of facts and events by reason, was Renan's substitute for both philosophy and religion.

The Political Elitist

It would be a mistake to suppose that, devoted as he was to scholarship, he lived exclusively the life of the mind. At times, it is true, he wrote as if he had no interest in other activities. "The critic is too aware of difficulties to be energetic in action. Even when he joins a party, he knows that his opponents are not altogether wrong. Now, in order to act with vigor, you must be a bit brutal, believe that you are absolutely right, and that those opposed to you are blind or wicked."[78] But Renan was too deeply concerned about the state and fate of France, particularly during the Franco-Prussian War, to follow his own warnings. He twice ran for the National Assembly, though he was both times defeated. His thought on politics swung in almost as wide an arc as his thought on religion. In his early years he looked to religion for guidance, but the teaching of Jesus seemed essentially anarchistic, since it was indifferent toward government and never depended on it for the reforms it proposed.

A little later he accepted the principles of the French Revolution, "Liberty, Fraternity, Equality," and considered himself a liberal. But as he watched the violent insurrection of the Commune that followed the Franco-Prussian War, he lost his faith in democracy. He wanted to believe in it, and did believe in it in theory, but only where the mass of the people were restrained and responsible, and that, unfortunately, they never were. So he became, like the elder Burke, an elitist, who believed in the government of an aristocracy of brains and merit. During the war of 1870 he had a sorely divided mind. France was by far the more democratic of the two enemies, Germany far more efficient; indeed Germany under Bismarck was one compact regiment, before which France had no chance. "Military organization is founded on discipline," Renan wrote sadly; "democracy is the negation of discipline." He believed in government from the top down, but not from a top consisting of coarse and brutal militarists. His theory of government was essentially Platonist, with the defect of the whole Platonic line that it has evolved no acceptable way of selecting the elite who are to govern. In a lively exchange of letters with the German whom he called his master, David Friedrich Strauss, he anticipated his countryman of the next century, Monnet, by arguing that both sides should work for a United States of Europe, which could settle such disputes by joint counsel and joint power.

In his view of society too, Renan was an elitist. He felt something like contempt for the life of the average Frenchman of his day, narrow in his interests and tastes, conventional in his thought and action, intent on material advantage, blind to so much that made life worth living. Renan was eloquent for freedom of thought, speech, and vocation, but was clear that equality of opportunity would never turn baser metals into gold. He disliked "what he called Americanism, the greedy, pushing, self-advertising tendencies in daily life and in politics";[79] and would probably have said, as Newman did, that what the word "American" first suggested was vulgarity. Dr. Barry remarks that if Renan were asked whether democracy would prevail he would have answered that "culture, discipline, progress, are incompatible with an American suffrage. The leveller is condemned by Nature and Darwin."[80] We need hardly bridle at this. France has not been forward in its understanding of the outside world; it has valued few American writers except, for some strange reason, Edgar Allan Poe; and besides, this view of us has some truth. Renan thought that the French Academy had done much to save France from the sort of democracy that levels down. Matthew Arnold, who had similar views, quotes him in one of his *Essays in Criticism* as saying: "All ages have had their inferior literature; but the great danger of our time is that this inferior literature tends more and more to get the upper place. No one has the same advantage as the Academy for fighting against this mischief."[81] The image of America as a rough-and-ready frontier of culture dies slowly. But when anyone—Frenchman, Englishman, or other—makes a plea for standards, we may forget his accent and listen with profit to what he says.

The Historian under Criticism

It is not as a philosopher or a politician that Renan will live, but as a historian of Christianity. Does his work here stand up? His history, particularly its first volume, the *Vie de Jésus,* was met with howls of vilification from Catholic France, and some of his neighbors sprinkled with holy water the chairs he had sat in to exorcise his demonic influence. But some critics who were better informed also found defects. Albert Réville pointed out two of them. Renan had taken the Gospel of John as having been written by the apostle and being historically on a level with the Synoptics. In the thirteenth edition of his work, bowing to the weight of critical opinion, Renan retracted both views, though he retained the conviction that this gospel was written by a person who must have been in contact with an eyewitness at Golgotha. Réville also objected to Renan's intimation that Jesus may have acquiesced in deception in the raising of Lazarus, and argued that the incident was explicable as a popular legend without compromising the Master. This too Renan accepted. Some persons objected to his continuing to speak of God and immortality as if they carried their old meaning, particularly in his book about Henriette. This persistence in an old habit is natural enough; but if a man has ceased to believe in what a term has traditionally meant, it does seem better that he should find new words, and not trade confusingly on the connotations of the old.

Renan has also been taken to task, as are the humanists of today, for substituting a feeble makeshift for the religion that has traditionally served as the sanction of morality. If people are told by imposing authority that living in one way will take them to eternal happiness and living in another way to unending misery, they are likely to take heed. When this powerful sanction is removed and they are told that they should do right just because it is right and reasonable, many of them will take this as equivalent to Mr. Punch's remark, "The Devil is dead; we can now do as we please." The question at issue here is not whether ethics depends for its validity on religious belief, for philosophers have shown convincingly that it does not. The question is whether the desire to be reasonable is a force that as yet compares with fear as a motive for doing right. I think we must admit that it is not. And that implies that root-and-branch attacks on religion, without regard to time or place, are not to be approved by socially minded persons, however negative may be their view on theology. For where the level of education is low, it may be better for the community that men should do right with the wrong motives than do whatever is right in their own sight. On the other hand, where the respect for reason and justice (which Leibniz thought the most intellectual of the virtues) is strong, surely the philosopher or the scientist may feel at liberty to speak out. Truth, though not the only value, is for him the greatest, and as men slowly ascend the stair of intelligence, it becomes important for them, too. Renan, though daring, was therefore right in defending a religion of reason and reasonableness, which provides firmer sanction for right doing than any system of theology. Truth may be less inciting and exciting than fiction, but would not most men rather live in a real world with less happiness than in illusion with more?

But the charge most frequently heard against Renan is that he is a sentimentalist. Sidgwick, always formidable as a critic, wrote, "His most orthodox assailants in England felt for the most part that their strength lay in showing not that the Jesus of Renan was a mere man and ought to have been more, but that he was not the right man."[82] Others went further and said that Renan read himself into his subject. What made the Jesus of the early Galilean days so irresistible was his "charm," a term of which Renan never tires; "as often happens in natures of great refinement," he wrote, "tenderness of heart transforms itself into infinite sweetness, into misty poetry, into universal charm."[83] We read of a "subtle and joyful moralist" whose "conversation was full of gaiety and charm," of "gentle joy and amiable bantering," whose "preaching was suave and gentle, running over with the life and perfume of the open fields," uttering his "innocent aphorisms" in his own "delicious way" of teaching in parables. He was "the charming doctor who pardoned all if only they loved him." He lived in "joyous Galilee" where nature was "ravishing" and where everything about the Galilean Sea had an "idyllic and charming touch." Christianity at its birth was "a delicious pastoral," "an idyll," lived in "intoxicating surroundings."

Jesus was the center of "a band of joyous youths," "a gay and vaga-bond group." The outward scene, the pronouncements of the Mas-ter, and his "theology of love" are all described as delicious.[84] (I have here put in English some of the phrases gathered from the critical pages of Dean Church.)

This was the youthful Jesus conjured up by Renan's imagination as he followed the steps of the Master from Capernaum to Jerusa-lem. How true it is, or how wide of the mark, no one knows. The first thirty years of Jesus' life are a virtual blank left to the historian to fill in as best he can. Renan filled it in with a personality that was congenial to himself. Probably most readers will feel that in the powerful character that stands behind the mist of twenty centuries and changed the course of all of them there was a great deal more than the charming, gay, and gentle moralist that Renan has given us; they may feel as Marlowe did in contemplating some faded like-ness of Helen of Troy,

> Was this the face that launched a thousand ships
> And burnt the topless towers of Ilium?

But one also feels that if Jesus was much more than this he was not wholly unlike this. We should surely misconstrue his power if we did not also understand that it was the power of a profound gentle-ness, and this Renan drives home with masterly strokes. He may be wrong in much. Writing so largely in the dark, he probably was. But at least his figure lives; it is not that of a wooden theologizing moralist; and perhaps no book has done so much, the world over, to make the Founder a credible, at times mistaken, but heroic em-bodiment of the power of love.

The Magic of Style

No small part of the immense influence of Renan's *Life,* as well as that of his other books, was their superb style. On style his practice was better than his theory. In his acceptance address to the French

Academy, he said: "Human intelligence is a whole of parts so closely bound together that a great mind is always a great writer."[85] Kant, Hegel, Dewey, Wittgenstein great *writers*? It would take more courage than taste to defend that thesis. What seems to be true is that one who thinks clearly, if willing to take pains, can also speak and write clearly. In respect to clarity, Renan is not the equal of his contemporary, Macaulay, but neither is any other historian. Renan was portraying a time and place where such clarity was more difficult, and he did take immense pains with his writing—erasing, interlining, correcting his script incessantly, and pursuing the unhappy printer, as Burke did, with persistent changes in the printed proof. The result was worth the trouble. "Reading the Germans," says J. M. Robertson, "one sighs for the Renan sentence"; and he goes on: "His style is as consummate as his scholarship; and his books remain 'literature' in the higher sense."[86] At the same time, it is hard to say how his effects are achieved. His biographer Barry writes: "M. Bourget tells a pleasant story of the critic who could analyze every great style and lay bare its secret; when the talk fell on Renan, he shook his head. 'Ah, that man's phrase,' he exclaimed; 'one sees not how it is made.' "[87]

A little more than this can be said, however. For one thing, Renan was blessed in early life with two admirable editors. He wrote many articles for the *Journal des Débats,* of which Ustazade de Sacy was the fastidious editor-in-chief. De Sacy was a scholar devoted to the classic French of the seventeenth century. He "went over my articles with the greatest care," says Renan. "I read them to him, and he made comments on them which formed the best lesson in style that I have ever had."[88] From that time forward, Renan carried a distaste for any word not in use in the seventeenth century, and thus a preference for established usage. His second editor was his sister Henriette. "For my style," he wrote,

I owe her an infinite debt. She read proofs of all I wrote, and her precious criticism hunted out with perfect delicacy the negligences I had overlooked. . . . She convinced me that everything might be said in the simple and correct style of good writers, and that neologisms and violent images always spring from misplaced pretension or ignorance of our real riches. Hence from my reunion with her dates a profound change in my manner of writing. I got used to composing in view of her comments, hazarding many points to see what effect they would produce on her, and prepared to sacrifice them at her demand.[89]

The young Renan was given to strong satire and irony; his sister dissuaded him from inflicting unnecessary wounds and moulded the scholar in him away from pedantry and toward readability by the common man. Scholarly jargon is easy, but is too often lazy, uncouth, and discourteous to the reader. "Full maturity of mind," said Renan, "is not really reached until it becomes plain that everything may be said without any scholastic apparatus, in the language of the people . . . ."[90] His simple, limpid prose delighted both those who never normally opened a book of history and the white heads of that parliament of purism, l'Académie Française.

There are two kinds of prose writing. If we use Pater's distinction, we have the literature of the mind and the literature of the soul. If we follow the similar distinction of DeQuincey, we have the literature of knowledge and the literature of power. In the first of each division falls the statement of fact, or of inference or generaliza tion from fact. In the second what is dominant or prominent is the writer's *sense* of fact, his moral and aesthetic response to the facts presented. The difference becomes clear at once in illustration: to take two scientific men, compare Darwin with Sir Thomas Browne; to take two historians, compare Hallam with Carlyle. Renan belongs in the second group. His prose is saturated with that unique personality, himself. Hence the dyes in which his prose is dipped are dyes of rosy colors. His optimism, his admiration of goodness, his sympathy with suffering, his sunniness of temper that hovers like a quiet benediction over the persons and places he portrays, the joie de vivre, the thankfulness to whatever gods may be for merely being alive in so fascinating a world—all these unite to give his prose its atmosphere. Did this strong *sense* of the facts affect his report of the facts themselves? Probably it did occasionally; one thinks particularly of his filling in of the thirty-year blank in the life of his greatest subject, and perhaps also of his account of Paul, whom he, exceptionally, disliked. But he was aware of the danger and tried to avert it. "What I never do," he protested, "is to add a material circumstance to the texts, a detail to the portrayal of manners, a stroke to the landscape."[91] With a scholarship as careful as his, the reader is glad at times that he let his vivid imagination loose to portray his subject in the round.

The Paradox of Renan

We may close on a major paradox in Renan's life. On the one hand he was an Orientalist; in the twelve volumes of his *History of the People of Israel* and *The Origins of Christianity,* he was studying persons who knew nothing of science, whose heroes were lawgivers like Moses or men of the sword like Joshua or mystical psalmists like David or prophets who spoke in aphorisms and parables like Isaiah and Jesus. On the other hand he was a rationalist, who believed that truth was gained only by intellect, and who early discovered that the Oriental theologies dissolved at the approach of reason. It was really truth, the revelation that came through reason, that he worshiped, from his seminary days at Issy to the end. So the statement on his tombstone is true: *Veritatem dilexi.* ". . . Truth," he wrote in his book on *The Apostles,* "is not for the man who is full of passion. It reserves itself for those who, without partisanship, without committed devotion or committed hate, seek it with entire liberty . . . ."[92] And sometimes, from the depths of his immersion in mysticism and prophecy, there comes a *cri de coeur* from Renan that perhaps he had missed his calling, that perhaps it lay in an entirely different tradition. In middle life, after two visits to Palestine, he for the first time visited Athens. He sat on a fallen stone and looked at the Parthenon, which, with the drums of its columns lying around it, is still the most moving monument ever raised by human hands. For Renan it was even more: suddenly he recognized that here was his true church, the church for which he had left that of his childhood and youth, a church dedicated to reason and the life of the mind. Nothing in his experience, he said, had made so strong an impression.

On a visit to Athens just a century later I too sat on a fallen stone and looked with such eyes as I had at that same temple, in which all the intellect and art of Greece seem to be embodied. At the foot of the hill, in a little store among some cheap and gaudy trinkets, I noticed a pamphlet, *Prière sur l'Acropole,* by Ernest Renan. It was inspired as he sat looking at the Parthenon from perhaps the same place a hundred years before, and for long it lay unused among his papers, appearing at last in his recollections. Since it is quintessential Renan, and reveals so vividly the tension within him between Greece and Palestine, I give a few sentences from it. It plumbs the depth of the chasm between his loyalties to Greece and Palestine and voices the doubt whether, in giving his life to Palestine, he had not taken the wrong road. He is addressing the goddess of wisdom, Athena, whose statue by Phidias stood in the Parthenon where her diadem caught the rays of the rising sun.

O noble spirit! O beauty simple and true! Goddess whose worship is of reason and wisdom, whose temple is an eternal call to conscience and sincerity . . . .

Priests of a foreign cult, come from the Syrians of Palestine, had charge over my teaching. These priests were sages and saints. . . . Their temples soared three times as high as yours, O goddess of order, and were built like the forest; only they were not solid; in five or six centuries they fell in ruin; they are the fantasies of barbarians who imagine that something good can be made outside the laws that you have laid down for those you inspire, O Reason. But these temples pleased me; I had not studied your divine art; I found God in them. Canticles were chanted there that I remember still . . . . Yes, Goddess, when I recall those chants, my heart melts; I almost become an apostate. Pardon me this folly; you cannot conceive the charm these rude magicians put into their verses, and what it has cost me to follow a stark reason. . . . O Princess, ideal that the man of genius incarnates in his masterworks, I would rather be the last in your house than the first in any other. More, I will bind myself to the base of your temple; I will forget every discipline but yours; I will make myself a stylite atop your columns; my cell shall be in your architrave. . . .

. . . the visions of all the sages hold part of the truth. Everything here below is a symbol only, or a dream.

The gods pass as men pass; it is well that they are not eternal. The faith men bore should never be a chain. They have fulfilled their duty to it when they wrap it tenderly in its purple shroud and lay it where the dead gods sleep.

HENRY SIDGWICK

Henry Sidgwick
Photograph by Samuel A. Walker   National Portrait Gallery, London

Henry Sidgwick

"Pure white light!" exclaimed a British philosopher in my hearing some fifty years ago when the conversation turned to Henry Sidgwick. That sums up pretty well what his contemporaries thought of him. He stood in their view as the exemplar of objectivity in thought, of clear and passionless understanding. The light he threw on his subject was uniquely uncolored by feeling, prejudice, or desire.

This very impersonality, however, has left his readers with little knowledge of Sidgwick the man. If philosophy students of today were asked what they knew of him, the answer would probably be that he was an English utilitarian who wrote an important big dull book period. Regarding the man who wrote the book even the graduate students in ethics know little or nothing. In *The Methods of Ethics* the austerity of the style and the author's insistence on keeping himself out of the picture have left the man Sidgwick scarcely more than a ghostly presence lurking behind the curtain of impersonal prose.

One is the loser if one leaves him there. In my own view he is one of the most attractive figures in philosophic history, not because he exhibited arresting individual traits, but rather because he did not. Philosophers have often been odd creatures. Ever since the father of their line, Thales, fell into a well while his head was in the clouds, their contemporaries have laughed over their eccentricities; and many of these singular figures—Socrates, Schopenhauer, Nietzsche, Spencer, Wittgenstein, for example—have shown such marked idiosyncrasies that legends have clustered about them. Sidgwick is not one of this company. If he stands out, as he does for some of us, it is not because there is anything about him that would strike the general eye or attract reporters. It is rather because he was so free from anything capricious or eccentric, because for once a philosophy that was itself exceptionally sane got embodied in the life of its creator. Of all the persons in this little gallery of mine, he is, I suspect, the nearest approximation to the fully reasonable temper, while being also the least known. Unfortunately reasonableness is not news.

Schooldays

Henry Sidgwick was born in 1838 at Skipton, a little town in Yorkshire, in which his father, a Church of England clergyman, was headmaster of the grammar school. He was one of six children, but, losing his father when he was three years old, he was brought up by his accomplished and devoted mother. He early began to show his own extraordinary gifts. He learned to play chess at the age of five, and became so excited by his successes at the game that he had to give it up at doctor's orders; perhaps in consequence of this over-excitement, he developed a stammer that remained with him for the rest of his life. His mother taught him Latin herself and did not send him to school until he was ten. At twelve, in Blackheath School, his career nearly came to a sudden end. Blackheath was the only school in England where the game of golf was played. One day when a senior student was driving, Henry stooped down too near for safety and was caught full in the face by the force of the drive, which might have killed him. He carried the scar for life.

When Henry was fourteen, his mother moved her family to Rugby and entered the boy at Rugby School, which had been made famous by the recent reforms of Thomas Arnold. This entry was in violation of her late husband's wish that his sons *not* be sent to a public school by reason of its corrupting influence. Arnold was a great headmaster (despite Lytton Strachey's malicious portrait of him) and had changed the moral climate of the school. Henry was fortunate enough to have as one of his masters an able young scholar who came to live in the Sidgwicks' house and to exert a strong and salutary influence on him. This was Edward White Benson, who later married Sidgwick's sister, and was destined to become Archbishop of Canterbury. Benson was a stimulating teacher; Sidgwick was the keenest boy in the school; and his feeling for the young master fell just short of idolatry. In the biography of the archbishop by his son Arthur Christopher Benson, Sidgwick wrote many years later:

his grasp of concrete details in any matter that he studied with us or for us was remarkably full, close and vivid: and his power of communicating his own keen and subtle sense of the literary quality of classical writings, and also of using them to bring the ancient world lifelike and human before our minds, was unrivalled. In these points I felt that the occasional lessons he gave the Sixth far surpassed any other teaching I had at Rugby—or indeed afterwards.[1]

On one important matter Benson's influence was decisive. A year before finishing his course at Rugby, Sidgwick was already equipped for university work. A scholarship at Balliol College, Oxford, was open; it was a tradition for the best boys at Rugby to compete for it; his headmaster wanted Sidgwick to do this; and if he had done so, it is almost certain that he would have won. He went to Benson for advice. Benson tried to be objective, but he was himself a devoted alumnus of Trinity College, Cambridge. Sidgwick ended by declining the Balliol opportunity and going to Trinity instead. This raises one of the intriguing minor *ifs* of history. T. H. Green had just gone from Rugby to Balliol, where he became a fellow, and founded the school of idealism that dominated British philosophy for the next half century. Sidgwick was a more brilliant scholar than Green, and an acute opponent of idealism. If he had supplanted Green at Oxford, what course would its philosophy have taken? Much may hang on a schoolboy's decision.

Cambridge

Sidgwick's career at Cambridge accorded almost monotonously with expectations. At his first opportunity, in his freshman year, he won the Bell scholarship; and again at the first opportunity the most prized of all Cambridge scholarships, the Craven, which was open to competition by all undergraduates, and carried with it the odd emolument of seventy-five pounds a year for seven years. Trinity had a set of examinations for its advanced students, with special prizes for high performance in each of its various fields. In his junior year Sidgwick swept five of these at once. He wound up by trying his hand at both the classical and mathematical triposes, winning the distinction of Senior Classic (the number one classical scholar), along with the Chancellor's Medal and a first class (though not the first position) on the mathematical side. Shortly afterward he was elected to a fellowship at Trinity, which was to be his home for the next forty-one years. Indeed he missed only one of more than 120 successive terms of teaching.

Such a record may raise the picture of an appalling gradgrind. But there is good evidence that he was nothing of the sort. To be sure, no one attains his kind of mastery of ancient languages without hard work. But his friend C. H. Tawney wrote of him, "he was always full of fun and in a sunny frame of mind. . . . My recollections of him at Bishop's College, and Rugby, and Cambridge are that he was a most amusing companion. He seemed to possess an inexhaustible fund of merriment."[2] Here there was some contrast, as we shall see, between the inner and outer man. But he was no recluse. He liked to attend the theater and to act in amateur plays himself; he enjoyed long walks across the countryside and had a lively sense for landscape; he was a popular guest because, with no desire to dominate, he was a ready and witty talker.

In his second year at Cambridge he had the good fortune to be elected to a club where his gifts in exchanging ideas were given full scope. It was a small society of long standing called the Apostles. Sidgwick said that his membership in this group had "more effect on his intellectual life than any one thing that happened to him afterwards" (*Mem.*, p. 32). The club met for discussion in a member's room every Saturday night of the term. One of the group read a paper, whereupon each of the others in turn took his stand before the fire and gave his opinions on the views of the reader or the earlier speakers. Gradually, Sidgwick wrote, the spirit of the club

absorbed and dominated me. I can only describe it as the spirit of the pursuit of truth with absolute devotion and unreserve by a group of intimate friends, who were perfectly frank with each other, and indulged in any amount of humorous sarcasm and playful banter, and yet each respects the other, and when he discourses tries to learn from him and see what he sees. Absolute candour was the only duty that the tradition of the society enforced. No consistency was demanded with opinions previously held—truth as we saw it then and there was what we had to embrace and maintain, and there were no propositions so well established that an Apostle had not the right to deny or question, if he did so sincerely and not from mere love of paradox. The gravest subjects were continually debated, but gravity of treatment, as I have said, was not imposed, though sincerity was (*Mem.,* pp. 34–35).

The influence of these discussions shows itself throughout Sidgwick's later writing—in its steady placing of truth above argumentative success, in its skill in analysis, and in its ease and simplicity of expression.

A Theological Cloud on the Horizon

Sidgwick took his degree in 1859. It was the birth year of some great books and some influential men of thought: of Darwin's *Origin of Species* and Mill's *Liberty*, of John Dewey and Henri Bergson, Samuel Alexander and Edmund Husserl, Graham Wallas and Havelock Ellis. The year ushered in a decade of rapid intellectual change, both in the world of thought and in Sidgwick's own attitudes. Hitherto his religious views, accepted automatically from the Church of England and confirmed by Rugby, had been on the whole orthodox. This orthodoxy began to fray in the debates and discussions of the Apostles. It was frayed still more under the influence of Mill, who for many years was his hero; indeed at the end of his life, dictating in illness a fragment of autobiography, Sidgwick remarked: "No one thinker, so far as I know, has ever had anything like equal influence in the forty years or so that have elapsed since Mill's domination began to weaken" (*Mem.*, p. 36). And he followed with keen interest the debates over the Darwinian view of the origin of man, and the discomfiture of the bishop of Oxford by Huxley before the British Association. When he was twenty-four he came across Renan's *Etudes d'histoire religieuse,* of which he would write: "I . . . derived from Renan's eloquent persuasions the conviction that it was impossible really to understand at first hand Christianity as a historical religion without penetrating more deeply the mind of the Hebrews and of the Semitic stock from which they sprang" (*Mem.,* p. 36). In accounting for the redirection of his studies that Sidgwick was about to make, it must be remembered that he was not as yet a professional philosopher; the fellowship to which he was appointed in the year of his graduation was for teaching ancient languages, in which his proficiency seemed to lie. So he followed Renan's lead and decided to immerse himself in the ancient languages of the Near East by way of clearing up the problems that were haunting him about the meaning and credibility of the Christian teaching.

In his determination to master Eastern languages, Sidgwick was abetted by the academic calendar, with Oxford and Cambridge in session for less than half the year. In the vacations he devoted himself almost feverishly to his new enterprise. He went to Dresden and Berlin, studied German intensively, and found eminent German scholars, including Ewald, who were ready to tutor him, sometimes refusing a fee, in Hebrew and Arabic. This continued for two or three years. When he wrote to his sister, "I have nearly got through the Old Testament," he meant that he had read it in Hebrew. He became so proficient an Arabic scholar that he considered standing for one of the two Cambridge professorships in this field.

But slowly he came to realize that, helpful as Renan's method was, it would never solve the problems that were really troubling him.

Was Jesus incarnate God, miraculously brought into the world as a man? Were his utterances of divine authority? Did he actually rise from the grave with a human body glorified, and therewith ascend into heaven? Or if the answers to these questions could not strictly be affirmative in the ordinary sense of the term, what element of truth, vital for mankind, could be disengaged from the husk of legend . . . ? (*Mem.,* pp. 37-38.)

These were the questions of importance, and though a knowledge of the text of Scripture and the circumstances of its writing was relevant, it could never by itself provide the solution. This was a matter of reflective thought, of a philosophy that could read between the lines and put the disjointed fragments of the Gospels together. Here he found himself torn between pragmatism and science. He was convinced, as Renan was, that Christian belief was a powerful support for morality. The assumption that the moral law was the will of God, who would reward obedience and punish wilfulness, did make for a harmonious society, in spite of encouraging morality for dubious reasons. Nor was he insensitive to the personal charm of churchmen like Benson—to their persistent hopefulness, to the cheerfulness, affection, and service that the Christian life at its best tended to produce. Still, truth and goodness were very different things; pure hearts do not always go with clear heads; and it is the business of the truth-seeker to see that goodness is not based on illusion. Speaking long afterward in the *Life* of Archbishop Benson of those who would apply to the Bible the same principles that they would to other historical works, Sidgwick said:

What was fixed and unalterable and accepted by us all was the necessity and duty of examining the evidence for historical Christianity with strict scientific impartiality; placing ourselves as far as possible outside traditional sentiments and opinions, and endeavouring to weigh the pros and cons on all theological questions as a duly instructed rational being from another planet—or let us say from China—would naturally weigh them (*Mem.,* p. 40).[3]

As a result of his biblical studies, Sidgwick was tempted to write a book dealing with Christianity on historical and philosophical principles. How one wishes that he had! He was one of the few Englishmen who had immersed themselves in the wave of biblical criticism that had swept over Germany; he would no doubt have had help from his friend George Eliot, who had translated the greatest product of such criticism, Strauss's *Das Leben Jesu*; and his combination of scholarship with philosophy would have produced a superb critical work. But he was haunted by the harm that such a work might do to the foundations of a church that he valued highly, and the book was never written. We get some idea of what it would have been from an article printed in the *Westminster Review* in 1866 and entitled "Ecce Homo." It was the review of a book of that name published anonymously a year before, which offered a fresh and eloquent defense of a supernaturalist position. It was evidently written by a man of no ordinary powers, and Sidgwick happened to know who he was: he was to become Sir John Seeley, professor of Modern History at Cambridge. But the review showed that the reviewer was a far more sophisticated critic than was the author. Sidgwick did not fully disclose his own position, but he said enough in the opening pages to show that, for himself at least, Strauss and Renan had not written in vain. Like them, he saw that the occurrence of miracles was the hub of Christian apologetics. Reports of miraculous suspensions of scientific law are scattered through the four Gospels. They cannot be rejected without bringing the whole text into question; they cannot be accepted without placing Christianity in conflict with science at numerous points. Sidgwick was a thorough believer in scientific method, which had achieved its triumphs through the assumption that every event is preceded by a cause from which it follows in accordance with law. He saw that if this were abandoned numberless miracles claimed by saints and sects the world over would have to be accepted also, since they were often attested by evidence as strong as that of the biblical miracles. The question was one of probability. Which was the more likely, that nature was actually invaded from some nonrational realm or that some error had been made in understanding or reporting the event? In the light of what he knew of human credulity, especially where passion was deeply involved and the line between legend and history vaguely drawn, he could hardly hesitate. In his opening pages he exposed Seeley's lack of clearness on this point with damaging effect.[4]

The contrast is striking between Renan's case and Sidgwick's in the length of their struggle over belief. Renan's crisis was over in about two years. Sidgwick's lasted at least a decade, and in one form or another to the end of his life. We find him writing when he was twenty-four: "At present, however, I am only a Theist; but I have vowed that it shall not be for want of profound and devoted study, if I do not become a Christian." And again a little later: ". . . I still hunger and thirst after orthodoxy: but I am, I trust, firm not to barter my intellectual birthright for a mess of mystical pottage." At twenty-nine he was exclaiming: "Oh, how I sympathise with Kant! with his passionate yearning for synthesis and condemned by his reason to criticism. . . ." In the main, criticism triumphed with the years. "I am glad," he wrote in maturity, "that so many superior people are able to become clergymen, but I am less and less able to understand how the result is brought about in so many thoroughly sincere and disinterested and able minds" (*Mem.*, pp. 82, 90, 177, 455).

Sidgwick Resigns His Fellowship

His doubts came to a head in 1869, when he was thirty-one. At that time it was still the custom of the Cambridge colleges to require their fellows to sign the articles of the Church of England. Most of them did so mechanically, taking the process of signing as a mere formality, not as a considered expression of assent. Sidgwick was more conscientious. He asked himself whether he had any right to accept a position and pay granted on the express condition that he profess belief in dogmas that he knew he did not believe. Did he believe, for example, that Jesus had no human father? Did he believe that at his death Jesus still walked the earth with a human body of flesh and bone, and that this body was taken up into heaven to sit at the right hand of God the Father? Or was it a lie to say that he believed these things? He thought it was. So, quietly and without publicity, he sent a letter to the master of Trinity saying that since he found himself unable to comply with one of the conditions on which his fellowship depended, he was, with great regret, resigning it. The shock to Trinity, and soon to the university, was profound. That Cambridge should cut off one of its most brilliant scholars merely for being more honest than others seemed absurd. Some of his friends expostulated with him, but found that he had thought the matter through more thoroughly than they had. "After all," he wrote, "it is odd to be finding subtle reasons for an act of mere honesty: but I am reduced to that by the refusal of my friends to recognise it as such." "I happen to care very little what men in general think of me individually: but I care very much about what they think of human nature. I dread doing anything to support the plausible suspicion that men in general, even those who profess lofty aspirations, are secretly swayed by material interests" (*Mem.,* p. 201).

Honesty proved the best policy. The fellows could not change the rules, for they were requirements set by Parliament, but they promptly voted to create a special lectureship in moral science which allowed Sidgwick to stay in Trinity without being a fellow, and to turn, as he wished, from classics to philosophy. Since his act brought suddenly to light a long series of past injustices, it served to wake Parliament up. Several Cambridge students from such churches as the Methodist and the Presbyterian had become senior wranglers at Cambridge only to have fellowships denied them on religious grounds. Two years after Sidgwick's action, the religious tests for fellowships were finally abolished by parliamentary statute.

But the issue of religious liberty was not so easily set at rest in the public mind. As doubts spread about ancient dogmas, questions inevitably arose whether laymen have a right to belong to churches, or clergymen to officiate in them, who do not accept their creeds. Sidgwick argued the case with his usual skill in an article in the American *International Journal of Ethics* in 1896. He maintained here too his exacting standards of honesty. In January of the next year Hastings Rashdall, who was to become a distinguished don at Oxford and dean of Carlisle (and was an admired teacher of my own), published a reply, presenting the curious scene of a clergyman arguing for a laxity in these matters that a layman could not approve. A year later Sidgwick replied in his book on *Practical Ethics* with an essay on "Clerical Veracity," in which Rashdall's liberalism was courteously but firmly rejected. It is evidence of the fairness that Sidgwick's critics felt in him that when, some years later, Rashdall published his admirable two-volume work, *A Theory of Good and Evil,* one of the two men to whom he dedicated it was his old opponent, Sidgwick.

Sidgwick's defection from orthodoxy was already apparent at twenty-eight, when he wrote the article earlier mentioned on Seeley's *Ecce Homo.* His skepticism deepened with the years. When he paid visits to his brother-in-law the archbishop, as he frequently did, the two men, who retained much affection for each other, avoided religious discussion by an unspoken understanding. The archbishop was rather frightened of Sidgwick, the more so because of his total freedom from fanaticism, and Sidgwick regarded Lambeth Palace in the age of science as a curious survival. After a visit to the busy and efficient primate, he wrote about the Church of England: ". . . I feel rather as if I were contemplating a big fish out of water, propelling itself smoothly and gaily over the high road" (*Mem.,* p. 396). "Bishops individually," he said, "represent everything that I find most agreeable; collectively, everything that I most detest."[5]

His alienation from Christianity, however, was purely intellectual, and he continued to regard religion as the strongest of influences making for the good life. This left him in a dilemma. Should he attack dogmatic religion as untrue and thereby help to undermine its moral force, or dissemble his disbelief in it for the sake of preserving that force? One would expect him to find some middle way, and he did. He refused to carry on open or aggressive warfare with religion while always ready to state and discuss his views with interested persons. His own reason, with its confident assurance about values, gave him quite enough light to live by, but he knew that for many others the zest and the values of life were so bound up with their faith that its loss would cloud their lives, and while he thought they were mistaken, he had no heart for wrecking happiness.

Arthur Christopher Benson, the archbishop's son, who was a student at Cambridge, is a witness to his uncle's scrupulousness in these matters. Sidgwick was fond of the young man, but saw him only occasionally. Shortly after his graduation, his nephew writes,

He made me a gentle apology for not having seen more of me as an undergraduate. . . . he added that he had always known and felt that my father was uneasy about his possible influence on my religious views, and that he had therefore made up his mind that he would not raise such questions at all, and that he would not encourage me to discuss such things; and that this had ended in his seeing less of me than he had wished. He added that he hoped that I should not misunderstand it, or put it down in any way to a lack of affection; for indeed it was rather the reverse. I do not think that I ever heard such a thing said more feelingly and delicately, and it gave me a sense of justice and high-mindedness which was intensely impressive.[6]

Though Sidgwick was not a militant critic of Christian belief, he was in another and paradoxical way a thorn in the side for Christian apologists. How could they maintain with any plausibility that religious belief was indispensable to high character with such a man about? G. G. Coulton reported as the common feeling about him that he showed "every Christian virtue except faith."[7] Even his opponents bore similar testimony. "His irony never hurt, it was so kindly," said Maitland; "and, of all known forms of wickedness, 'Sidgwickedness' was the least wicked."[8]

The Education of Women

I have already noted Sidgwick's admiration for John Stuart Mill, and it is hardly surprising that after reading Mill's book of 1869, *The Subjection of Women,* the ardor of his support for women's "liberation" should have taken fresh flame. He thought, as did Mill, that the public had never known what women were capable of, since they had so generally been held in some kind or other of subjection. Victorian England was no exception to this rule. Herbert Spencer recalled having lived near a girls' school, and having observed the pupils reflectively during their hours of recess. For athletics they walked quietly arm in arm around the school yard. We now know that they can, with encouragement, run a marathon, play a formidable game of tennis, and make expert opponents in karate and judo. I should have much enjoyed taking my grandmother, who was convinced that her sex were frail vessels, to a women's final at Wimbledon, where young Amazons in shorts put on breathtaking exhibitions. Victorians were likewise inclined to think that women were cut off by nature from the higher reaches of scholarship and intellect. Sidgwick knew better than most people the danger of generalizing about women, but he was clear that if they had scholarly ambitions, they should at least have the chance of showing what they could do.

Cambridge University in the 1860s had no women students or teachers. By way of exploring the interests of women living in the city of Cambridge, he announced and in 1870 delivered sets of lectures more or less parallel to those he gave for men. To his surprise between seventy and eighty women attended, and he proceeded to co opt other volunteer dons for like service. He next gained the consent of the authorities to allow some of these women, largely self-educated, to sit for university honors examinations. One high hurdle in their way was the requirement of Greek and Latin, since the girls' schools did not teach these languages adequately, if at all. Sidgwick, a distinguished scholar in both, was opposed to this requirement, even for men, and he persuaded the authorities to let the women substitute the Higher Local Examination for the "Little-Go," the entrance examination, a boon that was no doubt the more readily granted because no degrees were involved. Many women recommended by girls' schools applied for the privilege of at least this taste of the university. The doubts whether women were capable of rigorous work were soon removed when two of these students gained honors in the Moral Sciences Tripos of 1874; and another in the following year took honors in both classics and mathematics. In December 1881, the year when the honors examinations were formally opened to women, two women candidates were the only ones the examiners thought worthy of first-class honors. Of course they did not get their degrees; these had to wait till 1923.

Since none of the colleges would take them, some of the women were welcomed into the families of local dons, and others were housed in a residence rented by Sidgwick at his own expense. Indeed so many well-qualified girls applied that a special hall of residence was plainly required. Sidgwick shortly had a committee which organized a campaign for funds. He notes that John Stuart Mill "has come forward like a woman" and promised forty pounds a year for two years. The modest hall, accommodating thirty students, was built in a part of Cambridge called Newnham, and was accordingly called Newnham Hall. Sidgwick was fortunate enough to secure as its first head an able administrator, Anne Clough, a sister of the poet Arthur Hugh Clough, who worked without fee and even paid her own board. Another building called Sidgwick Hall was added in 1880, and the two buildings became the nucleus of the present Newnham College. Behind the new building was a garden in which the philosopher liked to walk and meditate; after his death it was converted into a formal rose garden in his honor. I have visited this garden to pay my respect, and wished that I were not confined in so trivial a sense to following in his steps.

Sidgwick had much respect for women and worked with them harmoniously. It is worth noting that even here, however, he did not lose his critical sense. To his friend Frederic Myers he wrote:

I have been attending a North of England Council Meeting, and making observations on women. It seems to me that they have at present one defect in "action by means of debate," they have not quite enough practical self-assertion at the right place and time, and hence are more apt to nurse small jealousies than men. *Nous autres hommes,* if a President of a Committee shows a disposition to suppress one, one snubs him at once, says loudly the thing he doesn't like, and then is in good-humour afterwards (*Mem.*, p. 249).

At thirty-seven, Sidgwick married Eleanor Mildred Balfour, known to her friends as Nora; and the marriage was a lifelong source of strength and happiness. Nora was the sister of Arthur James Balfour, so Sidgwick had as brothers-in-law both the archbishop of Canterbury and the prime minister of England. Nora was an extremely able collaborator, particularly in his work for women and in his pioneering labors in psychical research. After the death of Miss Clough in 1892, Nora was appointed principal of Newnham College, and in some rooms in the new building the pair made their home for the rest of Sidgwick's life.

Though they had no children, Sidgwick captivated his nephews and nieces by his gift for improvising epic stories, which he could produce at will and protract to any length desired. His nephew A. C. Benson tells of the delight he felt one evening when all the family but his uncle and himself had gone out to dinner. Uncle Henry had begun some days before the story of a king who heard a gnatlike voice saying, "Dig." He dug, but the voice said, "Deeper." As he went down from level to level, he unearthed a succession of marvels till he came to a great green room. The final chapter was approaching, and the small boy felt that now was his chance. He tells

how I stole upon his secure hour, and demanded that the story of the Green Room should be *finished;* how he put his book aside with a laugh, and, while I played with the buttons of his waistcoat, the strange and beautiful *dénouement* unrolled itself—so that for a day at least I was in the proud position, among my envious brothers and sisters, of knowing what had really happened, and withholding the information.[9]

"White Light"

Though Sidgwick devoted much time and energy to women's education and, as we shall see, to psychical research, his heart lay in philosophy. Perhaps because of the very diversity of his gifts, Cambridge was slow to recognize the greatest of these. In 1866 he was passed over for the chair of moral philosophy in favor of Frederick Denison Maurice, an outstanding theologian; since Sidgwick was still known as a classicist rather than as a philosopher, this was no surprise to him. But when Maurice died six years later, he was again passed over in favor of a clergyman, the Reverend T. R. Birks, of whom nothing seems to be known but his name. Some nine years later Birks suffered a stroke, and the vice-chancellor of the university had to appoint a deputy for him. By then Sidgwick's great work on ethics had appeared and had made him the obvious appointee. Once again he was passed over in favor of one of his pupils named Cunningham. It was not until Birks died in 1883 that Sidgwick was finally appointed to the Knightbridge chair, which he filled with distinction till his death in 1900. His philosophical views were never the reigning views of the England of his time; rather the idealism of Oxford, as preached with eloquence by Green, Caird, and Bradley, dominated the last quarter of the century. Sidgwick's influence was attained less by his conclusions than by the manner of man he was—by his ways of thinking, writing, and teaching, and perhaps above all by the atmosphere of impartial reasonableness that pervaded his thought and his action. We must say a little more about these intangible things.

The "white light" that Sidgwick threw on things was drawn from his self-critical habits of thought. He was sometimes regarded by his colleagues as a fence-sitter unable to make up his mind. This was untrue. He was not lacking in decision; it was rather that he was less willing than others to form a decision before all the relevant factors had been taken into account. I remember turning to his *Principles of Political Economy* for an answer to the question whether free trade was a desirable policy or not. I could, no doubt, have got the simple answer I wanted from some economic journalist, but as I read on it became plain that from Sidgwick I should never get it. I was inclined, as James Bryce was in reading him, to cry out, "Do lapse for a moment into dogmatism." But this Sidgwick resolutely refuses to do. He will not say that free trade is a good thing, for that is too undiscriminating to be either true or useful. What he does say is that a protective tariff is not to be recommended under most circumstances, though under circumstances *a, b,* and *c* it has advantages *d* and *e* unless indeed these are countervailed, as they well may be, by drawbacks *f* and *g.* The validity of every qualification is apparent, and one learns slowly and sadly that the truth about free trade is not to be forced into any nutshell of formula. Sidgwick's writing is a continual inculcation of this kind of lesson.

It is not only the complexity of truth, however, that baffles the search for it; there is also the smokescreen of likes and dislikes thrown up by the searcher himself—personal aversion, religious odium, political prejudice, pride, fear, jealousy, and all the rest. The ablest of intellects have often become untrustworthy when their special devotions or detestations have been fanned into life. Macaulay remarked of Burke that he employed all the resources of a splendid intellect in proving conclusions dictated by his feelings; and Macaulay himself will bear watching when he is dealing with his hero William III. Luther wrote about Erasmus like an angry child. Kierkegaard rationalized his treatment of Regina in scandalous fashion; Nietzsche, when he set up as anti-Christ, was asimmer with pet hatreds. If Sidgwick ever felt such passions, there is no hint of them in his writings, and one is led to wonder whether he ever felt them at all. Bishop Gore, who could not have been happy about Sidgwick's religious attitudes, said of him nevertheless that he was as near as any man he knew to the character described in the text, "Blessed are the pure in heart." Less kindly critics would perhaps prefer the language of an Irishman about Lecky: "He was so irritatingly impartial that he provoked both friends and foes to conflict."

Was Sidgwick, then, an intellectualist, a man whose veins held ice water rather than blood? Some have felt that he reserved his warmth for ideas and was little concerned about his fellows as human beings; G. E. Moore, who had been a pupil of his, remarked to me that he thought Sidgwick interested himself in his students only in proportion to their ability. He had a curious habit of not recognizing people on the street. He did not seem to realize that this might give offense; it could hardly have been due to deliberate incivility. That he was alive to the feelings and impulses of ordinary men is clear from his acute analysis of them in his ethical writings and from his criticism of others who disregarded them. He writes of Taine's *Origines de la France contemporaine*: ". . . it seems to me essentially deficient in sympathy and therefore in real penetration. It is all very well to maintain a scientific attitude of mind: but the physicist must have his *senses* acute and alert to perform a fine scientific analysis accurately, and sympathy is an indispensable sense of the scientific historian" (*Mem.*, p. 397). He was devoted to poetry, an addiction not conspicuous in men whose blood is ice water. One of his pupils who became a bishop writes of him: "Not only, or perhaps chiefly, in intellectual things, but in practical matters of conduct, his wisdom, considerateness, unselfishness, and resolute impartiality were a constant help, a standard one put before oneself for guidance" (*Mem.*, p. 314). And Lord Bryce remarks of him that "the gravity of a Stoic was relieved by the humour and vivacity which belonged to his nature, and the severity of a Stoic was softened by the tenderness and sympathy which seemed to grow and expand with every year."[10]

In the light of his journal, in the light of his letters, in the reports of those who knew him best, the image of Sidgwick as an icicle seems grotesque. But the charge of coldness is not entirely without foundation; it is one of the charges most likely to be made against all the figures in this book, and it calls for more attention. As regards Sidgwick, perhaps the truth runs something like this.

First, he belonged to that small class of men who are possessed by an overmastering love of truth. He showed this in action as well as in thought. He resigned his chief means of livelihood rather than subscribe, even as a formality, to what he thought untrue. In 1860 seven eminent Anglicans published a book of *Essays and Reviews,* in which it was gently suggested that if one took reason seriously, some elements of the creed must be revised. The book went through nine editions in a year and raised a storm of orthodox criticism. Sidgwick, aged twenty-two, wrote a letter to the *Times* that might have come from the pen of Renan. His own position was clearly summed up in a line he quoted from Bishop Westcott: "they love their early faith, but they love truth more" (*Mem.,* p. 65). A little later he says in replying to a criticism of the Stoics by Sir John Seeley:

He speaks of "reason" as if it meant only logic; as if its supremacy kept the man entirely cold; as if it were impossible to feel ardour and enthusiasm for abstractions. . . . But how was the Stoic himself made and kept honest, and pure, and self-sacrificing? Not by his logic, but by the enthusiasm that he felt when he contemplated the true law, the right reason, the wisdom that became dearer to him than any pleasure, the idea of good that rose up in and absorbed his soul, casting into shade the *prima naturae,* the lawful objects of the earlier natural impulses. . . . to deny this efficacy to those *incredibiles ardores* that the inner vision of truth and wisdom excited in a few is worse than a mere historical error: it implies a psychological deficiency.[11]

Bishop Gore remarked, "There was in him an extraordinary belief in *following reason*—a belief and a hopefulness which continued up to the last" (*Mem.,* p. 557). In the fragment of autobiography dictated at the end of his life, Sidgwick says that his experience in the Cambridge Apostles "really determined or revealed that the deepest bent of my nature was towards the life of thought—thought exercised on the central problems of human life" (*Mem.,* p. 35). In this devotion to reason, Sidgwick, like Spinoza and Kant, was a modern Stoic.

An icy intellectualism is usually arrogant; Sidgwick's "intellectualism" was the opposite. He resorted to constant and almost excessive self-criticism. Perhaps John Morley was thinking of his modest self-estimate as well as his passion for truth when he said,

"If any Englishman ever belonged to the household of Socrates, Sidgwick was he."[12] "I am not an original man," Sidgwick said, "and I think less of my own thoughts every day" (*Mem.,* p. 93). Nor was his self-criticism a mock modesty that declines to admit its points of strength. To a close friend he wrote: "I like criticising myself, and have formulated the following on it:—*Pro.*—Always thoughtful, often subtle: generally sensible and impartial: approaches the subject from the right point of view. *Con.*—Inconsequent, ill-arranged: stiff and ponderous in style: nothing really striking or original in the arguments" (*Mem.,* p. 177). At times his self-depreciation was more sweeping. To the same friend he wrote: "Do you know, if I was quite sure that every one whose opinion was worth having regarded me as a very commonplace person, it would be an indescribable relief. . . . By commonplace I mean simply as regards power and performance" (*Mem.,* p. 121). Even when he was working on his great book on morals, he wrote to George Eliot: ". . . I feel rather dull from the task of weaving a sieve to hold the water of life in—for a book on Morals often seems like that; however tight one tries to draw the meshes, everything of the nature of Wisdom seems to have run through when one examines the result— that is, if it was ever there" (*Mem.,* pp. 283–84). He would have enjoyed the freedom in writing of those who were not haunted by such self-doubts, but he did not envy them. In his late forties he entered in his journal:

Have been reading Comte and Spencer, with all my old admiration for their intellectual force and industry and more than my old amazement at their fatuous self-confidence. It does not seem to me that either of them knows what self-criticism means. I wonder if this is a defect inseparable from their excellences. Certainly I find my own self-criticism an obstacle to energetic and spirited work, but on the other hand I feel that whatever value my work has is due to it (*Mem.,* p. 421).

A factor that strengthened the impression of his being a cold intellectual was his sheer subtlety of mind. When a thinker has a system to which he is committed, he can march straight forward along the road laid down for him by that system. Sidgwick had no such system. He dealt with particular problems as they arose, and as all objections had to be dealt with before they were dismissed, he often seemed to move at a snail's pace. Being singularly open-minded, he was ready, like William James, to hear all sides of a case, whether presented by the philosopher or by the man in the street. An amusing instance arose at a meeting of the Economic Section of the British Association in 1888. The economists were having a field day on socialism, which Sidgwick had minutely examined and for the most part rejected in his books on economics and politics. "The Committee had invited a live Socialist, redhot 'from the Streets,' as he told us, who sketched in a really brilliant address the rapid series of steps by which modern society is to pass peacefully into social democracy." Sidgwick had never heard of the man, but he outlines his argument in his journal and takes pains to point out just where it failed. "Altogether a noteworthy performance " he concludes; "the man's name is *Bernard Shaw*" (*Mem.*, pp. 497–98). A man "from the Streets"! In those days Shaw was just that, but Sidgwick took him in all critical seriousness.

Sidgwick was neither the prosecuting attorney nor the counsel for the defense, but the judge on the bench. And judicial decisions are not the preferred reading of the many. ". . . I feel more in my element," he wrote, "when I feel called upon to weigh and balance and mete out so many ounces of blame and so many of praise, than when enthusiasm and sublime flights are wanted" (*Mem.*, p. 213). Mrs. Sidgwick quotes the description of him by an old friend as a person

whose fairness in controversy almost led him to be unfair to his own side; who seldom made a statement or expressed an opinion without qualifying it; who was commonly reputed to have a mind so subtle and evenly balanced that it never pronounced a decision; and yet whose counsel guided practical men, and whose wisdom was recognised by men of every school of thought and religion (*Mem.*, p. 204 n.).

She adds to the sketch:

in practical affairs he generally acted consciously on a balance of advantages, not on any overpowering conviction that the course he adopted must certainly be right; there was no element of fanaticism in anything he did. . . . The result was not indecisiveness in action. When he took up any matter—for instance, the education of women—he worked at it with a deliberate zeal and unwavering single-minded self-devotion which made up for lack of enthusiastic and unhesitating conviction . . . and perhaps his balanced temperament prevented his being a very inspiring leader, except to those who knew him well. . . . He was at no time the leader of a party. But he often led the leaders . . . (*Mem.*, pp. 203–4).

He may have given some color to the charge of cold intellectualism by his conviction that feeling never *knows*. Though he loved poetry, he was impatient of the idea that poetic feeling, however exalted, is somehow revelatory of the nature of things. Wordsworth's "Ode: Intimations of Immortality from Recollections of Early Childhood" has been taken by many a reader as expressing a profound insight into truth. And that the eagerness, innocence, and joy of the child should be an inheritance from an earlier life is a striking conceit, beautifully expressed.

> Our birth is but a sleep and a forgetting:
> The Soul that rises with us, our life's Star,
> Hath had elsewhere its setting,
> And cometh from afar:
> Not in entire forgetfulness,
> And not in utter nakedness,
> But trailing clouds of glory do we come
> From God, who is our home . . . .

But to pass from the beauty of the thought and the expression to their truth, from the charm of childish innocence to its birth in another existence, is itself childish in its use of evidence, as we see at once if we let intelligence break the spell. Poetry, even great poetry, is not science, and we confuse quite different functions of our mind if we are lax about this. Commenting in his journal about the *Essays on Poetry* of a friend, Roden Noel, Sidgwick writes: "the fundamental difference between him and me is that he thinks the Poet has Insight into Truth, instead of merely Emotions and an Art of expressing them. . . . I feel rather angry when I am asked to take a poet as a philosopher" (*Mem.,* p. 458).

He was particularly sensitive, as a result of his own experience, to the claim of the religious zealot to reach by the mystical route truths that were unattainable and unverifiable by reflective thought. He made something of an exception of Tennyson, for whom nature meant the nature accepted by science and who saw more clearly than Wordsworth did the limitations of feeling in apprehending it. In a long letter to Tennyson's son, he expressed his view discriminatingly:

for your father the physical world is always the world as known to us through physical science: the scientific view of it dominates his thoughts about it; and his general acceptance of this view is real and sincere, even when he utters the intensest feeling of its inadequacy to satisfy our deepest needs. . . . I always feel this strongly in reading the memorable lines . . .

A warmth within the breast would melt
The freezing reason's colder part,
And like a man in wrath the heart
Stood up and answered, "I have felt."

At this point, if the stanzas had stopped here, we should have shaken our heads and said, "Feeling must not usurp the function of Reason. Feeling is not knowing. It is the duty of a rational being to follow truth wherever it leads." But the poet's instinct knows this; he knows that this usurpation by Feeling of the function of Reason is too bold and confident; accordingly in the next stanza he gives the turn to humility in the protest of Feeling which is required (I think) to win the assent of the "man in men . . ." (*Mem.,* pp. 540–41).

Sidgwick's faith did not match Tennyson's. But this letter is the more memorable because he goes on to admit that if feeling has its limits, so has reason. He speaks from a mind still curiously divided. Of the poet's lines he says: "I feel in them the indestructible and inalienable minimum of faith which humanity cannot give up because it is necessary for life; and which I know that I, at least so far as the man in me is deeper than the methodical thinker, cannot give up" (*Mem.*, p. 541).

"Labor Improbus"

One further comment is called for on the charge that "the freezing reason's colder part" held Sidgwick firmly in its grip. A reader of his journal rises with something of the same feeling that Matthew Arnold carried away from a reading of Marcus Aurelius. The imperial Stoic was a great and good man whose mind, nevertheless, was pervaded by a secret melancholy, or if this is too strong, a man whose spirits were habitually low. Too often one finds the words "Labor improbus," worthless toil, entered in Sidgwick's journal in summary of his day's work. At thirty-one, after resigning his fellowship, he wrote to a friend:

Just now I am much depressed, with no particle of regret for what I have done, but depressed at the thought of being so different from my friends.
>   Why should a man desire in any way
>   To vary from the kindly race of men?
There is nothing in me of prophet or apostle. The great vital, productive, joy-giving qualities that I admire in others I cannot attain to: I can only lay on the altar of humanity as an offering this miserable bit of legal observance (*Mem.*, p. 199).

At forty-seven he wrote: "Am fighting against a general depression of mind; conviction that I am not likely to write anything that will interest myself or any one else, and that my work here is a failure" (*Mem.*, p. 438).

How is one to account for this persisting malaise in a life so active and so successful? No doubt in part its root was physical. He had a serious and prolonged attack of dyspepsia in his second year at Trinity, and had recurring spells of it throughout his life. One can see in Carlyle how profoundly this may affect one's disposition. Furthermore, Sidgwick, like Spencer, suffered from a chronic inability to sleep. At fifty-eight he wrote to his friend the psychologist

James Sully: "As for insomnia, I have been rather alarmed: but five days at Brighton have brought me up to 6 hours again: so I do not feel qualified to ask for sympathy. At Cambridge I am liable to run down to 5 1/2, 4 1/2, 3 1/2 . . ." (*Mem.,* p. 548). For a time this led him "to make a rigid rule of abstinence from all reading after dinner which tends to hard thinking" (*Mem.,* p. 483). But he refused to take drugs, and contented himself with lying still and (he seemed unable to avoid this) meditating. It is surprising that with so little sleep he could achieve so much work, and invariably of a high level.

Again, his classes were small, and he felt his philosophical influence also to be small. To this must be added his conviction that the news of the world he had to communicate to his students was not good news. Religious faith he believed to be an important buttress of happiness, and the tendency of his thought was to break this buttress down. In a letter to Frederic Myers he wrote:

as to you, I have another sadness in feeling that during the years in which we have exchanged thoughts I have unwillingly done you more harm than good by the cold corrosive scepticism which somehow, in my own mind, is powerless to affect my "idealism," but which I see in more than one case acting otherwise upon others (*Mem.,* p. 283).

If he lacked exuberance there were reasons then, however well concealed from others, which were apt to creep up on him in the long hours of the night.

The Methods of Ethics

While Sidgwick was promoting the education of women and was deeply involved with university affairs, he was even busier writing his main work, *The Methods of Ethics* (1874). C. D. Broad, who later held Sidgwick's chair and was the most acute philosophic critic of his time, devoted half of *Five Types of Ethical Theory* (1930) to Sidgwick's volume, and begins his discussion of it with the arresting statement: "Sidgwick's *Methods of Ethics* seems to me to be on the whole the best treatise on moral theory that has ever been written . . ." (p. 143). Its author had approached a publisher with diffidence. "The book," he remarked to a friend, "solves nothing, but may clear up the ideas of one or two people a little" (*Mem.,* p. 284). He got up enough courage to send the manuscript to Macmillan. To his surprise and delight, the company accepted it and offered him half the profits. But Sidgwick doubted whether there would be any profits. ". . . I was afraid," he wrote to his mother, "that it was really unfair on Macmillan to ask him to take the risk. So I urged him to show a portion of the MS. to Mr. John Morley . . ." (*Mem.,* p. 292). Fortunately Morley knew a good thing when he saw it. The book came out in 1874, and remains one of the classics of British and modern thought. Let me sketch the drift of its argument.

The main question of ethical theory is how to tell what it is right to do. Moralists had differed widely and even wildly in their answers to this question. Paley said that the right method was to find the will of God as revealed in Scripture. Kant said that it was to set out the abstract principle of a proposed action, for example a lie, and then to ask whether one could will consistently that everyone should obey it. Hume said that it was to find the action which, because of its tendency to produce happiness, aroused the most general approbation. Samuel Clarke said that the rules of conduct, such as the Golden Rule, were as self-evident to our reason as the multiplication table. Sidgwick held that all such proposals really reduced to two, the appeal to rules and the appeal to ends. The first tells us to look for self-evident maxims of conduct; the second tells us first to define the end or ends of life, and then ask what actions will best conduce to those ends. The second method can be seen to break into two subkinds: egoism, which says that the end is one's own good, and utilitarianism, which says that it is the greatest good of men generally.

The question then becomes, which of these methods, or what combination of them, best comports with the judgments we actually make? This sounds as if Sidgwick were using common sense as his court of final appeal, and he did sometimes refer to himself as a common-sense philosopher. But this does not mean that he took common sense at its face value. No one has exposed with a sharper scalpel the vagueness and inconsistency of our common-sense moral judgments. But every science must have its data, and the data of ethics were the judgments of actual men. These judgments were not arbitrary but the end result of a long trek by humanity from savagery to civilization; and, as such, they were the deposit of a vast experience. They were the necessary point of departure for any theory that did not hang in the air. The business of ethical theory was to find out what were the methods implicitly used in arriving at the judgments, and whether there was any method that would make them into a consistent and credible whole.

Probably most plain men are intuitionists. They have early learned such maxims as "Don't lie," "Don't kill," "Don't cheat," "Keep your promises," "Don't steal," "Be fair in your dealings with others." They would think it strange to be asked for reasons for these rules, which have been accepted so long and so unthinkingly that they seem to be self-evident. Sidgwick has no difficulty in showing that while there would be very general agreement about them in ordinary cases, they are hopelessly vague and inconsistent in extreme cases. "Don't lie"—but if a Nazi officer asks if you know of any Jews in the neighborhood, and you are hiding one in your attic, is it self-evident that you should tell the truth? If you do, you will be in essence violating the second maxim, "Don't kill." Indeed all the maxims that begin by seeming certain turn out, if made universal, to be false guides.

Now if none of these common-sense maxims is certain, is there any test that shows us we are laying hold of certainty when we seem to see it? And if so, are there any maxims that pass this test? To both questions Sidgwick answered Yes. As for the first, he laid down four requirements that any maxim claiming self-evidence must fulfill. First, its terms must be clear and precise; on this, the two widely differing founders of modern thought, Bacon and Descartes, had agreed. Second, the proposed rule must be really self-evident; that is, it must not be warranted merely by influences that make it appear so, such as that of a respected authority, or of acceptance by our community, or our own desire, which is especially likely to distort our views on morals. Third, any maxim that we take as self-evident must be consistent with all others that we take to be so; otherwise one or other of the conflicting rules must be untrue, if not both. Fourth, what is self-evident should be accepted by all who can grasp it, and a failure in this consensus must so far make against its certainty. These rules apply to the claims of self-evidence in other fields than ethics; and if we find ourselves saying "it stands to reason" that something is true, it is helpful to pull from our pocket this little quadrant of Sidgwick's and apply it to our dogma.

Suppose now that one submits the common-sense rules of morals to this fourfold test; are there any that survive? All the ordinary ones such as we have cited fall at once. But Sidgwick holds that half a dozen truly self-evident rules remain. However, they are so purged of excrescences as to have an almost mathematical abstractness. Take, for example, Sidgwick's assay of the Golden Rule: Do to others as you would have them do to you:

This formula is obviously unprecise in statement; for one might wish for another's co-operation in sin, and be willing to reciprocate it. Nor is it even true to say that we ought to do to others only what we think it right for them to do to us; for no one will deny that there may be differences in the circumstances of two individuals, A and B, which would make it wrong for A to treat B in the way in which it is right for B to treat A. In short the rule strictly stated must take some such negative form as this: "it cannot be right for A to treat B in a manner in which it would be wrong for B to treat A, unless we can find some difference between the natures or circumstances of the two which we can state as a reasonable ground for difference of treatment." Such a principle manifestly does not give complete guidance; but its truth, so far as it goes, is self-evident . . . .[13]

Sidgwick was, then, an intuitionist in morals, though the rules he would admit as intuitions are so few and so attenuated as to give little guidance in particular cases. He was also a rationalist in morals, for self-evident rules are a priori rules, and such concepts as "ought" and "right" are a priori concepts in the sense that they are not drawn from, and do not refer to, anything given in sense. He says indeed: "I regard the apprehension, with more or less distinctness, of these abstract truths, as the permanent basis of the common conviction that the fundamental precepts of morality are essentially reasonable."[14]

But Sidgwick was not primarily an intuitionist. Indeed the last of his six self-evident rules was that one should seek the greatest good. This takes him at once into another method of ethics, in which, in order to find out what I ought to do, I must consider the consequences of the actions open to me. Now, as we have seen, there are two places of residence for this greatest good—self and mankind. If egoism is offered as a method for expressing and coordinating the judgments of common sense, it plainly will not serve. It holds that all we should concern ourselves with is our own good, and since the good of others does not count, we may sacrifice any amount of the good of others to gain even a small increase of our own. There is a general consensus against such action as callously insensitive and unfair.

Sidgwick therefore moves on to utilitarianism, which holds that one should be guided in one's action by the greatest good of all who are affected by it. And apart from the first five wispy abstractions that he borrows from the intuitionists, this is the method in which Sidgwick comes to rest. His line of argument for it is characteristic. It is an elaborate attempt to show that this is the position which underlies and unifies the great mass of our common-sense judgments of conduct. Similar attempts had been made earlier, notably by Hume, but they had never been carried through with such a sweep of coverage of all the main virtues and vices, with such sharpness and sympathy in analyzing the plain man's meanings, and with a logical sense so alert to buried inconsistencies. That the generally adopted rules of truthfulness, honesty, and unselfishness make for the general good can be shown easily enough. But Sidgwick saw that it was the borderline cases that were logically crucial. What is our ultimate resort when community mores conflict, or when we make qualifications or exceptions to them, or when different persons interpret the same rule differently, or when different cultures adopt standards that seem fundamentally at odds with each other? Sidgwick had a keen eye for these crucial cases, and showed that when we try to solve them rationally, we turn inevitably to the general good. Truthfulness conduces to this good; yes, obviously; but even when we make exception to it for the doctor or the detective, we justify the exception itself in the same way by appeal to the greater good of the whole.

One day a young Finnish anthropologist named Westermarck, who was inclined to an extreme subjectivism and relativism in ethics, appeared in Sidgwick's study to ask for advice. He went away disappointed. He was the sort of social scientist who thought that if a Fijian made his father at a certain age climb a tall palm tree and shook him down to his death, that indicated a concept of filial duty in flat conflict with ours. But he knew (or at least came to know) that the Fijians also held the belief that one carried into the next life the set of faculties, lively or debilitated, with which one left the present life. Was the act of the Fijian youth, then, one of the most callous cruelty or one of sympathy and kindness? Sidgwick would no doubt have pointed out that if the youth's belief were sincere, his apparent cruelty was an attempt to save his father from a life of decrepitude, and he would have added from a study of the records that the act was sometimes done in tears. If Sidgwick had lived a few decades longer, we can imagine the plowshare he would have driven through the "cultural relativism" of the Sumners and the Benedicts.

Ultimate Difficulties

Sidgwick's defense of a joint method of ethics, combining the rational intuition of a few abstract truths with the appeal to consequences for particular acts is (with certain refinements that need not be raised here) extraordinarily convincing. But two elements remain puzzling. First, he was a hedonist. He thought that the one feature that gave intrinsic value to any experience was its pervading feeling-tone. Experiences that were pleasant were, so far, good; experiences that were unpleasant or painful were, so far, bad. Most men would no doubt agree that pleasure is intrinsically good, and its opposite bad. But they would for the most part also agree that pleasure is not the only thing that makes an experience good. Of course Sidgwick saw the logical futility of Mill's suggestion that some pleasures have a higher quality than others, which must be counted in the reckoning as pleasure though it is clearly not pleasure. How he would have dealt with Broad's objection that the pleasures of malice would have to be called intrinsically good I do not know. I have attempted to deal with the difficulty in my own way in my book *Reason and Goodness* (p. 310). Sidgwick showed uneasiness at times with his theory, but in the main that theory was a straightforward quantitative hedonism. Hedonism has been so often and so decisively refuted, from Butler's time forward, that to rehash the arguments is needless. The main argument for it is that Henry Sidgwick believed it. And that argument, potent as it is, will hardly save the hedonist's case.

The second difficulty with Sidgwick's position is also one that has proved puzzling to his readers and apparently to himself, since he states it differently in different editions of his book. The difficulty has to do with the reasonableness of egoism. He thought it self-evident that the course of conduct which, so far as we could see, would produce the greatest good was the one we ought to choose. But he admitted that when he looked at the matter from the egoist's point of view, it was also self-evident that his own good alone was relevant in the calculation. For consider: a young man is asked in wartime to risk his life for his country. He agrees that if his country prevails, the world will be much better off than if it failed. Should this be decisive for his choice? He may say, "No. For if I die, the advantages for which I have died will never be experienced by *me*.

They may be of immense value in other lives, but they will be ciphers in mine. What you are asking of me is to place my good at risk and perhaps throw my own away to gain something that for me amounts to nothing at all." Place yourself in the egoist's position, said Sidgwick, and his argument is unanswerable. The philosopher was faced, therefore, with what for a rationalist was the intolerable position of having two rational insights conflict. The position of the egoist was self-evident; the position of the utilitarian was self-evident; but together they canceled each other out.

Sidgwick felt that unless this contradiction could be somehow exorcised, it meant failure for his system as a whole. And being an extremely conscientious man, he actually considered for a time resigning his chair. He was being paid to teach young Englishmen the foundations of morality, the rational grounds for doing their duty. But it looked as if these foundations were incoherent, and that for doing an unpleasant duty there was no rational ground at all. So far as he could see, there was only one way out. If theism were true and the world was governed by a Deity who was just, the young man could be assured that he was not giving his all for nothing, for a just Deity would so order things that his sacrifices in this world were compensated in another. To be sure, this did not prove that there was a just Deity, but since it seemed to be the only way of making duty rational, Sidgwick thought we were justified in accepting theism as a postulate.

Now this position falls short of conviction; it grants too much to the egoist. It is true that the egoist himself is never going to enjoy the values that his sacrifice will bring to others. But is he therefore justified in regarding others' values as no values at all? Sidgwick has emphasized that to be reasonable one must grant that experiences of the same quality and intensity are self-evidently of the same value, whether they occur in A's mind or in B's. If A is a rational egoist, he must recognize this as much as anyone else; and if he first recognizes it and then denies it, he is contradicting himself and so ceasing to be rational. He may say that he is not contradicting himself "from his own point of view." But in true rationality there are no points of view. One cannot in the same breath say that the experience of another with a quality and intensity the same as one's own has equal value, and yet no value; no "point of view" will make the contradiction rational. The egoist may fall back on his last desperate question, Why should I be rational? But it is to be doubted whether this question has any sense. To ask Why? is to ask for a rational answer, and that is to admit, if one is serious, that one is already accepting rationality as the final court of appeal.

Adventures in Psychical Research

This reply did not wholly satisfy Sidgwick. For even if self-sacrifice were sometimes clearly called for by reason, was it just that a person should be penalized for being rational? He could not see that a world so ordered could be just. Was it just that a person who sacrificed his good for that of others should lose that good forever, should never be compensated for that loss? That surely would be unjust and reflect its injustice upon the creator who so arranged things. And since ordinary life did not supply such compensation, it must occur, if at all, in another life. But was there such a life? In part it was questioning of this kind that drove Sidgwick to his long adventure with psychical research. It was also in part his concern about the credibility of the miraculous and the supernatural in religion generally. In his study of Christianity and other religions, he had found that their histories swarmed with accounts of the intercourse of normal minds with a supernormal and indeed supernatural order; and in the greatest of the Christian churches miraculous events were supposed to be of daily occurrence. Sidgwick was astonished at the combined credulity and inconsistency of the trained scientists who surrounded him at Cambridge. Many of them were ready to accept without question the miracles of the New Testament while they would reject with scorn the claims to similar events today; or if they did accept such events as occurring in their own communion, they would reject without hesitation events equally well attested in other communions. They made no attempt to justify their beliefs by the sort of evidence they demanded in their professional work, but rested them either on faith or on reported mystical experience. Neither justification was convincing. If faith followed the scriptural "Blessed are they who have *not* seen and yet have believed," it was at odds with their scientific principles; and as for mysticism, strong mystical evidence could be cited for contradictory religious convictions.

"Spiritualism" was an unlikely field for such a man to enter—full as it was of gross superstition, wishful thinking, the hysterias and hallucinations of unbalanced minds, and scientific illiteracy, to say nothing of downright fraud. Yet the issues involved in these swamps and quagmires of the mind were of the utmost theoretic importance, nothing less than the relation of mind and body and the survival of human personality. Sidgwick's attitude toward the phenomena of "spiritualism" might be summed up, as Bryce suggests, by saying: "If they are false, it will be a service to have proved them so. If they contain some truth, it is truth of a kind so absolutely new as to be worth much effort and long effort to reach it. In any case, science ought to take the subject out of the hands of charlatans."[15] Sidgwick saw that if a single case could be found of information purporting to come from a deceased person which was plainly unaccountable on natural grounds, the doctrine that personality could survive death would be established. In view of this fantastic possibility, the investigation should surely be pressed.

He began to press it as early as his undergraduate days by joining "The Ghost Society," which devoted itself to running down and examining tales of haunted houses and apparitions of the living and the dead. In this he later had the support in Cambridge of his pupil Frederic Myers and of Edmund Gurney, and, on occasion, of Arthur Balfour, of Lord Rayleigh, professor of physics who had married a sister of Balfour, and, above all, of his wife. His early inquiries were not rewarding. In 1878, after years of investigating spiritualism, he wrote to a friend, "I have not quite given it up, but my investigation of it is a very dreary and disappointing chapter in my life" (*Mem.*, p. 336).[16]

The experimental work was disappointing because it had to be done with mediums who usually turned out to be either stupid or fraudulent; and it was disagreeable because one had to be constantly suspicious of them. And thought transference, of which Sidgwick believed he had some genuine cases, proved an obstacle in examining the most important cases of all, alleged communications from the dead. For instance, there might be, and occasionally appeared to be, cases in which the subconscious self of one person transferred ideas to the subconscious self of another. Now if one was to show that suggestions such as the whereabouts of a lost key or a lost will came from a deceased rather than a living person, one had to rule out this hypothesis along with others of a natural kind; and this was exceedingly hard to do.

Still, in view of the issues, religious, philosophical, and practical, Sidgwick felt that the investigation should go on. In 1882 Sir William Barrett, professor of physics at the Royal College of Science in Dublin, reported success in experiments in telepathy, and called a conference of interested persons to discuss them. At this conference the Society for Psychical Research was born. Myers and Gurney said they would join only if Sidgwick would consent to serve as its first president. The fact that the British Society had such a sponsor as he, and the American Society had not, goes far, I think, to explain the comparative success and standing of the two branches. As C. D. Broad says,

the fact that Sidgwick, whose reputation for sanity, truthfulness, and fairness was well known to everyone who mattered in England, was at the head of the Society gave it an intellectual and moral status which was invaluable at the time. It was hardly possible to maintain, without writing oneself down as an ass, that a Society over which Sidgwick presided and in whose work he was actively interested consisted of knaves and fools concealing superstition under the cloak of scientific verbiage.[17]

His work with this society, though intermittent, absorbed a substantial part of his time for the rest of his life. Since he was repeatedly elected to its chair, he gave a series of presidential addresses in which he made clear the aims, the uses, the appropriate procedures, and the perils of such research. He and Mrs. Sidgwick invited to Cambridge, and frequently entertained in their home, the more notable mediums and psychical researchers of the time, including Madame Blavatsky, whose theosophical adventures in India had been dramatic, and whose chain-smoking and stevedore language were calculated to raise Victorian eyebrows; one of the Fox sisters from America; Mrs. Piper; and Eusapia Palladino, who so impressed William James. The most significant service the Sidgwicks rendered in the way of research was their work on a census of hallucinations. Everyone has heard stories of how, at the death of an absent relative or friend, some person who knew him has had an apparent perception of him that was so vivid as to seem real. These stories, taken uncritically, have little value. If they are to count as evidence, we must know how common they are and what proportion of them coincide in time with the death of the person perceived. Sidgwick, who was among other things an expert statistician, headed a committee to investigate these matters statistically. Over a period of five years, the committee distributed a questionnaire to great numbers of people, following up the more striking cases with personal interviews. Its report, written chiefly by Mrs. Sidgwick, occupies about four hundred pages in Volume 10 of the society's *Proceedings*. One interesting conclusion was this. If a period of twenty-four hours is taken as marking a rough coincidence, then the chance of such coincidence, assuming the events to be unconnected, would be about one in 19,000. In fact the coincidences worked out as one in 63. The suggestion that there is some connection stronger than chance is therefore reinforced.

There was some difference between the Sidgwicks as to what their research established. Nora Sidgwick was fully convinced, and Henry somewhat less so, that telepathy at least was a fact. It seems likely that Sidgwick would have been of his wife's opinion if he had lived to read the recension made by herself and Mrs. Verrall, another acute critic, of the 763 experiments, made through parlor games, by Prof. Gilbert Murray of Oxford, himself a later president of the society.[18] It may be said that the proof of telepathy has no bearing on the case for human survival. This is not true. If direct thought transference occurs, then the view of most psycho-physicists that all states of consciousness are the by-products of brain states is itself untrue. If so, mind is not wholly dependent on the brain, and since this dependence is the main argument against survival, the case against it is sensibly weakened.

On the issue of survival, Mrs. Sidgwick, whose skill as a researcher her husband thought greater than his own, came out with the conviction that it had been established beyond doubt. Sidgwick could not follow her here. His principle was that the supernatural conclusion could be made out only by excluding all natural possibilities, and in no case could this be done to his full satisfaction. It may be that his admitted wish to believe and his fear of prejudice made him lean over backward. Incidentally, those pontificating critics of such research who hold that all believers are victims of their own desires should be faced with Professor Broad, who hoped that he would not survive, but was unhappily convinced by the evidence that he would.

Sidgwick was under no illusions about his powers to contribute to psychical research. "I feel equal," he said, "to classifying and to some extent weighing the evidence, so far as it depends on general considerations," but he knew that a sleight-of-hand performer such as Houdini would be much more effective in exposing irregularities than a trained physicist, let alone a philosopher. His work has been well summarized by Broad:

His main contribution to psychical research . . . consisted in the weight which his known intelligence and integrity gave to the serious study of the subject, in the tact and patience with which he handled the very difficult team which he had to lead rather than to drive, in the extremely high standard of evidence which he inculcated both by example and by precept, in his courage and persistence in face of repeated failure when success seemed almost within reach, and in the general maxims which he laid down in his various addresses to the S.P.R.[19]

Broad's testimony is fortified by Frank Podmore, one of the more skeptical minds of the S.P.R.: "That the term 'psychical research' is not even now a bye-word and a reproach is due mainly to Sidgwick's character, his unquestioned sincerity, and his practical wisdom."[20] He faced the doubts that were sure to be raised about his honesty with courage and humor. He knew that on the legal maxim, "When you have no case, slander the prisoner's attorney," such attacks usually mean desperation; so he said, "My highest ambition in psychical research is to produce evidence which will drive my opponents to doubt my honesty or veracity."[21] To his frustration, people continued obstinately to revere him.

Sidgwick as a Writer

Most of Sidgwick's works arc in print, though it must be admitted that they are not widely read. Perhaps an exception should be made for *The Methods of Ethics,* but J. B. Schneewind has shown that even this great work is not well arranged to bring out the sequence of the author's thought. Other readers have voiced difficulties with Sidgwick's books. His unhurried, evenhanded, unimpassioned treatment of all questions, some of them deeply emotional, is not to everyone's taste. L. R. Farnell speaks of "the drab dreariness of Sidgwick's *Methods of Ethics.*"[22] Leslie Stephen, who wrote the account of him for the *Dictionary of National Biography,* said to Morley, "I think it a very weak book in substance—an everlasting bother about metaphysical puzzles that are not worth bothering over. . . ."[23] Roy Harrod recalled in his *Life of John Maynard Keynes*: "I remember Alfred Whitehead telling me that he had read *The Methods of Ethics* as a young man and found it so stodgy that he had been deterred from ever reading any book on ethics since."[24] As a literary judgment coming from the author of *Process and Reality,* this has its irony. Even Broad, a better judge, speaks of "the uniform dull dignity" of Sidgwick's prose. And this band of critics was joined by Sidgwick himself. On one occasion, Lord Rayleigh asked him what books he should read for a fellowship examination in economics. Sidgwick offered a number of suggestions. "You have not mentioned your own book," said Rayleigh. "Well, no," said Sidgwick; "I have recently been going over it for a new edition, and the truth is that I find it so very dull that I cannot honestly recommend it."[25]

One cannot read such strictures on his writing without asking whether they are valid. Dull? Yes, but dullness is one of the most subjective of all qualities. Darwin found Shakespeare dull; Spencer found Homer insupportably dull; everything is dull to someone or other, except perhaps imminent execution, which presumably bores no one. It is true that a person with no prior interest in ethical theory should not begin with *The Methods of Ethics.* One who thinks that a New York daily tabloid is more interesting than the *Times* should give the book a wary berth. Sidgwick is dull in the sense that he never drums up interest by devices extraneous to the argument. He never dramatizes his matter (like Macaulay), never raises his voice to the exclamatory (like Burke) or to the imprecatory (like Nietzsche), never carries his reader along with humorous overstatement (like Mencken and Shaw). He keeps his thought on the even keel of a judicial impersonality. But if the reader happens to be that rare character, a person interested in the truth about ethics and nothing but the truth, if he wants the essential issues precisely stated, if he wants an argument carried through without looking to left or right for the smallest glitter of irrelevant adornment, he will find Sidgwick's pages both illuminating and attractive reading.

As could be said of Russell and many others, his first strong enthusiasm for a philosophical writer was for Mill. He confided of Mill in his diary: "What I really envy him is his style; whenever I have by accident tried to say something that he has said before, without knowing, his way of saying it always seems indefinitely better" (*Mem.,* pp. 420–21). He analyzed Mill's style as only an exceptional scholar could have done: "Mill goes extraordinarily well into Aristotelian Greek with the same kind of shortening that puts Macaulay into Tacitean prose" (*Mem.*, p. 132). But he realized that philosophy labors under a great handicap when it offers itself as literature. Literature commonly has to do with persons—with Odysseus, Othello, Dr. Johnson, Faust; that is its fascination. Philosophy deals with abstractions and their abstract relations, lifted bare out of experience; and to most men these cannot compare in interest with persons. "Am trying to write chapters for a book on Politics," Sidgwick notes, "but it will not be literature any more than my other books. Yet I should like to write literature before I die, if only the substance of what I have to say would adapt itself to form" (*Mem.*, p. 407). But form is abstract, and the form of philosophy is eminently so. In fitting his thought to that form, he had to put constraints on the man of letters that was also within him. "The shades nowhere speak without blood," said Bradley, "and the ghosts of Metaphysic accept no substitute. They reveal themselves only to that victim whose life they have drained, and, to converse with shadows, he himself must become a shade."[26] That mood appears occasionally in Sidgwick too. But he never became a recluse, as Bradley did; he kept in touch with practical life by being a university administrator, a chairman of numberless committees (including the Cambridge Mendicity Society), a frequent traveler, and a canvasser of the ordinary mind, even in its darker corners.

In his writing, as in his philosophy, he tried not to wander too far from common sense. He admired the clarity that is an outstanding merit of the British philosophical tradition. He studied the German tradition in its own country, and his lectures on Kant place in salient contrast German ponderousness and English straightforwardness. He even immersed himself for a time in Hegel. But his attempts to find footholds on what Burke would have called the nodosities of that formidable philosophical oak always ended in slipping and falling, and he carried away a permanent aversion to what he regarded as Hegel's pedantic jargon and needless obscurity. One of his students, McTaggart, was more successful than he in understanding the great German and rendering him in intelligible

English, but there were those who doubted whether McTaggart's Hegel was the real Hegel. As it happened, Sidgwick was one of the examiners appointed to read McTaggart's dissertation, submitted in application for a fellowship at Trinity. There is a well-known story of his having remarked to his fellow examiners, "I can see that this is nonsense, but is it the right kind of nonsense?" He personally thought it was, and McTaggart got his fellowship. John Morley comments on the story: "To comprehend that nonsense can ever be right in kind is one of the many keys to genuine richness of nature."[27]

"I have found that I write slowly and with great labour," Sidgwick noted (*Mem.,* p. 252). For many years he imagined an ideal reader of his books and wrote for him; but he came to think that he had set this reader on too high a pedestal of sophistication, and began to aim at his probably actual readers. From that time he thought his style had improved in simplicity and directness. "Decidedly nature intended me to read books and not to write them," he once said (*Mem.,* p. 463), but here as often he underestimated himself. The fact is that he was a master of lucid argument and exposition. He tried to write in such a way as to convince the specialist but also to carry the intelligent layman along, and he had the practiced perception of the skilled teacher for what such a reader needs if he is to follow the train of thought. Not that the argument is always easy, but if it is difficult, it is because of its own subtlety or complexity, not from any lack of expertise in presenting it. And Sidgwick had what many philosophers seem to lack altogether, a writer's ear. If one reads him aloud (an excellent test of any writer, H. W. Fowler thought), one finds that the rhetorical emphasis corresponds very well with the emphasis required by the sense. His English is standard English; he prefers the simple word; he detests pedantry; he has dropped his anchor in common sense and is reluctant to shift from that mooring in either thought or speech.

It is sometimes forgotten that Sidgwick was both a literary critic and a poet. "He might, I think, have been the first of contemporary critics," said Leslie Stephen, "had he not devoted his powers to better things."[28] Sidgwick wrote in his thirties: "I always feel that I should like to [be] as many people as possible . . . . Practically one has to kill a few of one's natural selves (between the ages of twenty-five and thirty-five) to let the rest grow—a very painful slaughter of innocents" (*Mem.*, p. 249). Among the innocents so slaughtered were a novelist and a poet. To a friend he reported from Dresden: "I have written a good deal of poetry, and have at present the plots of two novels and one long poem in my head" (*Mem.*, p. 41). Of these only one short poem seems to have seen the light.

Though Sidgwick soon gave up writing poetry, he never lost his love of it or his alert eye for new poets of quality. He thought Christina Rossetti's sonnet "Remember" "perhaps the most perfect thing any living poet has written" (*Mem.*, p. 215). And he had both a retentive memory and a remarkable gift for reciting poetry. He did not need to have poems or excerpts that he meant to quote entered in his written lectures; he left vacant spaces for them and filled them in from memory as he spoke. He made the odd discovery that poetry was a good remedy for seasickness, from which he used to suffer on his trips to the Continent. For these he developed his own therapy, which was to retire to an unfrequented part of the deck, take his stand there, and recite poetry by the hour with appropriate gestures. This worked admirably until some ladies reported to the captain that a madman was talking vehemently to space.

As a talker Sidgwick had a physical defect that for many would have been serious: the stammer that came on in childhood. He was embarrassed and worried by it, but it made surprisingly little difference, and his friends even thought that he used it to his advantage. Leslie Stephen said that "His skill in using his stammer was often noticed. His hearers watched and waited for the coming thought which then exploded the more effectually" (*Mem.*, p. 315). His wife would not have it that he did this consciously. She says that "the hesitation often came at the pointed word because it was the point, the desire to bring it out producing the nervous effect to which the stammer was due" (*Mem.*, p. 316).

"Write *at* somebody," he once advised, "as you always talk *at* somebody." But he could hardly live up to his own advice, for in spite of the handicap just noted, he was probably the best talker in Cambridge, and his conversation had a freedom of play that his writing never overtook. His nephew Benson, who, as president of Magdalene College, had been exposed to much good talk, said, "I always felt my uncle to be the best talker I ever met" (*Mem.*, p. 316). "He had an excellent memory," says J. N. Keynes, "and there seemed to be no limit to the range of his knowledge. He was a capital story-teller; his supply of apposite stories—they were always pertinent to the previous conversation, never brought in merely for their own sake—seemed inexhaustible. And all his talk was touched by a subtle, delicate humour that added to its charm" (*Mem.*, p. 316). The testimony of Alfred Marshall, the economist, is the more convincing because he could be severely critical of Sidgwick, as we shall see.

If I might have verbatim reports [he wrote] of a dozen of the best conversations I have heard, I should choose two or three from among those evenings [at the Grote Club] in which Sidgwick and [W. K.] Clifford were the chief speakers. Another would certainly be a conversation at tea . . . in which practically no one spoke but [Frederick Denison] Maurice and Sidgwick. Sidgwick devoted himself to drawing out Maurice's recollections of English social and political life in the thirties, forties, and fifties. Maurice's face shone out bright, with its singular holy radiance, as he responded to Sidgwick's inquiries and suggestions; and we others said afterwards that we owed all the delight of that evening to him. No one else among us knew enough to keep on again and again arousing the warm latent energy of the old man: for he always looked tired, and would relapse into silence after two or three minutes' talk, however eager it had been, unless stimulated by some one who knew how to strike the right chord (*Mem.*, pp. 137–38).

Sidgwick had the resources, as was said of Macaulay, to talk freely "on subjects *not* introduced by himself," and his readiness in adapting to them made him a social favorite.

. . . I remember a party at Cambridge [says A. C. Benson], at which a lady was present whom it was thought desirable to ask, but who was little used to social functions. She suffered at first from obvious nervousness; but it fell to Henry Sidgwick to take her in to dinner, and he began to talk to her at once about the education of her children. The bait proved incredibly successful: it was probably the only subject in the world on which she had both views and experience; and she left the house with the manifest consciousness of having had an agreeable evening, having held her own with an eminent man, and having appeared in the light of a brilliant educational theorist, with the additional advantage of having been enabled to put her theories to a practical test.[29]

Ready though he was in conversation, Sidgwick could meet defeat even here. Once a hostess introduced a young lady who had expressed a wish to meet him, and left the two together. Sidgwick tried to think of something to say. Nothing came, and the young lady was too shy to begin. After this silence, he must say something pointed, interesting, if possible humorous. Still nothing came. The two stood silent in the protracting vacuum, until the hostess took the young lady away. Sidgwick, at home, worked out a remark that he could use to any person at any place or time. But no one could ever drag the precious secret from him.[30]

This disaster seems to have been unique, and if Sidgwick could have written as he talked, there would have been no complaints about his style. In his books he follows the argument closely and austerely; he did not give his mind free play as he did in talk. His friend James Bryce, a master of conversation himself, puts it so well that I borrow a paragraph from him.

Sidgwick did not write swiftly or easily, because he weighed carefully everything he wrote. But his mind was alert and nimble in the highest degree. Thus he was an admirable talker, seeing in a moment the point of an argument, seizing on distinctions which others had failed to perceive, suggesting new aspects from which a question might be regarded, and enlivening every topic by a keen yet sweet and kindly wit. Wit, seldom allowed to have play in his books, was one of the characteristics which made his company charming. . . . Though fond of arguing, he was so candid and fair, admitting all that there was in his opponent's case, and obviously trying to see the point from his opponent's side, that nobody felt annoyed at having come off second best, while everybody who cared for good talk went away feeling not only that he knew more about the matter than he did before, but that he had enjoyed an intellectual pleasure of a rare and high kind. The keenness of his penetration was not formidable, because it was joined to an indulgent judgment: the ceaseless activity of his intellect was softened rather than reduced by the gaiety of his manner. His talk was conversation, not discourse, for though he naturally became the centre of nearly every company in which he found himself, he took no more than his share. It was like the sparkling of a brook whose ripples seem to give out sunshine.[31]

The Economist

It is strange that of this would-be poet and critic it should also be said that he would have been happy as chancellor of the exchequer. He would indeed. When the colleges of Cambridge, some of them richly endowed, some of them poverty stricken, were trying to work out a scheme for joint fund-raising and equitable distribution of the product—an extremely delicate business—Sidgwick was on the committee to devise a fair fiscal plan. He duly drew up such a plan and placed it before the committee. While it was universally admired for its fairness in taking everything into account, it was rejected because the Cambridge dons, not being chartered accountants, could hardly understand it, let alone administer it. Sidgwick was at home in economics, Carlyle's "dismal science," which combines in baffling proportions the exactitude of equations for some of its central laws with a muzziness about the edges that enabled generations of "sophists, economists, and calculators," as Burke called them, to play Kilkenny cats with each other.

One of Sidgwick's three greatest works was *The Principles of Political Economy* of 1883. The book was the product of a series of oscillations in the respect paid to economics. Adam Smith had virtually founded the science with *The Wealth of Nations* in 1776. In the half century that followed came the industrial revolution in

Britain, which put Smith's system to a severe test of practice, and produced a host of camp followers, criticizing it, supplementing it, and in part codifying it into more precise laws. Chief among these was David Ricardo, who sought to demonstrate an "iron law of wages," to the effect that wages tend to fall to, and remain at, a level that covers the bare subsistence of the workers.

The next true landmark of the science was the magisterial work of John Stuart Mill. Starting with the assumption that each man is seeking his own advantage in buying and selling his labor and products, Mill showed that an elaborate system of clear-cut laws could be deduced, though qualifications had to be added, themselves clearly statable, to adjust them to particular circumstances. Economics was therefore a mainly deductive, though partly inductive, science. For many years after it was published in 1848, Mill's work remained the standard. But it produced its own crop of critics, just as *The Wealth of Nations* had. They pointed out that many of its conclusions were more than qualified, they were nullified, by the refractory facts, and that, like the conclusions of Ricardo, they condemned much of the race to permanent poverty. Mill himself contributed to the doubts by changing his view in successive editions from an individualist to an almost socialist position. Faced with the failure of laissez faire and the industrial revolution to make prosperity general, he at last made the lugubrious statement that it is doubtful whether all the labor-saving devices ever invented have lightened the day's toil of a single human being. The criticisms and divisions among economists in the forty years following Mill became so serious as to increase the doubt whether economics was a science at all.

Here Sidgwick entered the scene and did for economics something comparable to what he had done for ethics. In neither field, perhaps, could he be called profoundly original; his achievement was rather to rethink older positions into full clarity, to show with inexhaustible patience where, how, and how much the actual facts required their amendment, and to bring conflicting positions into harmony by credible compromise. Both Adam Smith and Mill had left it less than clear to what degree economics was a deductive and to what degree an inductive science, in what sense exactly it was a science, and in what sense an art. Sidgwick answered the first question by saying that the theory of production must be mainly inductive and analytic, and by dealing with the subject in this fashion in his Book I. On the other hand, the laws of distribution and exchange must in the main be derived deductively, which was lucidly done in his Book II. Economics proper he insisted was a science with laws of its own; and these one should master before raising the momentous question how far it was permissible for government to interfere with those laws. The rules governing such interference form the *art* of economics; and to this he devotes a third book, full of the wisdom of the moralist. *The Principles of Political Economy* seems to me masterly and as well written as *The Methods of Ethics*. If it is less interesting, it is because it deals with a more abstract and impersonal subject matter; and if it receives today little attention, it is because the revolutions and depressions of the last century have shifted our attention to issues that had not arisen in the comparatively idyllic days before 1914.

A Contretemps with Marshall

Sidgwick's lectures on political economy supplemented those of the blind professor, Henry Fawcett. On Fawcett's death, Cambridge University in 1884 appointed Alfred Marshall to the chair of Political Economy. Four days after his election he gave Sidgwick a totally unexpected dressing down. Sidgwick's account of this, and still more his way of receiving it, provide one of the best examples to be found of that reasonableness which led to his inclusion in this book. Here is the incident as he sets it down in his journal.

The story begins on December 13, when we elected Alfred Marshall Professor of Political Economy. He came here on December 17, called on us, heard my view of the lectures required, then suddenly broke out. I had produced on him the impression of a petty tyrant "dressed in a little brief authority" (Chairman of the Board of Moral Science) who wished to regulate, trammel, hamper a man who knew more about the subject than I did. I tried to explain, and we parted friends; but the explanation was imperfect, correspondence ensued, and on Tuesday (23) I received from him a long and very impressive letter, analysing my academic career, and pointing out that the one source of failure in it was my mania for *over-regulation*. The result of this had been that my energies had been frittered away on details of administration, and on the effort to give a wretched handful of undergraduates the particular teaching that they required for the Moral Sciences Tripos. He contrasted my lecture-room, in which a handful of men are taking down what they regard as useful for examination, with that of [T. H.] Green, in which a hundred men—half of them B.A.'s—ignoring examinations, were wont to hang on the lips of the man who was sincerely anxious to teach them the truth about the universe and human life. I have left out the partly courteous, partly affectionate—for Marshall is an old friend—padding of the letter, by which he meant to soften the pressure of these hard truths, but this is the substance.

I was much interested by this letter: reflected on my own life and career: and came to the conclusion that I would write down my own view of the causes of my academic failure—I mean my failure to attract men on a large scale.

First, My Character and Opinions. Once, in reading Bagehot's article on Clough, I noted a few sentences which struck me as applying also to myself. As follows:—

"Though without much fame, he had no envy. But he had a strong realism. He saw what it is considered cynical to see—the absurdities of many persons, the pomposities of many creeds, the splendid zeal with which missionaries rush on to teach what they do not know, the wonderful earnestness with which most incomplete solutions of the universe are thrust upon us as complete and satisfying." (This represents my relation to T.H.G. [Green] and his work.) ". . . Undeniably this *is* an *odd* world, whether it should have been so or no; and all our speculations upon it should begin with some admission of its strangeness and singularity. The habit of dwelling upon such thoughts as these will not of itself make a man happy, and may make unhappy one who is inclined to be so."

I, however, am not unhappy; for Destiny, which bestowed on me the dubious gift of this *vue d'ensemble,* also gave me richly all external sources of happiness—friends, a wife, congenial occupation, freedom from material cares—but, feeling that the deepest truth I have to tell is by no means "good tidings," I naturally shrink from exercising on others the personal influence which would make men [resemble] me, as much as men more optimistic and prophetic naturally aim at exercising such influence. Hence as a teacher I naturally desire to limit my teaching to those whose bent or deliberate choice it is to search after ultimate truth; if such come to me, I try to tell them all I know; if others come with vaguer aims, I wish if possible to train their faculties without guiding their judgments. I would not if I could, and I could not if I would, say anything which would make philosophy—my philosophy—popular.

As for "over-regulation," it seems to me that there is an element of truth in it and an element of error. I have no desire to have my own way—not knowing sufficiently what way is my own; still less to coerce others. But I have a great desire in all social relations for definite understandings; not knowing what road is best for humanity to walk in, I want all roads that claim to be roads to be well made and hedged in. This impulse may no doubt mislead to pharisaism and mere schematism that devitalises the courses that kind nature keeps—perhaps it has misled me (*Mem.*, pp. 394 96).

There speaks what I mean by the reasonable man. The temperance of this response to a raking criticism, the readiness to seize what was just in it and to throw the husks away without undue friction or resentment or loss of friendship—these show, I think, a kind of character which, if it became general, could change the course of human affairs. It was after this incident, I think, that the testy Marshall wrote of Sidgwick's *Political Economy*, in its discussion of the functions of government, that it was "by far the best thing of its kind in any language." To remain an enemy of Sidgwick was not an easy task.

The Teacher

His reference to himself as an "academic failure" calls for some comment. There was indeed a curious contrast between the two friends who dominated philosophy at Oxford and Cambridge respectively in Sidgwick's time. T. H. Green expounded an idealist system in which all the divisions of philosophy fell into places appointed by the system and all problems were solved in the light of it. Sidgwick had no system to offer. Green spoke and wrote with a strong undercurrent of moral and religious feeling. Sidgwick took the concern of the philosopher to be with light, not edification, and ordered his teaching accordingly. Green had a school of disciples who before long were promoting his doctrines throughout the British universities. Sidgwick founded no school, and we have heard him saying that he would not do so if he could. Green addressed packed halls at Oxford. Sidgwick lectured to tiny classes; Arthur Balfour recalled attending one in which he and one other were the only students. This disparity in numbers was at least partly due to the different roles that philosophy played in the Oxford and Cambridge curricula. At Oxford, philosophy has long been part of several academic programs, so that it is pursued as a supporting subject by many students whose primary interest is in classics, politics, or economics. At Cambridge it is commonly pursued as one's major subject or not at all. The result is that at any given time Oxford will have perhaps five times as many students and teachers of philosophy as Cambridge has. By Oxonian or American standards, such Cambridge greats as Sidgwick, Moore, and Broad lectured to audiences that were pathetically small.

Sidgwick did not regard this as wholly a disadvantage. He believed that only persons of marked ability and intellectual interest should be encouraged to study philosophy at all. Furthermore, he did not believe that lecturing was the best method of teaching philosophy: his "Lecture against Lecturing" in *Miscellaneous Essays* is a vigorous and pointed criticism of this method. He thought small classes in which question and answer were possible provided far better conditions for teaching philosophy than crowded lecture halls. Philosophy for him consisted in intense and active reflection, and the aim of teaching it was to arouse this process in student minds. During or after his lectures he would ask whether the argument was clear and beg his hearers to state their difficulties either orally or in writing.

. . . I have found it hard [he said] to convince my pupils of the importance, for progress in philosophy, of stating perplexities clearly and precisely. The art that has to be learnt in order to achieve this result has been called the art of "concentrating fog." . . . An intellectual fog, like a physical fog, is very pervasive, and liable rapidly to envelop large portions of a subject even when its original source really lies in a very limited and not very important difficulty. The great thing, therefore, is to concentrate it; and the most effective way of concentrating it is for the student to force himself to state the difficulty on paper.[32]

When he could influence students to do this, he was tirelessly patient in dealing with their difficulties. His stress on crystallizing out the precise questions reminds me of the similar insistence of Moore, who may indeed have learned this important lesson from Sidgwick.

Though Sidgwick did not found a school in the sense of a body of proponents of his philosophical views, he was in fact the principal founder of "the Cambridge school." Cambridge philosophers have stood out for certain characteristics, particularly clearness, precision, and rigor. These were the traits of Sidgwick himself. The minds that he had a part in forming—Moore and McTaggart, for example—are evidence of the strength and nature of his influence. And it extended to many others who did not go into philosophy professionally, such as the economist Maynard Keynes, the statesman Arthur Balfour, the classical scholar Lowes Dickinson, and the historian F. W. Maitland.

. . . I believe [Maitland wrote of him] that he was a supremely great teacher. In the first place, I remember the admirable patience . . . which nothing but pretentiousness could disturb. Then there was the sympathetic and kindly endeavour to overcome our shyness, to make us talk, and to make us think. Then there was that marked dislike for any mere reproduction of his own opinions, which made it impossible for Sidgwick to be in the bad sense the founder of a school. I sometimes think that the one and only prejudice that Sidgwick had was a prejudice against his own results (*Mem.,* pp. 305–6).

Maynard Keynes's father, the logician J. N. Keynes, makes a similar estimate of him and goes on:

In dealing with the exercises submitted to him for criticism he was always quick to perceive and ready to enter into the point of view of the writer . . . . He was at the same time relentless in laying bare inconsistency and slovenliness of thought; and in his power of supplying a discipline in clear unprejudiced thinking he was unrivalled (*Mem.*, pp. 307–8).

"He never claimed authority," wrote his pupil Arthur Balfour, "he never sought to impose his views; he never argued for victory; he never evaded an issue." "Of all the men I have known he was the readiest to consider every controversy and every controversialist on their merits" (*Mem.*, p. 311).

Though Sidgwick deprecated lectures, it was part of his business as Knightbridge Professor to deliver them. On the effectiveness of his lecturing opinions differ. He did not spare his audience.

However small the class might be [said Maitland], Sidgwick always gave us his very best; not what might be good enough for undergraduates, or what might serve for temporary purposes, but the complex truth, just as he saw it, with all those reservations and qualifications, exceptions and distinctions which suggested themselves to a mind that was indeed marvellously subtle, but was showing us its wonderful power simply because even in a lecture-room it could be content with nothing less than the maximum of attainable and communicable truth (*Mem.*, p. 306).

Sometimes truth at its maximum is not easily communicable, and if one looks at Sidgwick's posthumously published lectures *The Ethics of Green, Spencer, and Martineau*, one can see that first- or second-year students in philosophy might find the going hard. They are clear, as always, but they record the collision of first-rate minds on points of ultimate difficulty. To the expert such collisions are exciting, like a chess game between masters, while to the layman unacquainted with the niceties of strategy the performance may be dull. Indifferent students did find Sidgwick's lectures dull. So, I was surprised to hear, did Moore; I have no idea why.

Sidgwick did not think much of the history of philosophy as an introduction to the subject. If students had raised for themselves the questions answered by Spinoza or Hegel, they would be eager for answers given by the masters; if, as was more likely, they had not, they would be perplexed and probably repelled by refinements in which they saw no point. He once burst out uncharacteristically:

. . . I hate the history of philosophy even more than any other history; it is so hard to know what any particular man thought, and so worthless when you do know it. . . . we don't want to know what particular black stones the aborigines adored—at least I don't. . . . I am very jealous for the free exercise of the human intellect (*Mem.,* p. 140).

He could not get interested in *Gelehrsamkeit*. A knowledge of what men had said and thought was very different from the process of active reflection in which philosophy proper consisted, and it was the latter that he was concerned to arouse and direct in his students. When in his *History of Ethics* he did devote himself to history, the critical mind is still active and the reader feels an unerring sense at work for the crucial points in each successive theory.

His thought about women's education modified his thought about men's. He came to think it absurd that Oxford and Cambridge should demand at entrance a knowledge of two dead languages from boys who perhaps knew nothing of French or German. It is interesting to recall that two of the leaders in the abandonment of compulsory Greek in Britain should have been among the finest Greek scholars of their respective generations, Sidgwick at Cambridge and Gilbert Murray at Oxford. Sidgwick developed his views in a fifty-page essay on "The Theory of Classical Education,"[33] which is the most discerning study I know of the place of language in a liberal arts curriculum.

The Political Philosopher

Of the last and largest of Sidgwick's three principal works, *The Elements of Politics,* I have a pleasant personal memory. I wanted the book, and seeing a secondhand copy advertised at eight shillings

in a British catalog, I ordered it. To my delight it turned out to be
Sidgwick's own copy, bearing his autograph, and having inserted
between its leaves a set of sheets in his minute handwriting that
supplied additions for a second edition, as well as two letters of advice from Lowes Dickinson to Mrs. Sidgwick on how the additions
might be used.

The book is too modestly named. It is not a statement of elements
merely, or of elementary considerations, but a systematic discussion
of the principles on which states should be formed and conducted,
just as his other two main works are discussions of the principles of
ethics and the principles of economics. T. H. Green's *Principles of
Political Obligation* is in some ways a greater book, but it approaches
the subject by considering historical views, whereas Sidgwick's book
is a single, closely reasoned system.

Like every other political thinker who is not befuddled, he sees
that the ultimate justification of the state is moral. Just as a particular
act of yours or mine is to be judged by whether or not it contributes
to the greatest happiness, so must a state be judged. For the state is
a device, constructed or accepted by a group of people to promote
the common good. To a teleologist in ethics, as I am, it makes curiously little difference to the line of argument in politics whether
one takes the good to lie in happiness, as Sidgwick does, or in a
simple, indefinable quality possessed alike by all that is good, as
Moore does, or in a combination of self-realization with happiness,
as I have elsewhere proposed. A government is a means to an end
assumed to be desired by all normal persons. To the fundamental
question of politics—Why should I obey the law?—the answer is
that only by so doing can we move toward an end that we want in
common. Political obligation, though not the same as moral obligation, thus rests on the same ultimate ground.

So do rights of all kinds, for rights are merely obligations looked
at from the other end. If I claim a right to vote, to write and speak,
to walk the streets in safety, to make contracts and have them kept,
that means that other people have obligations to grant me these

privileges. Civic rights and duties thus derive from the same source and are to be justified in the same way. Similarly of laws. Legislation to spend public money to build a bridge, a hospital, or a public library is often defended on the grounds of local convenience, public clamor, or the need to right a wrong, but these again are only means to an end beyond them. That ultimate end is the general good.

Sidgwick inclines in his politics, as in his economics, toward laissez-faire individualism; that is, a theory that is based on two assumptions, one psychological, the other sociological. The psychological one is that a man is more likely to provide effectively for his own welfare than the government is. The sociological one is that even if each man does seek his own welfare, the joint product will be the common welfare. Neither of these, as Sidgwick admits, is self-evident or always true, but he holds that they are approximately true, or tend to be true, and that the best government is therefore a hands-off government, whose main business is to give its citizens freedom to fashion their own destinies, so far as they do not interfere with the like freedom of others.

The great alternative to this is socialism, which, with the same ultimate end as individualism, claims that this end is best served if the lives of the citizens are more or less completely regulated by government. Sidgwick has dealt with this at length in his *Political Economy*; he discusses it again more briefly in his *Politics*. Refusing to accept the dilemma, either individualism or socialism, he ends in a characteristic compromise. For the most part, the government should leave the individual alone. But there are indispensable enterprises that would be done badly or not at all if left to the individual; for example, the building of roads, bridges, and dams, the general education of the young, provision for the national defense, care for the hopelessly poor and elderly. If one compares his discussion of these issues with that of such socialist advocates as Shaw or the Webbs, one is struck again by the special qualities of his treatment. He is invariably ready to see both sides of a case, but he combines the sympathy of the moralist with the technical competence of the trained economist. Above all he moves in an atmosphere of quiet, unprejudiced reasonableness that is unsurpassed among writers on politics.

Minor Works

I have made some comment on each of Sidgwick's three chief books, but these are only a fraction of his published work. The editor of the *Britannica* asked him to write the historical part of its article on ethics. The article was at once so compressed and so comprehensive that he was urged to round it into a book. This he did, and the book, his *History of Ethics,* has been a great boon to students who want the essentials of all the main ethical theories. Unlike many ethical histories, it includes a statement of Christian ethics considered as a purely human system and divested of its supernatural background. Readers accustomed to hearing this ethics taught as revealed, and therefore errorless and final, receive some shock from the respectful but cool objectivity of Sidgwick's assessment.

As a noted moralist, he was also in frequent demand by the London and Cambridge Ethical Societies, in both of which he was a leader; and late in life he published the addresses given before these societies in a book on *Practical Ethics*. Included in this book is the essay on "Unreasonable Action," which I have mentioned in connection with Marcus Aurelius. It raises in modern form the old question of Socrates whether knowledge is virtue. Do we ever, with full and clear awareness of the evil involved in a wrong action, do it nevertheless? Socrates and Aurelius both thought not, that our wills follow our insight, and that if we go wrong it is because we are ignorant of the consequences or have allowed our minds to dwell on one part of them to the neglect of others. Sidgwick holds that in general Socrates was right. But he brings to light with his accustomed insight the half-conscious forces that tend to cloud our vision—the impulses, excuses, and desires that make the worse appear the better reason and push us along the irrational road. There remains a residue of cases, however, that do not yield to this analysis, cases in which we see clearly the dominant good involved in *A* and the dominant bad involved in *B,* yet deliberately choose the bad. Regarding such tragically pure wrongdoing Sidgwick makes two comments that tend to uphold our belief that man is not an irrational animal, but a brokenly rational one. Such acts are usually sins of omission rather than commission: we lazily fail to do what we know we ought to do more often than we deliberately do what we know we ought not to do. And again,

even a man who said, "Evil, be thou my good," and acted accordingly, might have only an obscured consciousness of the awful irrationality of his action—obscured by a fallacious imagination that his only chance of being in any way admirable, at the point which he has now reached in his downward course, must lie in candid and consistent wickedness.[84]

At Sidgwick's death there was found among his papers material for five more substantial volumes, which were edited by his wife and some Cambridge colleagues. It sobers an American professor to realize that these close and sustained analyses were lectures given to undergraduates in tiny groups—lectures on *The Philosophy of Kant,* on *The Ethics of Green, Spencer, and Martineau,* on *Philosophy: Its Scope and Relations,* and on *The Development of European Polity.* The fifth volume was a miscellany of papers on theology, literary criticism, economics, and education. For the most part these books are edited according to the pattern he had used himself; they are prefaced by an analytical table of contents in which the argument is presented in condensed form. They are all bound by Macmillan in the same sober brown, but when they stand on the shelf alongside his three master works and his *Memoir,* all in similar costume, they make a massive testimony to the extraordinary mind behind them.

Personal Characteristics

Such a mind one is eager to see at close range. Fortunately it was not so perfect as to cut off all possibility of nit-picking. Sidgwick was absentminded, indifferent to dress, and as his wife had to admit, showed a "habitual want of order in the smaller material concerns of life," such as the neatness of his room and desk (*Mem.*, p. 279). Once when talk about murder mysteries turned to the difficulties of getting rid of the corpse, he remarked that a small body could be effectively hidden in the mountain of papers on his desk. He had no ear for music, could not tell one tune from another, and could not "learn to dance because he could not catch the time" (*Mem.*, p. 432 n.). This combination of sensibility to rhythm in poetry with deafness to it in music has been shown by many great writers of prose and verse and, to me at least, remains something of a puzzle. He was not the best of correspondents, for though he wrote excellent letters, he was impatient of the time they took, and in his later years tried to keep them to one side of a sheet of notepaper (*Mem.*, p. 320). Even in this small space he could say a good deal, since his handwriting was minute.

What was he like physically? He was rather small in stature, and commonly wore a broad-brimmed soft black hat. A full ambrosial silken-textured beard set off the large brow and clear-cut nose. Benson says of him: ". . . Henry Sidgwick was the only man I have ever seen who had something of the nobleness of mien, the kindly dignity, and the unapproachable antiquity of the elders in Blake's designs of the Book of Job."[35] He was physically sturdy, played a respectable game of tennis, and at sixty-two was playing golf with Maynard Keynes, aged seventeen, who "enjoyed Sidgwick's talk as much as his golf."[36] He recorded his recreations in *Who's Who* as "novel reading and a little walking." Told by his doctor that he needed regular and vigorous exercise, he followed this advice in his own way. He ran. With a charming freedom from Victorian self-consciousness, he ran through the streets of Cambridge to and from his lectures, his gray beard flying and his gown bellying in the breeze.

He was inclined to think of himself as lazy. "*Really* busy, I suppose I never was in my life" (*Mem.*, p. 270), he says—though how a lazy man could have produced that row of volumes is less than clear. The fact is that he was deeply contented with the academic life, since his joy lay in the activity of thought, and composing lectures was for him relatively easy. He did not long for change, and when invited to stand for a seat in Parliament, he declined. In a letter to his mother he wrote: "one of the puzzling things to me is to conceive how human beings whose lot is cast in such an age as this can want 'change'. I seem to get more variety than is good for my brain every day of my life. Change! What I want is uniformity . . ." (*Mem.*, p. 290). He knew the danger, in such a life, of self-absorption. To his sister, who was ill at the time, he wrote:

When I found out how selfish I was, I used at first to try and alter myself by conscientious struggles, efforts of Will. But that does not answer for an invalid; one has not to fight oneself in open battles, but to circumvent oneself by quietly encouraging all the various interests that take one out of self. Botany was something, the *Times* something; but to me the *great* artifice was the direct and sympathetic observation of others. I used to try and think how they were feeling, and sometimes to prophesy what they would say. I think most of my little knowledge of my fellow-creatures comes from that period of my life (*Mem.*, p. 271).

During the same period he sent his sister a few rules

(which you won't find in copy-books on the subject), by means of which I manage to worry along—as: (1) Always save yourself as much trouble as possible, as, *e.g.*, by doing anything that can be done any time when the *first* impulse occurs, etc. (2) Always do that part of your duty that you *don't* dislike—then you can think over the rest, which at any rate has by that time been reduced into a more manageable shape. Then it seems clear that one should (3) always do at once whatever being disagreeable yet must be done, and will only get worse by putting it off (*Mem.*, pp. 269–70).

Except for a few minor untidinesses, he practiced the discipline he advised. His needs were simple and he lived austerely. Even in early days of straitened income he gave liberally to Newnham, and after attaining his professorship he habitually gave away much of his income. For some years he provided £300 annually to help establish a Readership in Law, whose first occupant was Maitland. At the same time he was giving £200 a year to Indian students who were preparing for the Civil Service examinations in Cambridge. In 1889–90 he contributed £1,500 for new buildings for the department of physiology. At the creation of a chair in Mental Philosophy and Logic for James Ward, Sidgwick gave £200 annually for several years to help in getting it established.[37] When, in 1892, Alexander Bain could no longer support the chief British journal of philosophy, *Mind,* Sidgwick took financial responsibility for it, and in 1900 founded the "Mind Association," which today has members throughout the world. The root of this generosity did not lie in a series of compassionate impulses; it sprang from his reflection that after the necessities of life were fulfilled, increasing expenditure tended to bring diminishing returns in happiness, and free funds might better be used in meeting the necessities of one's fellows. But while demanding of himself, he was indulgent toward the luxury of others, especially of those who used it to maintain standards of taste, knowledge, and refinement. Such standards, he thought, tended to spread. He defended his conclusions on these matters in an address on "Luxury" to the Cambridge Ethical Society.

In these days when moral skepticism and diversity are so marked, it is dangerous to call anyone "good"; to many it smacks of the unctuous and the priggish. Sidgwick himself would no doubt have repudiated an imputation of goodness with laughter. But a sketch of him that failed to stress this quality would be false to fact. It is stressed all the more fittingly because both his utilitarian ethics and his theological skepticism have often been held to be incompatible with the higher levels of morality. But, as professional moralists know, utilitarianism, far from being a loose and permissive ethics, is an extremely exacting one. And as for his theological skepticism, it was somehow compatible with the comment from Benson, who, as son of an archbishop, had a wide acquaintance with the religious leadership of Britain, that he had "always considered Henry Sidgwick to be, on the whole, the one man I have known who, if he had been a Christian, would have been selected as almost uniformly exhibiting perhaps the most typical Christian qualities. . . . he is one of the few men to whom one could honestly apply in the highest sense the word 'saint'."[38] When he resigned his fellowship rather than subscribe to what he did not believe, one of his colleagues remarked, "though we kept our own fellowships without believing more than he did, we should have felt that Henry Sidgwick had fallen short if he had not renounced his."[39]

Leslie Stephen, who depreciated Sidgwick's greatest book, wrote this striking passage in *Mind*:

There was no merit in Boswell's good humour, said Burke, it was so natural. I had the same feeling about Sidgwick's unselfishness and high principle. I fancied that he could not really have a conscience—much as he professed to esteem that faculty—because I could not see that his conscience could ever have anything to do. He had plenty of scruples, because he saw the full complexity of any case; but when he had the facts properly arranged, the decision to act followed spontaneously.[40]

Few men, probably, feel a sense of civic duty so strong as to lead them to break off a vacation in Switzerland and take the long trip back to England in order to vote in a local election. Sidgwick did.

The Rational Temper

But it is not so much the practical virtues, great as they were, as the intellectual virtues that draw me to Sidgwick. He had a command of that "dry light" which Bacon longed for and in some measure attained. He was capable of profound sympathy with others while seeing their plight with the detachment of a scientist watching a butterfly. Though he had strong likes and dislikes, they did not discolor the "white light" of his intelligence. In his inquiries into psychical research, for example, his hopes and feelings were strongly engaged, but "no one," said Oliver Lodge, "however hostile to our inquiry, ever imagined that Sidgwick let his enthusiasm warp his judgment or his candour be coloured by his hopes."[41]

We have seen that his emotional attachments to religion gave him a long struggle. He once wrote, "the virulency of unreasoning ortho-doxy is getting to disgust me more and more daily" (*Mem.*, p. 47). And his skepticism, like Arnold's at Oxford, was well known among clerics. But the urbanity and understanding that he showed in discussions of religion were so disarming that some of his most cordial admirers were bishops. Westcott, for example, bishop of Lincoln, said of him: "Great in range and exactness of knowledge, great in subtlety of analysis, great in power of criticism, he offered the highest type of a seeker of the truth . . . ."[42] Indeed Sidgwick sometimes exasperated people who were on his side by his readiness to concede everything he could to an opponent. There is an example of this in a letter of Leslie Stephen to that devotee of outspokenness, W. K. Clifford: "We had rather a good meeting at the Metaphysical, in which [T. H. Huxley] trod rather heavily upon Sidgwick's toes, and Sidgwick displayed that reflective candour which in him be-comes at times a little irritating. A man has no right to be so fair to his opponents."[43]

Most of the philosophers who live in history have been system builders; Sidgwick was not. His place in history is not beside Kant or Hegel; still less is it with passionate romantics like Rousseau or Nietzsche. But his work will stand as a permanent implicit criticism of all such ways of philosophizing—of too facile a system-building on the one hand and of too ready a surrender to "reasons of the heart" on the other. His chief accomplishment as a philosopher was to carry methods of analysis that were approved by and intelligible to common sense up to new levels of thoroughness, subtlety, and clarity. His influence through this achievement has been widespread and strong. Schneewind is right in saying: "Sidgwick is often de-scribed as the last of the classical utilitarians. He may with as much accuracy be viewed as the first of the modern moralists."[44] He paved the way for such students of his own as Moore and Rashdall and for such successors as Broad, Prichard, and Ross.

But in a way that holds of none of these others, Sidgwick's great-

est work was himself, for even among philosophers he stands out
as perhaps the most perfectly balanced model of the reasonable temper. In his published work he never resorts to bluster, rhetoric, or
acrimony; never raises his voice; takes his own way, never bowing
to authority; pays readers the compliment of using standard English
and of making each step in the argument clear; never takes advantage of an opponent by twisting or understating his case; and above
all moves in an atmosphere of quiet objectivity that seems never to
be ruffled by any breeze of prejudice or partiality. He thus lifted
the moral level of controversy as well as its technique; "what, so I
think, we may all admire," said Maitland of Sidgwick, "is the watch-
ful honesty which will not suffer any hope, however ardent, or any
desire, however noble, to give itself the airs of proof."[45]

The End

In May 1900, when Sidgwick was sixty-two, he consulted a London
surgeon who diagnosed a cancer that might prove mortal and in any
case would require a serious operation. A week or two later he went
to Oxford and read a searching paper on the philosophy of Green,
apparently in his usual good spirits, and telling nobody but his
brother Arthur, an Oxford Fellow, what lay ahead. On May 30 he
left Cambridge for London, where the operation was to be performed the next morning. His wife writes: "He dined that night
with his brother-in-law, and never was his conversation more brilliant than at that little family party—only Arthur and Alice Balfour
and Sidgwick and his wife present—in the large dining-room at
10 Downing Street" (*Mem.*, pp. 589–90). After the operation he was
able to do a little dictation, but, as he predicted, it was a half-life,
and he died August 28. He thought it unsuitable to use the Church
of England service at his burial, and only these words were spoken:
"Let us commend to the love of God with silent prayer the soul of a
sinful man who partly tried to do his duty. It is by his wish that I
say over his grave these words and no more" (*Mem.*, p. 599).

THE ENEMY: PREJUDICE

The Enemy: Prejudice

The four persons whose lives have been sketched were not chosen merely because they were eminent. They were chosen because they all evinced in high degree a trait that I place at the top of human virtues, reasonableness. It is a rare virtue, unspectacular, unexciting, unpopular, gray, almost impossibly difficult. I have tried to show that in spite of this difficulty a reasonable life can be lived, since in these four men it actually was, that those who lived it did not find it gray, that on the contrary they found it fulfilling, satisfying, and richly productive of human good.

This chapter turns from biography to theory. What do we mean by reasonableness? Why is it so difficult? In the great army of prejudices it has to fight, which are the most insidious?

By reasonableness I do not mean intelligence, though that may be a great help. Attila, Torquemada, and Stalin were highly intelligent men, but they were not reasonable men. Nor is a reasonable man necessarily a learned man, for learning may be present without even ordinary common sense. No; the reasonableness of which I am speaking is a settled disposition to guide one's belief and conduct by the evidence. It is a bent of the will to order one's thought by the relevant facts, to order one's practice in the light of the values involved, to make reflective judgment the compass of one's belief and action.

Reasonableness and Education

Such reasonableness, unlike intelligence, is an acquired, not an innate, characteristic. In this respect it is like breadth of knowledge. But the knowledge gained by a student may have mostly vanished

247

by the time he gets his diploma attesting how vast it is. If you are like me, facts do not stay with you, while habits, for good or evil, do. And reasonableness, as I have defined it, may become a habit. It is a habit that, once acquired, can be kept permanently and applied in any field. Though not necessarily the product of education, it is the greatest benefit that education can confer.

Of course there are many such benefits. Education can make one an expert technician in electrical engineering or bone surgery; it can make one a leading authority in a field on which my own community has been lectured, the chronological stratification of vowel contraction in Greek. I do not deprecate such knowledge. But a supermole or a supermagpie is not necessarily an educated mind. What we hope from such a mind is a rational temper, a readiness to look before leaping, indeed to look at all sides of an issue and attach due weight to each, to see things not through rose-tinted or black-tinted or distorting lenses, but as they are. In short, what we want from education is the reasonable mind.

If seeing things as they are seems an easy business, let it be added that no one has yet fully achieved it, and probably no one ever will. Freud's contribution to psychology, which has been said to be greater than that of any other man since Aristotle, is mainly an insight into the ways in which thought veers and shifts under the control of hidden desires. "Many of us," says F. L. Lucas, "having read our Freud, have grown more sceptical than ever; seeing reason no longer as a searchlight, but usually as a gust-swept candle guttering amid the winds of emotion and the night of the Unconscious."[1] Nor is it the thought of ignorant people alone that gutters in the winds of prejudice. I once heard Dean Woodbridge of Columbia say that he had almost given up hope of the League of Nations because of his experience of Columbia faculty meetings.

The Divided Self

Why is it so hard to be reasonable? "Things and actions are what they are, and the consequences of them will be what they will be;

why then," asked Bishop Butler, "should we desire to be deceived?"[2] That is a fascinating and important question, but the general answer to it is not difficult. The answer is that we are all divided personalities, like the two girls of whom one said to the other, "I feel rather schizophrenic today; I hope you don't mind." "Oh no," said the other; "that makes four of us." We are lovers of truth, but also lovers of much else; and it is hard to keep the competing loves from interfering with each other. On the one hand, we all want to know. A. E. Housman said that the love of truth was the faintest of human passions, but it remains a passion nevertheless. How many of us, if offered as a gift an understanding of Einstein or of cancer or of the best cure for inflation, would turn the offer down? We should be more likely to agree with Dr. Johnson that there was nothing he would not rather know than not know. This interest in truth may flicker feebly in a bored student or rise to the passion of a life, as in Spinoza, but it is present in degree in everyone.

Along with this interest in truth, however, each of us has—or perhaps we should say *is*—a set of other impulses and interests: impulses to love, to fight, to seek company, to imitate, to run from danger, to eat, to drink, to laugh, and many more. Each of these impulses has its own end, which may appeal to us powerfully, and whose attainment may conflict with what reflection would suggest. This conflict is the root of human irrationality. Man is an irrational animal because he *is* still an animal. If we are to see the nature and depth of this conflict between rationality and the irrational, we must know a little more fully what human nature is like.

Human nature is best described for our purposes as a set of impulses, distinguished from each other by the ends that satisfy them, and constantly interacting with each other. Many attempts have been made, and are still being made, to reduce these impulses to stimulus-response reactions of a purely physical kind. John B. Watson in the twenties, B. F. Skinner in the fifties and sixties, and Gilbert Ryle from the forties to the seventies tried to exorcise consciousness as a "ghost in the machine" and to explain human nature in material terms.[3] They failed, and for a reason suggested by a

New Yorker cartoon. A perplexed little man in a white coat is standing before a mammoth computer which is exuding a typewritten slip saying, "I think, therefore I am." The point, which would be lost on some eminent psychologists, is clear enough to the plain man. The computer, however complex a machine, is not conscious. It does not think. It harbors no purpose. Only the scorned "ghost in the machine" could do any of these things. Only a *mind* is conscious, purposive, and able to be rational.

The Cognitive Drive

We have said that the great conflict in man's nature is between his rational and nonrational sides. What do we mean by calling him rational? We mean that he can think, and that he can to some extent control his beliefs and his actions in accordance with his thought. I have covered much space elsewhere in an account of the process and growth of thinking,[4] and shall not stay here even for an outline of this account. A few points must suffice.

The drive to know is central to human nature. Its roots are deep in the past of the race. The intense curiosity of the chimpanzee, the approach and scurrying retreat of the squirrel when offered a nut, the selection by the bird of one straw as suitable and another not in building its nest—we cannot deny that cognitive processes are going on here. But this is *bound* thinking, bound to perception on the one hand and to utility on the other. Thought in man is freed from both. Pascal considered the highest of human attainments to be the ability to sit in a room and think of the far away, the long ago, of essences and relations that have nothing to do with the here and now. No animal can do that, for its thought is tied to what its surroundings suggest. In man thought is free to pursue its own immanent end. That end is to understand. To understand anything—a triangle, a watch's keeping time, the eruption of a volcano, the French Revolution—is to see it in a system of relations that make it what it is. Spinoza thought, and I follow him here, that one cannot fully understand a pebble on the beach without following out the mouldings of it by wind and wave, the further causes of these causes, and so on to infinity. The growth of thought in the race is like the growth of a great tree whose branches are thrown out in all directions as if trying to embrace the universe in their grasp. Nothing less than such an embrace would bring the restlessness of reason finally to rest. Reason in its essence is a perpetual raising and reraising of the question Why?, and if there were no more whys to answer, its special work would be completed.

Reason, then, as reflective thought, is an attempt to grasp things in the relations that explain them. That is the work of the scientist and the philosopher. But in a more limited domain it is also the work of the plain man. If he would build a house or sail a boat, he must know something of nature's laws and adjust himself to them. And he must obviously use his reason if he is to live a good life. One may have a sweet disposition, to be sure, without being intelligent, but sweetness is not goodness in the sense of the moralist. Being good calls for doing what is right; and doing the right thing in the voting booth or the courtroom, in child-rearing or in business, demands the ability not only to think but to deal with problems of high complexity. And to do what is objectively right calls for at least three rational insights, all of which may be difficult in the extreme. We must forecast the consequences of our proposed act in the way of intrinsic goods and bads in the experiences of those affected by it; we must see the difference between facts and the values of those facts, which alone count morally; and finally we must be able to weigh values, and sets of values, against each other. It is no wonder that John Erskine felt moved to write an urgent essay on "The Moral Obligation to Be Intelligent."

The Nonrational Side of Human Nature

To be reasonable, then, means habitually to guide one's beliefs and actions by what reason prescribes. We have studied the lives of four

great men for whom reason was the dominant force in both belief
and conduct. Of course they all failed, as they would be the first to
admit; perfect reasonableness is as remote and unattainable as a
fixed star. Still, pursue it we must, for, as Aristotle said, men are
rational animals, however brokenly so. We have been examining
approximations to reasonableness; it is time to turn to the factors
that make us *un*reasonable. Some of these are mere failures to observe, or standard fallacies in argument. For these there are pre-
ventive aids, such as the admirable discussion of fallacies in Mill's
Logic or in Thouless's *Straight and Crooked Thinking.* But what
lies at the root of these fallacies themselves? As a rule, they are the
result of the invasion of our thinking by the nonrational parts of
our nature.

Besides the cognitive impulse, the-mind is a set of other propensities bound together by one consciousness. These propensities
used to be called "instincts" because they were taken to be inherited
from our animal forebears and to be present in everyone from birth.
But the work of enumerating and distinguishing them proved
thorny and controversial. Hobbes and Hocking recognized one such
instinct, the drive for power; Freud recognized two, sex and the
death instinct; McDougall distinguished twelve to eighteen, de-
pending on the edition of his *Social Psychology*; Thorndike enumer-
ated over two hundred. Since we have no need to get involved in
disputes over their heredity and number, we shall use the name
"impulse" for the entities we are discussing. Each impulse, in this
sense, involves all three sides of human nature as traditionally described—thought, feeling, and will. Fear, for example, is the emotional part of an impulse whose cognitive part is an object thought
of as dangerous, and whose conative part is a tendency to flee from
the object. And so of the other impulses.

Prejudice as Perverted Logic

What we are concerned with here is the outstanding enemy of reasonableness, namely prejudice. Prejudice is pre-judgment, the form-

ing of a judgment on insufficient grounds and for nonrational causes. Unfortunately the commonest cause of prejudice is a worm that lies at the heart of the thought process itself. Scientific thinking moves through identities; an event the same in character as some previous event will act in the same way—"same cause, same effect." But we must be sure the character is the same, or thought is bound to be derailed. Some time in early life we are given sugar; it is white, grainy, and sweet. We then see some salt, which looks and feels so like sugar that we take it to be sugar. We taste it and get a shock. We have made a primitive induction. We have also been guilty of pre-judgment and prejudice, though we should hardly call it that; for if the mind were not adventurous enough to make such identifications, it would never get started in thinking.

Logical induction is a process by which we pass from one or a limited number of cases of the conjunction of *A* and *B* to the conclusion that this conjunction holds generally. The swallowtailed butterflies I have seen may all have had dark wings; so I expect that the next one I see will also have dark wings. Do I *know* this? Clearly not. Does that imply that no generalizations from a few instances to a law are to be trusted? Here comes the point of divergence between science and prejudice. Both science and prejudice proceed by carrying over their past experience to their expectation of the future. But they do so in different ways. Prejudice carries it over uncritically and dogmatically, its expectations tinged by, and perhaps selected by, its likes and dislikes of what it has experienced. In our simple case, prejudice would insist that all swallowtails were dark-winged and drab. The scientist is more skeptical. That all the swallowtails he has seen have been dark-winged does arouse a presumption, but that is a hypothesis only; he sees nothing necessary about it; he reserves judgment till he can observe more cases. If he is fortunate, he will not have to wait long. He will see a swallowtail with bright yellow wings, and admit at once that his tentative generalization was wrong. Nor will he stop there. Acting on the great postulates on which all science rests, that every event has a cause and the same cause at every occurrence, he will want to know why some of his swallowtails were dark and others bright. And if he carries the inquiry to the point of dissection, he will find that the dark ones are female and that the bright yellow ones are male. He will have brought to light two new hypothetical connections that may turn out to be laws.

Thus science and prejudice spring from the same root; they are both attempts to draw conclusions from given experiences. But prejudice is crippled logic. It makes hasty generalizations from too few facts; it overlooks what others see; it imagines what for others is not there at all.

What leads us thus to distort the process of right thinking? Sometimes the answer is easy. If John has an unreasonable fear of dogs, we look at his past, and perhaps come upon a frightening childhood encounter with a dog, whose memory, as Freud has taught, may be none the less at work because repressed. The remarkable success in the seventies and eighties of the television series on "Archie Bunker," a ball of comic and outrageous prejudice, was largely due to the transparent emotionalism of Archie's absurd convictions, and no doubt to their viewers' satisfaction that they had escaped to a higher range of reasonableness.

Egoism

But what moves men to distort their thinking is not usually so obvious. John's one unhappy experience with a dog has cast a mantle of fear over dogs generally and is easily explained. But as a rule prejudice grows in a more roundabout way. There are certain central ideas round which, in everyone's mind, impulses and emotions tend to cluster. By far the most important of these is the idea of the self. We are all egoists, even when it would be absurd to call us egotists. Despite John Donne's "No man is an island," every man is an island, cut off from direct intercourse with everyone else in the world. All the sensations and percepts that form the objects of direct consciousness belong to that consciousness and are therefore a part of ourselves, as are our memories, feelings, and desires. Our field of consciousness, plus certain dispositions, *is* our self of that moment; indeed it is virtually our world, so that if the island of self should sink, the world we live in would sink with it.

No wonder, then, that the self should be the object of prime concern to us. Our happiness and importance, our self-respect and hope and fear, are all bound up with it; it is something of perpetual solicitude. Whatever favors and furthers this self we tend to like—people who approve or admire us, games or work that we are good at, doctors who have pulled us through, teachers who have encouraged us, places where we have been happy and made good. On the other hand, whatever belittles this self we tend to dislike—persons who criticize us or make us feel stupid or gauche, studies in which we are incompetent, rivals who sneer at us, hostesses who ignore us, neighbors who say that we treat our car or lawn or dog shabbily. Whatever threatens our self-love calls into action an imperial guard of impulses, ready to spring on the instant to its defense. The idea of self is thus an especially sensitive point on which converge from opposite sides two formidable bodies of pro and anti impulses.

That the common man is subject to egoistic impulses needs no proof. It is more surprising, but should be frankly admitted, that the same is often true of men of intellectual distinction. John Stuart Mill was one of our own examples of fair-minded men, but when his mother and sisters ventured to express some questions about his marriage to Mrs. Taylor, he virtually cut them out of his life. His must be one of the few autobiographies without mention of a mother. He would probably have admitted in the case of another that this was not a reasonable attitude, nor was it characteristic of himself. It no doubt had its origin in a relation with his wife that was singular to the point of abnormality. As another striking case of a splendid intelligence that was sometimes nullified by strength of passion, consider Burke. Edmund Burke was one of the greatest of philosopher-statesmen. But after serving for a time as secretary of the Irish Chancellor of the Exchequer, W. G. Hamilton, and being discharged by that official, Burke became hysterical in his enmity for the unfortunate man and emptied the copious vials of his wrath and rhetoric over Hamilton's head, describing him as "the most consummate villain that ever lived." Since Burke's successor seems to have been Samuel Johnson, who found Hamilton an estimable man, Burke's invective was pretty clearly an explosion of prejudice, set off by a wound to his public image. Indeed his capacious mind is a rare field for studying the conflict of reason and emotion. Macaulay commented that Burke often defended with incomparable intellectual skill positions provided him by his emotions. What his history shows is that even the best intelligence will not avail to keep prejudice in hand unless it addresses itself expressly and with self-understanding to the problem of control.

Take one further case. It came to the notice of Swinburne that Emerson had said something critical of him in an American paper. It expressed what a Puritan like Emerson would inevitably feel toward one who, in spite of his eminence as a poet and critic, sat as loose to convention as Swinburne notoriously did. The angry poet sat down and wrote the philosopher a letter describing him as a "gap-toothed and hoary-headed ape, carried at first into notice on the shoulder of Carlyle, and who now in his dotage spits and chatters from a dirtier perch of his own finding and fouling: coryphaeus or choragus of his Bulgarian tribe of autocophagous baboons, who make the filth they feed on. . . ."[5] Prejudice here has become sheer comedy. Swinburne was an able critic of others who was capable of abandoning all self-criticism when his own image was attacked. His intelligence was undisciplined in monitoring his own sometimes childish reactions.

These are all persons of intellectual distinction responding irrationally to wounds of their egos. But objections to such wounds are not always irrational. Sometimes when an ego is wrongly wounded, a sharp lesson is salutary. There was an occasion when a northern Michigan editor said something about Theodore Roosevelt, then president, that was gratuitously false. Mr. Roosevelt boarded a train, rode all the way from Washington to his critic's bailiwick, haled him into court, and won his case. When prejudice goes to the length of the malicious and harmful lie, the field should not be surrendered to it.

Except where there is malicious untruth, however, magnanimity seems clearly the better part. It is a rare quality. But persons who have it, even in high degree, do exist. It was said of Mirabeau that he found it hard to forgive the insults and meannesses done to him, for the reason that he had forgotten all about them. There is a story in point about Lincoln that bears the air of truth. Someone told the president of Secretary Stanton's having said angrily that in a recent decision Lincoln had acted like a fool. The teller presumably expected an explosion. Instead, Lincoln remarked thoughtfully that if Mr. Stanton had said that he was probably right, since he generally was. Most men, when they hear of criticism of what they have said or done, consume more energy in resenting the malice that must have inspired it than in considering whether it is true. So the response to reproach with understanding rather than resentment is all the more impressive. Prime Minister Asquith was once giving a political address when an enraged auditor shouted at him, "Why did you murder the miners at Featherstone in '92?"[6] Asquith's quiet response was, "It was not '92, it was '93." (A commission of inquiry had cleared him in the case.) It was my privilege long ago to hear both Asquith and the man who finally unseated him, Lloyd-George, that mercurial, eloquent Celt known as "the Welsh wizard." Asquith was a man so incapable of being carried away from his proud mooring in judicial reasonableness that he was called "the last of the Romans." Lloyd-George appealed to my youth. With the passing of years, Asquith has replaced him in the gallery of my admirations.

The Family

The idea of the self is by far the most sensitive point at which a wound may be inflicted. But there are other such points that lie outside the self. Each of us who lives a normal life is a member of a group that is in a way an extension of himself, whose members give each other support. A boy's gang, a baseball team, a college fraternity may form a group whose unformulated rule is "One for all and all for one." It is what the social psychologists call an "in-group," in which the members feel at home with each other, do not have to be on their guard, can banter and air their views and scoff at outsiders without fear of misunderstanding.

For most people the strongest of these in-groups is still the family, in spite of its widespread and sinister disintegration in this country. In a strongly bound family one learns in childhood to take one's troubles to father or mother for comfort and sympathy, and brothers and sisters, with all their bickerings, may be a unit against the noisy family next door or the families down the street that do not speak English.

Is it necessary to the cohesion of an in-group that it have an out-group to oppose? No; there are families whose children are brought up in an atmosphere of affection and considerateness that carries over into the treatment of those outside. The expectation of liking and being liked breaks down the fences of prejudice on both sides. Such happy family relations generally work to the advantage of its members. Sometimes indeed they go wrong. Nepotism and the perhaps too-famous Oedipus complex may result. One child may be habitually treated by his parents as a genius to be coddled, praised, and protected, with the result that he grows up conceited, confused, and unhappy, because he took his parents' words at their face value, looks down on others, and is detested in return.

Within the family the curious phenomenon called "projection" often enters in and provides a fertile root of prejudice. Suppose a child has a cruel and overbearing father who browbeats him unmercifully. The growing youth builds up a reservoir of hatred against his father, but for lack of strength he cannot let it overflow in action; indeed its very existence must be repressed. The hatred may fester in this repression, and not improbably he hates himself for hating his father. At this point, from which anyone would want to escape, projection comes to his rescue. It is not *he* that is mean and sullen. People generally are like that, or, if this is too improbable, a special group that is clearly more so than himself and beside whose anger his own is therefore innocent. This was evident on a large scale among Nazi youth who, treated with Spartan severity themselves, took out their anger on others. Brutality somehow became stern courage when the urge to escapist persecution came on. The bully is often the victim of his own unconscious frustrations, venting on others the anger he is too ignorant or too cowardly to vent on himself.

Whatever minor hostilities may develop within the family, it usually stands as a unit when any member is attacked from without. Mothers at murder trials are notorious witnesses that their sons are white souls incapable of such a deed; and the son whose mother has been insulted is not likely to pause for a reflective reply. Even in the "quarto and folio editions of mankind," as William James called them, wounded conjugal affection may react with violent prejudice. When Robert Browning read Edward Fitzgerald's remark after Mrs. Browning's death that now we should no longer have to read any more *Aurora Leighs*, Browning sat down and wrote a sonnet so scorchingly contemptuous as to give the unhappy Fitzgerald a permanent pillory in the anthologies of invective. He also gave Fitzgerald's remark a far longer and wider hearing.

This sort of instant, rattlesnake response to any critic of one's family has been thought by many, particularly in the West, to be a requirement of chivalry; and clearly it may be rooted in an admirable affection and loyalty. But genuine affection is not necessarily compromised by recognizing that its object falls short of perfection, that people have a right to an opinion of their own, and that the best retort may not be with a stiletto of steel or words. One is fortified in such reflections by finding that there are persons who can take criticisms of those near and dear to them with disarming humor and understanding. It is said of Lord North that once, in a theater, someone asked him, "Who is that plain-looking woman?" "That, sir," said the noble lord, "is my wife." "Oh no," said the inquirer, "I mean the one next her." "That, sir," said Lord North, "is my daughter. And let me tell you, sir, we are considered to be three of the ugliest people in London."[7] Of course not everyone can achieve such inner security, but a philosophical attitude toward such offenses is likely to stave off needless storms.

Religion

For many persons, the in-group that is closest after their family is their church. Here two questions arise. Is faith attended as a rule by prejudice toward those outside it? Is there anything in the charge that religious dogmas themselves are really prejudices?

First as to prejudices regarding out-groups. Some would say that it belongs to the essence of religion to regard all men as children of God, and therefore to treat them fraternally. And it is true that all the great religions of the world enjoin love and compassion for others; the Golden Rule is their common possession. The Christian Scriptures tell us that in Christ there is neither male nor female, neither Jew nor Gentile; and by those who have taken the character of Christ most seriously, even when, like Schweitzer, they have abandoned the creed of Christianity, the brotherhood of man is accepted as a valid insight of the moral genius of Jesus.

Still, the relation of religion and prejudice deserves a closer look. Besides a sweeping charity, the greater religions carry a different strain. Christianity, for example, is authoritarian; its creed is based on revelation, not reason; and hence differences with other creeds cannot be settled by sitting down and reasoning together. The claim of the Roman pontiff to speak with divine authority on belief and morals makes compromise difficult, for divinely appointed truth cannot be frittered away; and since the Roman creed embraces a great many carefully defined dogmas, nonarbitrable conflicts with other creeds are inevitable. Furthermore since the acceptance of certain dogmas is a condition of salvation for many Protestants as well as Catholics, and their rejection is taken to carry divine disfavor, these Christians cannot consider those outside the pale as standing ultimately on the same plane as themselves.

Many religious persons do not take such implications of their beliefs very seriously, and Western notions of equality would not permit the implacable old wars of religion. But the divisiveness inherent in religious absolutism is still present in many of the creeds, and the wars, persecutions, and outrages on reason and humanity that it has produced so abundantly should not be erased from men's memory.

Whether a religious person is made more tolerant and friendly to outsiders, or more hostile, depends on the part of his religion that he stresses. The matter is difficult to study with exactness, but in his comprehensive survey of prejudice Allport says:

We do have, however, some striking findings concerning the relation of the intensity of religious training in general to prejudice. Over four hundred students were asked the question, "To what degree has religion been an influence in your upbringing?" Lumping together those who report that religion was a marked or moderate factor, we find the degree of prejudice far higher than among those who report that religion was a slight or nonexistent factor in their training. Other studies reveal that individuals having no religious affiliation show on the average less prejudice than do church members.[8]

Dogma and Prejudice

It is time to turn from the practical to the theoretic question: Are religious dogmas themselves prejudices? The question is itself likely to arouse prejudice. But that it is a legitimate question is shown by obvious facts. There are millions of Moslems who believe that God is personal and one; there are millions of Christians who believe that God is three persons in one; there are millions of Buddhists who believe that God is not a person at all. These beliefs cannot all be true; indeed each is inconsistent with both the others. A central belief, then, of two of the great religions of the world must be false.

That implies, further, that it cannot have been arrived at by rational processes. It is dogma accepted for unsound reasons or for irrelevant causes. But that is almost the definition of prejudice. However strongly inclined we may be to make our own belief a rational matter, we can see that many or most of the religious beliefs of others are not, and that they do conform to the conception of prejudice.

Look at it in another way. You have been brought up, let us say, in the Anglican communion. You have recited the Apostles' creed Sunday by Sunday as far back as you can remember, so that you repeat it with as little reflection as doubt. Now reverse your religious environment. Suppose you were brought up from birth in a Moslem household. You were taught to unroll your prayer rug at the appointed hours, to kneel on it, face toward Mecca, and recite the creed. That under these circumstances your single eye for the truth would have led you to emerge a stouthearted Anglican is surely unlikely. Indeed we may be fairly confident that the man who accepts most unquestioningly the teachings of Canterbury would, if bred in Saudi Arabia, have accepted as unquestioningly the tenets of Mecca. That gives one to think. Strictly speaking, are men's religious conclusions rationally arrived at, or must they too be set down as reflecting prejudice? "Prejudice" as ordinarily used connotes a certain culpable wilfulness, and to attach this to religious belief generally would be obviously unfair. But if the term means more broadly the adoption of beliefs on nonrational grounds, then it is hard to see how religious beliefs can escape the classification.

Since this is a highly controversial matter, we should be as straightforward as we can. Consider the following. A Christian who pursues either the Catholic or the Lutheran line lives in two worlds at once and obeys two masters, revelation and reason. Of the two authorities, revelation, as eternal truth authoritatively communicated, must clearly take precedence. If it collides with reason, reason must give way. If one allows it to give way, how is one to escape the classification of prejudice? For prejudice consists in being carried on by desire, fear, or any other nonrational factor, beyond what reason warrants. And this seems to be what the religious man is supposed to do. "Blessed are they that have *not* seen and yet have believed."

It may be replied that what carries the Christian beyond reason is faith, and that this should not be put down among nonrational factors. But is this clear, when faith carries the Moslem to the belief in a monistic Deity and the Christian to the belief in a triune Deity? It may be said, again, that what carries the Christian on to his view is ultimately mystical experience, which must also be called rational evidence. But this is open to the same objection. Mystics have adduced their evidence to show that the world is good and that it is evil, that it is one and that it is not one, that personality survives death and that it is absorbed or destroyed at death. Beliefs so arrived at can hardly be held on rational evidence, for evidence that is genuinely rational cannot produce contradictory conclusions. It may be said that the appeal to revelation is itself held on rational grounds, which show that scriptural revelation is errorless, and that Christian dogma therefore must also be true. On this there are two comments. One is that it makes reason the supreme court, since the revelation is accepted only because it conforms to reason; and revelation as the ultimate authority has been superseded. In that case religious beliefs, like those of science, must be warranted by rational evidence, and if held in spite of this, must be a form of prejudice. The other comment is a mere reference to the history of biblical criticism from Strauss and Renan forward. (In my Gifford Lectures on *Reason and Belief* the issue is debated in detail.)

I do not mean to suggest that convictions on religious matters are necessarily prejudices. It is quite possible to think a religious problem through with all the sincerity and objectivity of which one is capable and arrive at theistic conclusions. But it seems clear enough that most persons do not reach their religious beliefs in this way. They adopt them rather through the strong suggestions of their time and place, the appeal to authority, the need for comfort or security, fear for their ultimate future. These are not rational factors, and a belief produced by them would seem technically to be a prejudice. Again, I am not saying that a prejudice must be untrue. It may of course be true, but if it is arrived at nonrationally, it can be true only by accident. Fine examples of the struggle of deeply religious men with the findings of their own reason are to be found in the lives of Ernest Renan and Henry Sidgwick. Their conclusion was that there could be but one standard of truth, and that if the integrity of either conscience or reason were to be maintained, this standard must be applied in all fields alike, in religion as well as science and philosophy.

Nationalism

Another node around which impulses and feelings collect, as insects around a streetlamp, is the idea of the nation. A threat to one's nation brings into action what McDougall calls the "most widely extended form of the self-regarding sentiment, which we call the patriotic sentiment." To call patriotism a self-regarding sentiment may seem strange in view of the sacrifice of self it often involves, but such sacrifice is possible because one has come to mingle one's pride and self-respect with the thought of one's country. The pride of the Athenian in his incomparable city is clearly audible in the Funeral Oration of Pericles to the people of Athens. Pride in being part of the world's most powerful empire came out in the *civis Romanus sum* of the Roman citizen. A Frenchman, though he may differ bitterly with other Frenchmen along class and party lines, is united with every other Frenchman in his pride in a noble tradition of art and letters, and in Paris as "the city of light." Rupert Brooke struck a chord of sympathy that was heard round the world when he wrote prophetically in the First World War:

> If I should die, think only this of me:
> That there's some corner of a foreign field
> That is forever England.

And Carlyle's abrupt query, "Shakespeare or India?" brought dramatically home to Englishmen that it could be better to own the greatest name in literature than to own an empire. It has been pointed out that what brought millions of Russians to the standard in the Second World War was not any conviction about Communism but loyalty to Mother Russia. And perhaps no one needs to be told how an American feels when, coming home from abroad, he first glimpses the Statue of Liberty.

On its positive side patriotism, this devotion to an idealized country, is a powerful force in enriching the human spirit. It awakes sympathy with minds larger than one's own, and with concerns that transcend petty preoccupations. The man without a country is a forlorn and crippled human being. But on its negative side it presents the face of Mr. Hyde, not Dr. Jekyll. Dr. Johnson defined it as "the last refuge of a scoundrel." It is one of the most fertile breeding grounds of the stupider kinds of prejudice. And in most of us there is a prejudice against the different as such. The western rancher does not take to the eastern "dude," nor does the southerner to the northern "yankee." To be at home with either calls for readjustment; and besides there is often felt in difference a subtle claim to superiority, a sense that one's own way of living is under implicit criticism, with all the animus that this tends to arouse. Further, though it is interesting to pay visits of curiosity to foreign countries, we should not want to live in them, and we come back with relief to where we can understand what people say and where there is assurance in the good familiar routine.

This prejudice against the foreign as such cuts us off from much that we could profit by. It does so in two ways. It deafens us to useful foreign criticism, and it arouses and sustains useless enmities.

We bridle when we hear our country maligned. We bristle at Cardinal Newman's saying that what the word "American" first suggested to British ears was vulgarity. We bristle at that, and perhaps retort with something about people who live in glass houses. But it might do us more good to take a long look at the intellectual house that Newman lived in, as described, say, in his *Idea of a University*. One may charge him, and justly, with some unpleasant traits, but never with vulgarity; he was a rare example of freedom from it. When Matthew Arnold visited this country, he gave us a lecture on "Numbers," in which he criticized our love of quantity as opposed to quality, particularly if the quantities were huge—the tallest buildings, the biggest companies, the longest bridges, the largest number of children in school; we paid too little attention to the unquantifiable things. He angered some hearers and readers. They would have done better to consider his point. Dean Inge came to us and attacked democracy with an incisiveness of which Arnold was incapable and which earned him enemies at home and abroad. But is it not true that democracy *is* an unwieldy and costly form of government, even if, as Churchill thought, it is the least intolerable form? The French and the Japanese contemplate us and find us artistically obtuse. The more thoughtfully we return their look, the more likely we are to agree with them. To Americans British speech often sounds affected, but where speech counts most, as in acting, British performers are much prized. In the days of now almost unimaginable peace and stability that preceded the First World War, the German-speaking peoples were the admitted leaders of the world in music and in philosophy; as a student of the latter subject I was myself among the thousands who swarmed to Germany as pilgrims to hear, for example, Wundt at Leipzig and Windelband at Heidelberg. In two needless and tragic wars the Germans threw away their cultural leadership and made the word "Kultur" itself a hissing. High schools in this country abandoned studying their language; the tide of students going abroad turned elsewhere; the Germans were hated as "Huns." Without raising bygone rights and wrongs, we may surely admit a loss in this reaction against all things German. Bach, Beethoven, and Brahms remained supreme; Leibniz and Kant and Hegel still stood out as monoliths against the sky. "You cannot draw up an indictment against a whole people," said Burke, and if you try, you pay a price.

The loss becomes far greater when patriotism passes over into nationalism. True patriotism is love of country accompanied by an alertness to its defects and a concern to put them right. Nationalism is patriotism gone blind to the virtues of other countries as well as to the defects of its own. Prime examples of such nationalism were Germany under the Nazis and Italy under the Fascists. *Deutschland über Alles,* when said by others, may be legitimate admiration, but when shouted by Nazis, it was the equivalent of a raised fist. And if the Roman Empire was to be revived, the new provinces might well have been consulted before being devoured. These particular crazed nationalisms are happily moribund.

What we have to fear today is in a sense not nationalism at all. Though it is not distinctively Russian, it has its capitol in the U.S.S.R. Communism is an avowed attempt to place all power in the hands of the "working class" and to expropriate the class of so-called capitalists. What makes it of special interest here is its refusal to permit free criticism of its doctrines and its resort to violence to sustain and spread them. Though it claims to be democratic, the government is in the hands of a fraction of the people called "the party," which attempts by forceful means to control both the thought and the action of the masses. To keep them in line, it has rewritten history, forced art, music, and even science to sound the "right" political note, and silenced even the most rational dissent. Americans have been charged with a stubborn prejudice against this system. Is the charge justifiable? Yes and No. A government that governs by excluding criticism is bound to be a government by prejudice; it is trying to make itself into a sort of dogmatic religion by repressing the means to its own correction. And a prejudice against a government by prejudice is hardly a prejudice at all.

On the other hand, a hostility based on clear perception of wrong may harden into an obsession, and then it is a real prejudice. Many think, with some reason, that this has happened in America, and among those who think so are some European peoples that live much nearer the Soviet Union than we do. Such an obsession may be exceedingly dangerous. It has led us to fight the Communists unsuccessfully on the other side of the world, to pour much of our resources into an attempt to outbuild them in the means of destruction and thereby to lead them into a determined effort to outdo us. Statisticians are now engaged in calculating how many times each of us could annihilate the other. This spiral of destructiveness is the most pressing problem of our day, since it threatens nothing less than the end of civilization. Einstein remarked that he did not know whether there would be a third world war, but predicted that if there were, the fourth would be fought with bows and arrows. To promote general destruction seems very like madness. This is no place for off-the-cuff proposals. But we need to remember that the Russians have felt the horrors of war more deeply than we have, that they do not want it, that they are as afraid of us as we are of them, and that their government has made repeated pleas, sincere or not, for total abandonment of nuclear arms. We should surely explore these to the limit. That would mean ridding ourselves of our obsession against them and assuming that below our antipathies there lies, as there certainly does, a common reason.

As for other nationalist prejudices, our record is on the whole not bad. America has been a promised land for the exploited everywhere; and we have tossed them into our big melting pot with hope of a new and fairly homogeneous brew. The hope has been largely justified. The media, warned against ethnic slurs, have helped. On radio and television there are no more "niggers," "wops," or "dagoes." American prejudices are likely to repeat old-world enmities, as of the Irish against the English, or to rise in waves, as in the witch-hunts of the McCarthy era or in the government treatment of the Japanese-Americans after Pearl Harbor. But Americans are becoming more cosmopolitan. They are to be found everywhere abroad. And when, in his own country, the cowboy meets the newcomer with his "Howdy, stranger," the "howdy" says as much as the "stranger."

Further, as the world too reluctantly acknowledges, Americans are a generous people. Churchill called the Marshall Plan the least sordid act in history. So far as we retain prejudices against other nationals, it is chiefly through ignorance, including a shocking ignorance of their historic cultures. Of course in this respect we do not sin alone. C. E. M. Joad, the English philosopher, wrote a book about America which he called *The Babbitt Warren*. It consisted of three sections, entitled "Truth," "Goodness," and "Beauty," and undertook to show that Americans did not know the meaning of any of these terms. Before issuing this comprehensive blast he had never desecrated his feet by setting them upon American soil. In a philosopher the prejudice of ignorance seems to me particularly culpable. Here he could have learned from that wise nonphilosopher, Charles Lamb. In talk with a friend, a third person was mentioned. Lamb burst out in his stammer, "I hate that man." "Why, Charles," said his friend, "I didn't think you even knew him." "I d-don't," said Lamb. "I c-can't hate a man I know." Xenophobes should take notice.

Race Prejudice

In the long run, however, perhaps our greatest problem is not nationalist prejudice but race prejudice. Blacks or Afro-Americans are no longer concentrated in one region, but are scattered throughout the country and form more than a tenth of our people. It is absolutely essential that some form of mutual appreciation be achieved if internally we are not to face a much troubled future, swept by unrest and crime, and externally isolated from the Third World. The subject is too large to admit of more than a few disjointed remarks. First, there are those who say that the so-called prejudice against blacks is not a prejudice at all, but a piece of well-founded knowledge. In a long series of "intelligence tests" from the Alpha test of the First World War to the SAT and MAT tests given to college applicants, blacks have scored lower than whites, and this result has been offered as decisive on the issue of comparative intellectual capacity. But none of these tests has produced a consensus of experts as to what they prove. Without denying that they show something important, psychologists have asked whether a low score on them is any proof of congenital incapacity. On this point no agreement has emerged, because performance in such tests has been shown to involve so wide a variety of factors. Unfamiliarity with paper work, the expectation of failure, homes where ideas are not discussed, nervousness in alien surroundings, linguistic difficulties, and a score of other factors cooperate to influence the outcome. No test yet devised has satisfied the experts that at long last they can draw the line between nature and nurture.

Second, even if such tests did show conclusively a lower average ability in blacks than whites, that would not prove that an individual white candidate should be preferred to a black, for the variation within the range of either blacks or whites is far greater than that between the averages. The only fair choice is between individuals. In the field of sports, black athletes, when nothing counted but individual ability, have repeatedly come to the top, as they have done in the ring, on the basketball floor, on the gridiron, and on the diamond. Since the Supreme Court's decision of 1954, the black youth's chance for an education has vastly improved, and though he has sometimes spurned this chance, he has made his way in the professions in a manner that shows how irrational the old prejudiced stereotyping was.

Third, race prejudice as a rule confuses race, ethnicity, color, genes, and ability. Racial differences are inborn and hereditary; ethnic differences are cultural; and it is a grave confusion to include the second among the first. And race is a much less important determinant of abilities than is commonly supposed. A careful anthropologist, Clyde Kluckhohn, writes:

The number of hereditary trait-potentialities *known* to differ (between groups, not individuals) is very small. Indeed one anthropologist, M. F. Ashley Montagu, has estimated that less than 1 per cent of the total number of genes is involved in the differentiation between any two existent races. Another, S. L. Washburn, expresses that same idea in terms of human evolution by saying, "If the time from the divergence of human and ape stems to the present be represented by an ordinary pack of fifty-two playing cards placed end to end, all racial differentiation would be on less than one-half of the last card."[9]

Gordon Allport remarks that color *is* linked to race, but "there is no evidence that the genes determining skin color are tied to genes determining mental capacity or moral qualities."[10] And even if the connection between race and color on the one hand and ability on the other were much closer than it is, we must remember that in America we are not dealing with a black race. In *The Anthropometry of the American Negro,* Herskovits estimated that more than three-fourths of our blacks are of mixed descent, and that the average black is as far from the pure Negroid type as he is from the Caucasian. "In short, the average American Negro is as much a white man as he is a black man. The label that we give is thus at least half purely social invention. Many times we apply it to people whose *race* is mostly white."[11] Thought on these matters is often about as impartial as that of the Scotsman who reported that when the Angles invaded Britain all the acute Angles went north while all the obtuse Angles remained in the south.

Fourth, the race problem is largely psychological. For hundreds of years blacks in this country have been at the bottom of the totem pole. They have been snubbed, made to go to the back door and take the back seats, hired last and fired first, given inferior schooling, segregated by real estate agents, socially excluded. People so treated are bound to develop internal defenses, though these vary from person to person. If they simply accept the labels of the master civilization, they think of themselves as lazy, stupid, made for hewing wood and drawing water. That makes things in some ways easier for them, but it freezes them into permanent subjection. Others go part way with these prescriptions and introduce into the black group a hierarchy based on color, with the lighter colored despising the darker, envying the whites, and contemptuous of themselves for both attitudes. Blacks' links to their ancestral cultures are more slender and difficult to trace than those of Greeks, Italians, or Chinese, and in a civilization to which they have never fully adjusted they feel alienated and insecure. Such appeasements as "affirmative action" have gone some way to reduce the hostility, occasionally leaning over backward and doing injustice to whites. But the inhabitants of our large cities are realizing that the race problem is far more than one of quotas, unemployment, or any outward rearrangements of society. It is the problem how to overcome the inveterate distancing of the majority from a minority of more than twenty million people, and the hostility of that vast minority, held because they have not been accepted into the American family. They feel like outsiders looking wistfully and angrily in.

Fifth, the problem can be solved only by a conquering of intellectual and visceral prejudice on both sides. Can this be done? That it can be done in individual cases everyone knows. The recently deceased black master of a Yale college was one of the most respected and beloved masters in Yale history. Can this obliteration of racial barriers be achieved generally? Unhappily, I can think of no case where it has been. Brazil has been cited, but it will not stand scrutiny. Hawaii is perhaps as near an approach as has been made. Separation as in South Africa, a doomed land if ever there was one, is out of the question on many grounds. The choice for the United States lies in the end between a general wiping out of prejudice from the public mind, which is theoretically possible, and a guerilla warfare so general and so destructive as to end the nation we know. Whites and blacks alike should face this alternative with far-seeing eyes, and in the light of it make their choice.

Sex Prejudice

In our expanding series of classes, race prejudice is outrun by sex prejudice, for this extends to half of humankind. If we follow Freud, we see sex at work in practically all love and hate; we see it

at work everywhere in literature, art, religion, even philosophy. That
Freud overstated his claims for sex is now widely conceded. But if
the strength of an impulse can be roughly measured by its evolu-
tionary depth, we should expect the sex impulse to have overmastering power. This we do in fact find. It would make an interesting
study in prejudice to list the persons of outstanding intellect and
judgment who have made fools of themselves when challenged by
this imperious impulse. Looking at the lives of the four men I have
chosen as exemplars of the reasonable temper, we find that three
out of four showed themselves at their weakest where matters of
sex were involved, though they manifested the weakness in very
different ways. How exactly Marcus and Faustina felt toward each
other will now never be known; but something was clearly amiss.
Perhaps the stern Stoicism of her husband had something to do with
that flightiness in his absence which has attached itself so firmly to
Faustina's memory. As we have seen, John Stuart Mill, one of the
true greats in the history of women's liberation, held a curious mis-
estimate of his wife, attributing to her capacities that the evidence
does not support. Perhaps under her influence, he froze his mother
and sisters out of his life when they ventured to disagree. And some
of the unhappiest moments in the life of Renan came when he fell
in love and, with strange incomprehension of his wife's and sister's
feelings, set up a ménage à trois—a mistake that was later rectified.
In Sidgwick alone of the four do we find the sort of settled reasonableness that remained unruffled by the competing claims of reason
and romance. He worked much with women; he was an early
champion of their rights; he married a woman who held a distinguished position of her own, and lived with her in apparently
unruffled harmony to the end.

The fact that three out of four exemplars of the reasonable temper
should falter over sex is surely significant. Sex, as biologists know,
is primeval, and the power to think is a comparatively recent acquisition which is easily overwhelmed by it. Romance and rationality
seldom go hand in hand. Reason attempts to see things as they are;

Romeo is not likely to see Juliet as she is. It is of the essence of the ecstasy and the fantasy of the lover to see his inamorata not as she is, but idealized, etherialized, and glorified. Schopenhauer thought that next to the instinct of survival itself, the sex instinct was the most powerful of human drives, and that its distortion of reason in romance was one of the subtle means adopted by nature to perpetuate the race. And no doubt this distortion has ruined countless lives by inducing able men and women to throw themselves away on those unworthy of them. Still, if all the world loves a lover, it is not because he is a deluded fool, but because his delusion is of so exalting a kind—he has seen visions and dreamed dreams that, even if they are untrue, all would wish to be true. Romantic love is a "great rich vine" on which have grown many of the finest fruits of literature and art. "It is not wisdom to be only wise," said Santayana; and, human nature being what it is, it belongs to rationality itself not to ignore the ancient undercurrents of our being. Yet, in romance the whisper of rational protest should not be wholly inaudible. One could wish that Keats's Fanny Brawne and Hazlitt's Sarah Walker had been more appropriate objects on which to heap all that eloquent idolatry.

Most prejudice is *against* some group, but we have been speaking here of prejudice *in favor* of one. Sex prejudice, however, does not operate in one way only; it is a special and tangled case. Built into the very instinct that exalts the other sex is a factor that tends also to belittle and restrict it. When this instinct blossoms into romantic love, it is prone to wrap its object, if female, in a cocoon of tenderness and protectiveness, in whose soft warmth she tends to bask in pleasure, without realizing at first the restrictions it carries with it. This accompaniment is perhaps the most tragic fact in the relation of men and women. On the one hand the instinct of which romance is the blossom is deeply rooted, powerful, and ineradicable; on the other hand it almost inevitably inhibits that freedom to be themselves which women so justly and urgently want. If it is natural for the lover to write sonnets to his mistress's eyebrow, it is also natural for him to cherish her, to be her guardian and stand between her and the world, to want her with him not only as an object of delight but as a helpmeet, playmate, and even plaything. At first she accepts and rejoices in this new status. What such reciprocity normally leads to is what both probably desire, a family. But a family imposes immense restrictions on the mother, not only in the months preceding the birth of her children but also for months and years that follow. To say that the father or anyone else can adequately substitute during these years for the mother's own care and devotion seems both antecedently improbable and actually untrue. While the man, if he is fortunate, is finding himself in his vocation, his wife is keeping house and dealing continuously with immature minds. That is an immensely valuable service which many who perform it prefer and regard as by far the most important service they could render. But an increasing number of others are rejecting it, both as unsatisfying in itself and as cutting down their future. When they return after ten or fifteen years of impressed labor to the field of their old ambition, they find themselves no longer competing on even terms with others, but burdened with the heavy handicap of having been long out of the race and off the field. No wonder that among modern women, and especially among American women, there should be so widespread a restlessness. They feel that they are living unfulfilled and frustrated lives.

No wonder, either, that their first reaction should be a wave of anger at the most obvious culprit, male prejudice, which they feel has put them down and kept them down. They call for legislation that would make it illegal to take official notice of sex differences. That there is a widespread prejudice against women as "the weaker sex"—weaker in understanding, stability, and endurance as well as muscular strength—seems undeniable. Women still have to fight their way as ministers, professors, lawyers, physicians, dentists, indeed in all the professions except nursing and acting. But the barriers are steadily falling. The old single-sex colleges have practically ceased to exist. There are now women policemen and firefighters.

Nowhere do women have more freedom to pursue their own vocations than in present-day America.

It must be added that if the divorce rates mean anything, one can hardly make similar claims about the happiness of American homes or American women. Nor can this be laid exclusively at the door of male chauvinism. If I am right about it, much of the frustration is of a less remediable kind, since it springs from the psychological ambivalence in the sexual relation. The romance idolized by men and women alike leads on to marriage, to family cares in which biology itself has appointed women to the most intimate and absorbing role, to their paying a heavy price for playing this role if it happens not to be their vocation, and therefore to the defeat of many a just aspiration.

The problem of sex prejudice, then, is a very complex and deep-rooted one to which there is probably no general solution. Day-care centers for children have helped many women to careers of their own; college and university courses for adults have equipped many others to return to teaching or the law or the marketplace; the sad solution for others has been the forgoing of marriage. But there is no sort of generalization or law that will solve a problem which is in no two cases the same. It must be solved, if at all, by the joint sympathy and understanding required by the individual case.

Prejudice and Abstractions

We have been dealing with the widening circles of prejudice that start with defensive resentment against whatever threatens the self. We have seen the community dividing into in-groups and out-groups, the in-groups standing together, though in larger and larger numbers, and regarding aliens with suspicion—first the family, then the sect, then the nation, then a group that includes half the world, the other sex. And operating throughout the series there is what we have called the central illogic of prejudice, the process of generalizing from one or a few instances to an entire class.

All this sounds as if prejudice were directed solely upon persons, or classes of persons. And these are the kinds of prejudice that are most likely to do harm. But prejudices may be directed against anything, even abstractions. Some people are prejudiced against change as such, no doubt because it offers some threat to their habits or security. Ruskin, Tolstoy, and Gandhi came to detest such essentials of modernity as railways, because they tore up the landscape and seemed to loosen the ties that kept men close to nature. Most people would agree to call this prejudice, on the ground that it was a misjudgment, based on feeling, of the gains and losses involved. Charles Lamb, Charles Darwin, Goethe, Macaulay, Whitman, Yeats, Asquith, and Dean Inge were all prejudiced against music; it is enough to add that all of them lacked an ear for it. In the United States there is widespread prejudice against the doctrine of evolution, chiefly because it is felt as a threat to religion, and therefore to security. In the schools there is an avoidance of mathematics on the ostensible ground that it is useless, but really because it is abstract and difficult. In many minds there is a prejudice against science itself on the real but unadmitted ground that it threatens pet convictions about UFO's, astrology, ghosts, miracles, or free will. In educational circles there is a prejudice against elitism, which is no prejudice at all if elitism means snobbery, but a fundamental one if it would place all subjects of study on a level, reject native differences in capacity, or refuse to admit standards in literature, music, and art. Sometimes a little self-analysis will help. If one finds oneself hating telephones or airplanes or science or music or nonobjective painting, a modest excavation in the field of one's own experience will often bring the real causes to light. If these are adequate to carry the weight of the aversion, the dislike is rational and no prejudice. If they are not, a true prejudice has been unearthed, and to recognize it as a prejudice is to have gone far toward freeing oneself from it.

Defenses of Prejudice: (1) The Subconscious

We have not painted prejudice in a happy light, so it may cause some surprise to learn that it has ardent defenders. President John

Grier Hibben of Princeton, a philosopher and logician, wrote a book called *A Defence of Prejudice,* whose first essay bears that title. For Dr. Hibben, prejudices are "judgments to which we give assent, but which we cannot prove."[12] He gives such examples as our belief in the Newtonian law of gravitation, the character of Saint Francis, or a forced and quick decision on a complex matter of practice. Take the sort of case Dr. Hibben is fond of dwelling on. A reflective and honorable man is invited to participate in a deal of whose moral character he is in doubt. He sleeps upon it and comes up with the strong conviction that he must have nothing to do with it. The decision has thus been made by a subconscious process of which he could give no clear account, and in Dr. Hibben's view it must therefore be called a prejudice. At the same time Dr. Hibben admits that the decision has been reached in a rational way, and we agree. Rationality is not confined to explicit reflection, and the subconscious habits of a thoughtful and conscientious man are apt to be an extension of his dominant habits. Dr. Hibben's cases are those of true beliefs, taken as prejudices because at the time they cannot be proved. But these are surely not what we commonly mean by prejudices. Prejudice involves going amiss. It is a diversion of rational thinking out of its course by nonrational factors such as feelings and desires. An appeal to intuition is not necessarily such a diversion, for this may be the upshot of much experience and much half-conscious rumination. The intuition of a Darwin on a Galapagos tortoise may be worth more than a doctoral dissertation on it by someone else.

Defenses of Prejudice: (2) Anti-Intellectualism

This brings us to another defense of prejudice, which really rejects our whole conception of the reasonable man. It may be true, the indictment runs, that a man who watches himself always to see that he is walking the straight line of truth and never taking a side step into prejudice will gain more truth. But truth is not the only value in the world. Your rational man, if he ever lived, would be an icicle or a stick. There would be no juice in him, nothing of personal idiosyncrasy or interest. Imagine a novel in which all the characters are rational men and women. Could anything be duller? It is the full-blooded people, with all their prejudices, that we are able to like or dislike. Think of Boswell's Johnson without his prejudices! At least the people who let themselves go are alive; they warm both hands before the fire of life; they make mistakes but do not beat their breasts about them; they are leaping flames of vitality—vivid, bright, and unforgettable. Is there not something to be said for freedom and even for abandon?

> My candle burns at both ends;
> It will not last the night;
> But ah, my foes, and oh, my friends—
> It gives a lovely light!

Now I should hate to be a party to snuffing Miss Millay's "lovely light"; and I am doing nothing so absurd as drawing up an indictment against impulses and feelings. I go so far as to think that without impulses and feelings there would be no values in the world at all, and therefore no point in living. I have admitted that a human being *is* chiefly a bundle of impulses to love, to fight, to play, to create, to know; and it is those of powerful impulses—the Saint Peters, the Luthers, the Leonardos, the Beethovens—who have the largest potentialities for lives of richness and enjoyment. If men were without these drives and the joy of fulfilling them, if they were mere computers, however errorless, life would have lost its savor. All this I grant.

But such freedom will be used differently by those whom the critics call classics and by those they call romantics, and I do not think the advantage is on the romantic's side. He takes the control of impulse as an infringement of his freedom; the classic thinks of it as an indispensable means to freedom. "In all things," said Dostoievsky, "I go to the uttermost extreme; my life long, I have never been acquainted with moderation." "Those who restrain desire," said William Blake, "do so because theirs is weak enough to be restrained." There speaks the pure romantic. The classic might intimate that both Blake and Dostoievsky were probably mad, to which the romantic might reply that he would be quite happy to be mad if he could be Blake or Dostoievsky. But he cannot; he must be his own modest self, ordered to some goal or not so ordered. And if he is not so ordered, he may be merely an unexhilarating squib, fizzing and sputtering its futility into the night.

Indeed, in the talk about the reasonable temper as imposing a yoke upon the life of feeling, there is much misunderstanding. Reason, to be sure, tells the angry or jealous or fearful man that if he lets all holds go and gives feeling its head, he will pay a heavy price. But control is not repression; it is the purchase of a larger good with a smaller present sacrifice. We may well heed Burke: "It is ordained in the eternal constitution of things that men of intemperate minds cannot be free." Plato reminded us that life is like a chariot race in which the driver, reason, is in charge of two spirited horses, appetite and emotion. It is only if, through an expert use of bit and reins, the driver can make them run together that he will ever manage to stay the course and avoid a pileup. Neither horse can win freedom by running off or hanging back or tripping up the other. Slavery, Plato went on, lay not in the dominance of reason over impulse, which was true freedom, but in the dominance of impulse over reason, which was anarchy. There was wisdom as well as wit in Adlai Stevenson's "Eggheads of the world unite; you have nothing to lose but your yolks."

I was once saying something like this to a historian colleague when he protested that I was not seeing things in perspective. We academics may admire quiet detachment, but it is not the people who trim away prejudices and try to live reasonably who have been the powers and movers in history. Asquith, fine judicial mind that he was, was turned out by Lloyd-George when a man was needed who would win the war. As Whitehead circumspectly puts it, "A certain element of excess seems to be a necessary element in all greatness,"[19] or, in Leo Durocher's ballpark Anglo-Saxon, "Nice guys come out last." The people who have turned the current of events have more often been flaming, dogmatic, one-eyed zealots than reasonable men: Genghis Khan, Mohammed, Luther, Napoleon, Hitler, Stalin, Mao. How far would Hitler have gone without his nationalistic prejudices?

The answer is, first, that he might never have been heard of, and that it might have been better for the world if none of these zealots had been heard of. Second, the mere fact of a person's changing history, without regard to whether the change is for good or evil, is no ground for hero-worship. (You may question my including such a hero as Luther in a list of zealots. He was a hero to me, too, until I read him, when I began to think there was something in Goethe's judgment, repeated by Froude, that "Luther threw back the intelligence of mankind for centuries by calling in the passions of the mob to decide questions which ought to have been left to thinkers." The pope was no saint, but was he really anti-Christ?) And if a leader does decide things by passion, it is an accident whether he turns out to be a blessing or a curse. Third, the notion that reasonable men must become Hamlets when given the reins of power is untrue; recall our glimpse of Marcus Aurelius. Fourth, men of reflection have often had men of action as their adjutants. It has been pointed out that the intellectual yeast of the four great revolutions of modern times came out of philosophers' studies. Behind the American Revolution lay John Locke; behind the French, Rousseau and Voltaire; behind the Russian and the Chinese the thought of a poverty-stricken exile, spinning his webs with intelligence and hatred in the British Museum Library. If these last two revolutions are failing, it is largely because, in the philosophies they embodied, reason and hatred were so inextricably mixed.

To the objection, then, that the reasonable temper freezes the spirit into an icicle and cuts off freedom and joy along with prejudice, our answer is that this idea is based on a gross confusion. It confuses the man of rational temper with the intellectualist. The intellectualist lives among his abstractions, and sacrifices the rest of life in order to maintain his hermitage there. The rational man too glories in understanding, but that very understanding makes plain to him that the richness of life lies in the fulfillment of varied interests and powers. To neglect these powers would itself be irrationality.

Defenses of Prejudice: (3) It Is Inevitable

There is a final objection to the view we have been pressing, and again it is fundamental. It is that rationality is an illusion because it runs counter to human nature. Freud has taught us that all human beliefs, especially if they leave the barest ground of fact, are non-rational gropings in the dark. Marx thought that all the defenses commonly offered of a capitalist society were rationalizations of class interest. J. O. Wisdom of New York University and Morris Lazerowitz of Smith College have worked out ingenious theories to show that the conclusions of speculative philosophers themselves are better explained by unconscious complexes than by logical thought; and W. T. Jones of the California Institute of Technology has elaborated a theory that human nature consists of biases which may be set out on a chart with their varying intensities, and used as indices of their owners' behavior.[14] The German psychologist Herzberg drew up a list, as objectively as he could, of about thirty of the greatest philosophers in history, and attempted to show that all of them were pathological cases.[15] Even William James suggested that what philosophers were doing was engineering the universe along the lines of their temperamental needs, coming out as rationalists if they were tender-minded, empiricists if they were tough-minded. Recall golfers making their final putts on the green, and how they twist themselves into fantastic shapes to help the ball into the cup. James thought of philosophers as putters on the green of life, trying by a little "english" to make the nature of things answer to their wishes.[16]

Macneile Dixon in his Gifford Lectures on *The Human Situation* has put the matter boldly:

'There never yet was a philosopher, whatever they may have said, no, nor man of science, whose conclusions ran counter to the dearest wishes of his heart, who summed up against them, or condemned his hopes to death. How honestly Darwin confessed the lurking presence of the desire to prove his theory true. "I well remember the time when the thought of the eye made me cold all over. . . . The sight of a feather in a peacock's tail whenever I gaze at it, makes me sick."[17]

Here we must demur. The mention of Darwin was an unfortunate one for Professor Dixon's case, for that great man is one of the finest examples on record of the honest and objective mind. He did, to be sure, want to find his theory true, but his statement of it, when at last he gave it to the world, carried conviction precisely because he was so fully aware of its difficulties; he had kept a journal of them over the years, and had answered them decisively before his critics had thought of them. "I have steadily endeavoured," he wrote, "to keep my mind free, so as to give up any hypothesis however much beloved (and I cannot resist forming one on every subject) as soon as the facts are shown to be opposed to it." Furthermore, it is perfectly possible to sum up against one's desires. Darwin's friend Huxley admitted that the thought of death as extinction was hateful to him, but he accepted it because he believed the evidence required it. On the other hand C. D. Broad concluded on the evidence of psychical research that he probably would survive death, though in such a form that he looked to his own survival with aversion.

None of us is free from unreasonable hopes and fears. But unless our thought can to some extent work loose from them, what is the point of philosophizing, even about this? Freud did not think that his theory of the id was itself a mere distortion by that id, or Marx that his theory of class determination was itself a by-product of his class, or Wisdom and Lazerowitz that their theory of philosophy was a nonrational vagary, or James that his theory of empiricism was merely congenial to his own temperament rather than true. And if thought is the puppet of feeling, what is the point of education? An educated malice and misanthropy would be more dangerous than the blundering kind—as with Satan, Stalin, and Iago. Surely the whole venture of education assumes that thought can be freed from slavery to feeling and desire, and can achieve some mastery over them.

But what of absolute relativism such as that advocated by W. T. Jones? If you meet his theory of universal bias by saying that then his own theory must be the expression of bias, he replies that he realizes this perfectly and is quite ready to accept it. He is offering a view congenial to his own nature, and would not expect me to accept his view on any other basis than its congeniality to my own. To say anything else would be inconsistent. But why avoid inconsistency? He would say, no doubt, that he has a bias against it, and so prefers to avoid it. This, I am afraid, will not do. The law of contradiction is not something you merely prefer to accept; it is something you *must* accept. As Bradley said, you may to some extent avoid the game of thinking, but if you sit down to it, there is only one way of playing. If you do play, you cannot even deny the law, for in denying it you reaffirm it. To deny the law is to assert that both sides of a contradiction may be true. But that is equivalent to saying that though the law may be false it may also be true. And then what exactly are you saying? Essentially nothing, for whatever you say does not exclude its own denial. Not all thought is biased, for Professor Jones's bias against inconsistency is plainly not a mere bias.

No one, then, can counter rationality with skepticism. If he offers this as only a preference, we prefer otherwise, and if he says he sees it to be true, he has already abandoned it. Men are rational, though, as Plato intimated, they are brokenly and imperfectly so. Even among philosophers we feel an immense disparity in the depth of their permeation by the spirit of rationality. Philosophers such as Nietzsche I find it hard to take seriously, for a philosophy that defies rationality seems like a pyramid trying to stand on its apex. Others, like Kierkegaard and the theologians in his train, use their reason to climb into a supernatural realm where reason and morality are left behind; then kick the ladder down. But if reason is so untrustworthy, how did it ever get them there? On the other hand, there are thinkers whose intellectual temper adds weight to everything they say. The father of this clear-eyed tribe was not Socrates, who was capable of arguing for victory, nor Plato, who was sometimes carried away on his own soaring wings, but Aristotle, that sober old gray eminence. He has sired a distinguished progeny. John Locke was one of them. I have often thought Locke's words a reflection of himself: "The love of truth is the principal part of human perfection in this world, and the seed-plot of all other virtues." And then there are the distinguished quartet whom I have sketched in this book.

The Reasonable Temper

I have tried to show that the reasonable temper is not the property of any one class of men, and therefore have cast my net widely. In its meshes are an emperor, a freelance reformer, an Orientalist, and a philosophy professor. They come from the top and near the bottom of the social order: the first was for many years the head of the civilized world; the third was the son of a poverty-stricken fisherman. They were alike indeed in all having to surmount physical weaknesses; the first did not reach sixty, and none of them reached seventy. But they varied even in their frailty. The first, though of immense wealth, lived the austere life of an ascetic; the second was for a time an apparently doomed consumptive, who had gone through a nervous breakdown that left him with the permanent tic of a twitching eye; the third was a man of unwieldy body who walked with difficulty; the fourth was tormented by allergies and was seldom able to get a night's sleep. In intellectual abilities they varied greatly. Mill and Sidgwick were among the most remarkable intellects on record. Renan was a fine scholar and historian, but hardly ranks as a philosopher; Aurelius was outstanding rather for character than for intellect. They differed widely in the manner of their education. The emperor had private tutors, who were showered with gratitude by their modest pupil. Mill said that he never suffered the handicap of a college education; his father supplied all. Renan had the full formal course for the Catholic priesthood, then used the logic with which it had equipped him to break from his cell. Sidgwick was a product of Rugby and Cambridge who could take any academic prize he cared to. But different as these men were in physique, in social advantage, in time, in place, in environment, and in education, they were alike in the rare trait celebrated in this book—devotion to reasonableness in life and thought.

For all of them conformity to reason was more than a special interest and delight. It was an integral part of duty and honor. For all of them prejudice was close to sin. All of them shared an ethics of belief that made carelessness in conviction or statement, surrender to superstition, fanaticism of any kind, personal attack in argument, dogmatism, the misstatement of an opponent's case or the concealment of weakness in their own seem like stains on their integrity. Not Mill alone but all of them were, in Gladstone's phrase, "saints of rationalism." In reading them one gives extra weight to their conclusions because of this felt intellectual probity. One does not have to be a skilled reasoner to be thus sensitive to waywardness and emotionalism in thought. And with these four the rational temper was not an intellectual virtue only. It was a spirit that irradiated practice, permeated feeling, and filtered down into illuminating talk and discerning taste.

It will be evident by now that this book is not merely a study of certain heroes of the mind, though of course it is that. It has a thesis. It is a tract meant for the times. "The irrational," says F. L. Lucas, "now in politics, now in poetics, has been the sinister opium of our tormented and demented century."[18] Two great wars, both preventable if the leaders had been reasonable men, have torn the world apart. A hell-bent race for explosives between two powers that can already exterminate each other threatens, unless halted by joint reason, to bring civilization itself to an end.

In our own country freedom has given us the priceless privilege of thinking and speaking as we will. How have we used it? We have produced some work that will live. We have also produced mountains of vacuous fiction, formless poetry, expensive but cheap drama, self-indulgence splashed on canvas, music that deafens and deadens us to silence as well as sound, violence in the streets, violence reaching out at us from boxes in our living rooms. Our educational levels have fallen. Confronted again by Arnold's choice between "culture and anarchy," we seem to have chosen anarchy. The failure is perhaps temporary and it is in ourselves, for we have come to tolerate and even to like these things. What would the quartet we have been studying have said of them? Of course no one can know exactly. But after spending an hour with them, one does draw the line differently between what is tawdry and what is not. They lived up in the hills where one can see farther and think more clearly than we usually do. If our ills are inward, as they largely are, we should do well to listen to what these men say. We should do even better to catch something of the reasonable temper in which they sought with such success to live their lives.

NOTES and INDEX

Notes

MARCUS AURELIUS

1. A. S. L. Farquharson, *Marcus Aurelius* (Oxford: Basil Blackwell, 1951), p. 120. He should have written "the tenth century."

2. Quoted by H. D. Sedgwick, *Marcus Aurelius* (New Haven: Yale University Press, 1921), p. 15, from Frederick's *Politische Correspondenz,* vol. 37 (letter of September 4, 1775).

3. Matthew Arnold, *Essays in Criticism* (London: Macmillan & Co., 1889), p. 354.

4. For a translation of some of the better letters, see Anthony Birley, *Marcus Aurelius* (London: Eyre & Spottiswoode, 1966), chap. 4.

5. G. H. Rendall, *Marcus Aurelius Antoninus to Himself* (London: Macmillan & Co., 1898), 1.7. Unless otherwise noted, quotations from the *Meditations* are from Rendall's translation, and the location is entered in the text.

6. It is given in Birley, pp. 207–9.

7. Edward Gibbon, *Decline and Fall of the Roman Empire.* 6 vols. (Milman ed., Philadelphia: Lippincott, 1867), 1:94.

8. Ibid., 1:95.

9. Birley, p. 108.

10. Ibid., p. 149.

11. Ibid., p. 218, translating a biographer, probably Marius Maximus, of the fourth century.

12. Ibid., pp. 257–58, quoting Cassius Dio.

13. Ibid., p. 287, quoting Dio.

14. Gilbert Murray, *Stoic, Christian and Humanist* (London: C. A. Watts & Co., George Allen & Unwin, 1940), pp. 102–3.

15. A. S. L. Farquharson, ed. and trans., *The Meditations of the Emperor Marcus Antoninus.* 2 vols. (Oxford: Clarendon Press, 1944), vol. 1.

16. See Henry Sidgwick's admirable essay on "Unreasonable Action" in his *Practical Ethics* (London: Swan Sonnenschein & Co., 1909), pp. 235–60.

17. William James, *The Principles of Psychology.* 2 vols. (New York: Henry Holt & Co., 1910), 2:522 ff.

18. Birley, p. 126.

19. W. E. H. Lecky is translating here from *De Clementia* 2.6, 7, in his *History of European Morals.* 2 vols. (London: Longmans, Green, 1882), 1:190. See his valuable account of Stoicism generally.

20. W. L. Davidson, *The Stoic Creed* (Edinburgh: T. & T. Clark, 1907), p. 149, following Cicero's *Tusculan Disputations* 2.61.

21. Spinoza, *Ethics,* 4.67.

22. Seneca, *De vita beata,* chaps. 8 and 9, cited from Lecky, 1:186-87.

23. Arnold, *Essays in Criticism,* p. 365

24. Birley, trans., p. 301, of *Meditations,* 2.1 and 6.48.

25. Lecky, 1:154.

26. Ibid., p. 251 n. Translation by Lecky.

27. Cited by Birley, p. 89.

28. *Meditations,* 7:55, slightly emended for clarity.

29. Ernest Renan, *Marcus Aurelius. The Origins of Christianity,* Book 7 (London: Mathieson & Co., n.d.), p. 154.

30. J. S. Mill, "Nature," in *Three Essays on Religion* (London: Longmans, Green, Reader & Dyer, 1875), pp. 28-29.

31. H. D. Sedgwick, p. 209. He devotes three chapters to discussion of Marcus's dealings with the Christians.

32. Ibid., pp. 215 ff.

33. Walter Pater, *Marius the Epicurean* (New York: Boni & Liveright, Modern Library, n.d.), pp. 178-79.

34. Cassius Dio 71.6, quoted by Birley, p. 246.

Linguistic note: My colleague Henri Peyre has reminded me of a curious fact: the Greeks, who introduced to the Western world the idea of reason had no word for it that corresponded to our own. In the *Oxford English Dictionary* "reason" is defined as "the guiding principle of the human mind in the process of thinking." Perhaps the nearest approach to that in Greek is λόγος, which is often used by Marcus. But the primary meaning of λόγος is speech or word, as in the opening of the fourth Gospel: "in the beginning was the Word . . ." (ὁ λόγος). Of the other more or less synonymous terms, σοφία means cleverness, skill, or shrewdness; νόησις means primarily thinking; διάνοια, discursive intellect, φρόνησις, good sense or prudence; and σωφροσύνη, temperance or moderation. It would be impossible to say in Greek, except by paraphrase, what Kant meant by *Vernunft.*

JOHN STUART MILL

1. Noel Annan, "John Stuart Mill," in *Mill: A Collection of Critical Essays,* edited by J. B. Schneewind (Notre Dame, Indiana, and London: University of Notre Dame Press, 1969), pp. 38-39.

2. J. S. Mill, *Autobiography,* edited by Currin V. Shields (New York: Liberal Arts Press, 1957), p. 32.

3. Ibid., p. 22.

4. Ibid., pp. 79-80.

5. Michael St. John Packe, *The Life of John Stuart Mill* (New York: Macmillan Co., 1954), p. 278.

6. Bertrand Russell, *Portraits from Memory and Other Essays* (New York. Simon & Schuster, 1956), p. 143.

7. Mill, *Autobiography*, p. 9.

8. W. L. Courtney, *Life of John Stuart Mill* (London: Walter Scott, 1889), p. 40.

9. Mill, *Autobiography*, p. 87.

10. Ibid., pp. 89, 90.

11. Ibid., p. 33.

12. F. A. Hayek, *John Stuart Mill and Harriet Taylor* (Chicago: University of Chicago Press; London: Routledge & Kegan Paul, 1951), pp. 31–32.

13. Mill, *Autobiography*, pp. 96–97.

14. J. S. Mill, "Inaugural Address, University of St. Andrews, February 1, 1867," in *Mill's Essays on Literature and Society*, edited by J. B. Schneewind (New York: Collier Books; London: Collier-Macmillan, 1965), pp. 354, 355–56.

15. Ibid., p. 363.

16. Ibid., p. 374.

17. Ibid., pp. 383, 384.

18. J. S. Mill, *Mill's Ethical Writings*, edited by J. B. Schneewind (New York: Collier Books; London: Collier-Macmillan, 1965), "Introduction," p. 31.

19. Alexander Bain, *James Mill: A Biography* (London: Longmans, Green, 1882), pp. 119–20.

20. J. S. Mill, "Utilitarianism," *Mill's Ethical Writings*, pp. 291–92.

21. Ibid., p. 313.

22. Packe, p. 81.

23. Hayek, *Mill and Taylor*, p. 287, quoting from *Letters of Charles Eliot Norton*. 2 vols. (London, Boston, and New York: 1913), 1:496–97

24. Mill, *Autobiography*, pp. 120–21.

25. Hayek, p. 85.

26. Ibid., pp. 275–79.

27. Ibid., pp. 165–66.

28. Alexander Bain, *John Stuart Mill: A Criticism* (London. Longmans, Green, 1882), p. 171.

29. Hayek, p. 98.

30. *Letters of C. E. Norton*, 1:400. September 13, 1870.

31. Packe, p. 131.

32. Hayek, pp. 177–78.

33. Packe, p. 413.

34. Mill, *Autobiography*, p. 169.

35. J. S. Mill, *On Liberty, Representative Government, The Subjection of Women: Three Essays*. With an introduction by M. G. Fawcett (London: Oxford University Press, 1969), p. 465. Succeeding quotations are from pp. 492, 494, 495, 496, 503, 505, 491 n., and 508.

36. Packe, p. 348.

37. Ibid., p. 492.

38. Ibid., p. 501.
39. Ibid., p. 500.
40. Mill, *Autobiography*, p. 162.
41. Noel Annan, in *Mill*, edited by Schneewind, p. 40.
42. Mill, *On Liberty*, pp. 14–15.
43. Ibid., p. 37.
44. Ibid., pp. 52, 53.
45. Ibid., pp. 75–76.
46. Courtney, p. 147.
47. J. S. Mill, *An Examination of Sir William Hamilton's Philosophy*, 4th ed. (London: 1872), p. 129.
48. J. S. Mill, "Theism," in *Three Essays on Religion*, 4th ed. (London: 1875), p. 255.
49. Mill, *Autobiography*, p. 105.
50. Mill, *On Liberty*, p. 46.
51. Ibid., pp. 67–68.
52. Alexander Carlyle, editor, *New Letters of Thomas Carlyle*. 2 vols. (London and New York: 1904), 2:196. May 4, 1859.
53. Hayek, p. 16.

ERNEST RENAN

1. Renan, *The Life of Jesus* (New York: Modern Library, 1927), p. 15.
2. Ibid.
3. Madame James Darmesteter, *The Life of Ernest Renan* (London: Methuen, 1898), p. 10.
4. Renan, *Souvenirs d'enfance et de jeunesse, Oeuvres complètes*, edited by Henriette Psichari. 10 vols. (Paris: Calmann-Lévy, 1947–61), 2:713. Translations from the *Oeuvres* are my own.
5. Ibid., 2:807.
6. Darmesteter, p. 43.
7. Ibid., 2:845.
8. Ibid., 2:822.
9. Ibid., 2:829.
10. Ibid., 2:851.
11. John Morley, *Recollections* (New York: Macmillan Co., 1917), 2:67.
12. "Nephthali," *Cahiers de jeunesse, Oeuvres*, 9:124, entry 9 *bis*.
13. Lewis Freeman Mott, *Ernest Renan* (New York and London: D. Appleton & Co., 1921), pp. 134–35.
14. Renan, *Souvenirs, Oeuvres*, 2:839–40.
15. Renan, *Les Apôtres, Oeuvres*, 4:458.
16. Ibid.
17. Renan, *Vie de Jésus, Oeuvres*, 4:244.
18. Renan, *De l'origine du langage, Oeuvres*, 8:119.

19. Renan, *Vie de Jésus, Oeuvres*, 4:244.

20. Ibid., 4:245.

21. Ibid., Introduction, *Oeuvres*, 4:75.

22. David Friedrich Strauss, *The Life of Jesus*, translated by Marian Evans (New York: Calvin Blanchard, 1860; republished St. Clair Shores, Mich.: Scholarly Press, 1970), 1:55.

23. Renan, *L'Avenir de la science, Oeuvres*, 3:767.

24. Renan, *Vie de Jésus, Oeuvres*, 4:363.

25. Ibid., 4:133, 132.

26. Renan, "Les Historians critiques de Jésus," *Études d'histoire religieuse, Oeuvres*, 7:116.

27. Renan, *Vie de Jésus, Oeuvres*, 4:262.

28. Renan, "Moi-même," *Cahiers de jeunesse, Oeuvres*, 9:216, entry 39.

29. Renan, *Vie de Jésus, Oeuvres*, 4:241.

30. Albert Schweitzer, *Quest of the Historical Jesus*. 2nd English ed. (London: Adam and Charles Black, 1911), p. 18.

31. Renan, *Vie de Jésus, Oeuvres*, 4:223.

32. Ibid., 4:230.

33. Ibid., 4:106.

34. C. S. Lewis, *The Case for Christianity* (New York: Macmillan Co., 1944), p. 45.

35. Renan, *Vie de Jésus, Oeuvres*, 4:293.

36. Ibid., 4:235.

37. Ibid., 4:363–64.

38. Richard William Church, *Occasional Papers*. 2 vols. (London: Macmillan & Co., 1897), 2:199.

39. Ibid., pp. 200, 201.

40. Quoted in French in ibid., pp. 201–2; no source given; my translation.

41. Darmesteter, *Life of Renan*, p. 15.

42. Renan, *Ma soeur Henriette, Oeuvres*, 9:156, 157.

43. Ibid., 9:464, 465.

44. Ibid., 4:470–71.

45. Renan to Marcelin Berthelot, September 12, 1861, *Correspondance (Renan-Berthelot), 1847–1892* (Paris: Calmann-Lévy, n.d.), p. 284.

46. Henriette Renan to Berthelot, November 30, 1860; quoted by Mott, *Ernest Renan*, p. 210.

47. Renan to the Editor of the *Constitutionel*, February 28, 1862, in Renan, *Correspondance, 1846–1871* (Paris: Calmann-Lévy, 1926), p. 211. My translation.

48. Hippolyte Taine, *Life and Letters*. 3 vols. (Westminster: Archibald Constable, 1902–08), 2:190; February 22, 1862.

49. Renan, "Les Peuples Sémitiques," *Mélanges d'histoire et de voyages, Oeuvres*, 2:319–20.

50. Renan to Grant Duff, March 10, 1862, *Memoir*, pp. 66, 67; quoted by Mott, *Ernest Renan*, p. 223.

51. Renan, Speech on being received into the French Academy, April 3, 1879, *Oeuvres*, 1:724.

52. Emile Faguet, *Histoire de la langue et de la littérature française* (Paris, 1899), 8:397; quoted by Herman G. A. Brauer, *The Philosophy of Ernest Renan* (Madison, Wisconsin, 1903), p. 209. My translation.

53. Taine, January 25, 1858, to J. J. Weiss, in *Life and Letters*, 2:132.

54. Taine, *Life and Letters*, 2:203.

55. Renan, quoted by Mott, *Ernest Renan*, p. 444, without source.

56. Renan, *L'Avenir de la science, Oeuvres*, 3:808.

57. George Saintsbury, *A Scrap Book* (London: Macmillan & Co., 1922), p. 229.

58. Renan, *Les Apôtres, Oeuvres*, 4:479, n. 3.

59. Mott, *Ernest Renan*, p. 362.

60. Darmesteter, *Life of Renan*, p. 273.

61. Ibid., p. 234.

62. Renan, "Nephthali," *Cahiers de la jeunesse, Oeuvres*, 9:149, entry 52.

63. Renan, *Revue des deux mondes*, August 15, 1889, p. 721.

64. Renan, *Souvenirs, Oeuvres*, 2:760.

65. Darmesteter, *Life of Renan*, p. 53.

66. Schweitzer, *Quest*, p. 4.

67. Renan, *Vie de Jésus, Oeuvres*, 4:83.

68. Mott, *Ernest Renan*, p. 452.

69. Ibid., p. 265.

70. William Barry, *Ernest Renan* (New York: Charles Scribner's Sons, 1905), p. 181.

71. Renan, *L'Avenir de la science, Oeuvres*, 3:1088.

72. Renan, *Nouvelles études d'histoire religieuse* (1884), *Oeuvres*, 7:707.

73. Renan, *L'Avenir de la science, Oeuvres*, 3:1049.

74. Renan, *Souvenirs, Oeuvres*, 2:909.

75. Ibid., p. 182.

76. Henri Peyre, *Literature and Sincerity* (New Haven and London: Yale University Press, 1963), p. 105.

77. Renan, *Les Evangiles, Oeuvres*, 5:13.

78. Renan, *L'avenir de la science, Oeuvres*, 3:1085–86.

79. Mott, *Ernest Renan*, p. 355.

80. Barry, *Renan*, p. 174.

81. Matthew Arnold, *Essays in Criticism* (London: Macmillan & Co., 1889), pp. 46–47.

82. Henry Sidgwick, *Miscellaneous Essays and Addresses* (London: Macmillan & Co., 1904), p. 23.

83. Renan, *Vie de Jésus, Oeuvres*, 4:131.

84. Church, *Occasional Papers*, 2:197–98.

85. Renan, Speech to the French Academy, April 3, 1879, *Oeuvres*, 1:730.

86. J. M. Robertson, *Ernest Renan* (London: Watts & Co., 1924), pp. 74, 76.

87. Barry, *Renan,* pp. 226–27.

88. Renan, "Souvenirs du *Journal des Débats,*" *Feuilles détachées, Oeuvres,* 2:1026.

89. Renan, *Ma soeur Henriette, Oeuvres,* 9:457, 458.

90. Renan, "L'Académie Française," *Journal des Débats,* January 22, 1859; *Oeuvres,* 2:232.

91. Renan, Letter to Mézières, *Journal des Débats,* April 10, 1879.

92. Renan, *Les Apôtres, Oeuvres,* 4:463.

HENRY SIDGWICK

Some passages in this chapter appeared in an article, "Sidgwick the Man," *The Monist,* 58 (July 1974): 349–70, and are reprinted here with permission.

1. A. C. Benson, *The Life of Edward White Benson, Sometime Archbishop of Canterbury.* 2 vols. (London and New York: Macmillan, 1899), 1:148.

2. Arthur and Eleanor Mildred Sidgwick, *Henry Sidgwick: A Memoir* (London and New York: Macmillan, 1906), p. 23. This memoir, which consists largely of Sidgwick's letters and journal extracts, is the most complete source of information about him. Quotations from it are identified in the text by (*Mem.,* p. —).

3. From a letter to A. C. Benson, in Benson, 1:250.

4. Sidgwick, *Miscellaneous Essays and Addresses* (London and New York: Macmillan, 1904), pp. 1 ff.

5. Lord Rayleigh, "Some Recollections of Henry Sidgwick," *Proceedings of the [British] Society for Psychical Research,* 45 (1938–39): 172.

6. A. C. Benson, *The Leaves of the Tree* (London: Smith, Elder, 1911), p. 65.

7. G. G. Coulton, *Fourscore Years: An Autobiography* (Cambridge: University Press, 1943), p. 350.

8. F. W. Maitland, *Collected Papers,* edited by H. A. L. Fisher. 3 vols. (Cambridge: University Press, 1911), 3:535.

9. Benson, *The Leaves of the Tree,* p. 61.

10. James Bryce, *Studies in Contemporary Biography* (London and New York: Macmillan, 1903), p. 341.

11. Sidgwick, *Miscellaneous Essays and Addresses,* pp. 27–28.

12. John Morley, *Recollections.* 2 vols. (New York: Macmillan Co., 1917), 1:124.

13. Sidgwick, *The Methods of Ethics* (London: Macmillan, 1874), bk. 3, chap. 13, sec. 3.

14. Ibid.

15. Bryce, p. 332.

16. Letter of June 24, 1878, to Roden Noel.

17. C. D. Broad, *Religion, Philosophy and Psychical Research* (London: Routledge & Kegan Paul, 1953), p. 94.

18. *Proceedings, S.P.R.,* 29 (1918): 64-110; 34 (1924): 212-74.

19. Broad, p. 103.

20. *Proceedings, S.P.R.,* 19 (1905-1907): 441.

21. Broad, p. 106.

22. L. R. Farnell, *An Oxonian Looks Back* (London: Martin Hopkinson, 1934), p. 44.

23. F. W. Maitland, *The Life and Letters of Leslie Stephen* (London: Duckworth, 1906), p. 250.

24. R. F. Harrod, *The Life of John Maynard Keynes* (London: Macmillan & Co., 1951), pp. 76-77.

25. Lord Rayleigh, "Some Recollections of Henry Sidgwick," *Proceedings, S.P.R.,* 45 (1938-39): 170.

26. F. H. Bradley, *Aphorisms* (Oxford: Clarendon Press, 1930), no. 98.

27. Morley, 1:124.

28. Leslie Stephen, "Henry Sidgwick," *Mind,* n.s., 10 (January 1901): 13.

29. Benson, *The Leaves of the Tree,* pp. 58-59.

30. Ibid., p. 59.

31. Bryce, pp. 338-39.

32. Sidgwick, *Miscellaneous Essays and Addresses,* pp. 349-50.

33. Ibid., pp. 270-319.

34. Sidgwick, *Practical Ethics,* 2nd ed. (London: Swan Sonnenschein, 1909; New York: Macmillan Co.), p. 260.

35. Benson, *The Leaves of the Tree,* p. 61.

36. Harrod, *Keynes,* p. 25.

37. These details I owe to C. D. Broad's *Ethics and the History of Philosophy* (London: Routledge & Kegan Paul, 1952), p. 58.

38. Benson, *The Leaves of the Tree,* p. 67.

39. Noel G. Annan, *Leslie Stephen* (Cambridge, Mass.: Harvard University Press, 1952), p. 199.

40. Leslie Stephen, *Mind* (1901), p. 14.

41. *Proceedings, S.P.R.,* 15 (1900-1901): 463.

42. Morley, 1:123.

43. Maitland, *Life of Stephen,* pp. 333-34.

44. J. B. Schneewind, *Sidgwick's Ethics and Victorian Moral Philosophy* (Oxford: Clarendon Press, 1977), p. 122.

45. Maitland, *Collected Papers,* 3:539.

THE ENEMY: PREJUDICE

1. F. L. Lucas, *The Greatest Problem* (London: Cassell, 1960), p. 145.

2. Joseph Butler, *Sermons,* VII.

3. For criticism of Watson, see B. Blanshard, *The Nature of Thought.* 2 vols. (London: Allen & Unwin, 1939), vol. 1, chap. 9; for Skinner: B. Blanshard, "The Problem of Consciousness," a debate with Skinner, *Philosophy and Phe-*

nomenological Research (March 1967), pp. 317-37; for Ryle: H. D. Lewis, *The Elusive Mind* (London: Allen & Unwin, 1969), chaps. 1-3.

4. In *The Nature of Thought*.

5. Given by Hugh Kingsmill, *Invective and Abuse: An Anthology* (London: Eyre & Spottiswoode, 1944), p. 189.

6. Roy Jenkins, *Asquith* (London: Collins, 1964), p. 69.

7. F. L. Lucas, *The Art of Living. Four Eighteenth-Century Minds: Hume, Horace Walpole, Burke, Benjamin Franklin* (London: Cassell, 1959), p. 139 n.

8. Quoted by Gordon W. Allport, *The Nature of Prejudice* (abridged; New York: Doubleday & Co., Anchor Books, 1958), p. 420.

9. Clyde Kluckhohn, *Mirror for Man* (New York: McGraw-Hill, 1949), p. 122.

10. Allport, p. 107.

11. Ibid., p. 108, reporting M. J. Herskovits, *Anthropometry of the American Negro* (New York: Columbia University Press, 1930).

12. J. G. Hibben, *A Defence of Prejudice and Other Essays* (New York: Charles Scribner's Sons, 1911), p. 5.

13. Alfred North Whitehead, *Dialogues,* recorded by Lucien Price (Boston: Little, Brown, 1954), p. 145.

14. For a full statement of Professor W. T. Jones's view, see his *The Sciences and the Humanities* (Berkeley and Los Angeles: University of California Press, 1965) and *The Romantic Syndrome* (The Hague: Nijhoff, 1961); also his essay and my reply in P. A. Schilpp, ed., *The Philosophy of Brand Blanshard* (La Salle, Ill.: Open Court, 1980).

15. Herzberg, Alexander, *The Psychology of Philosophers* (London: Kegan Paul, Trench, Trubner & Co., New York: Harcourt, Brace, 1929).

16. William James, *Pragmatism* (London and New York: Longmans, Green, 1907), pp. 6-13.

17. Macneile Dixon, *The Human Situation* (London: Edward Arnold, 1937), p. 17.

18. F. L. Lucas, *Style* (London: Cassell & Co., 1955), p. 68.

Index